QUEER ONLINE

Steve Jones
General Editor

Vol. 40

PETER LANG
New York • Washington, D.C./Baltimore • Bern
Frankfurt am Main • Berlin • Brussels • Vienna • Oxford

QUEER ONLINE

MEDIA TECHNOLOGY & SEXUALITY

Kate O'Riordan & David J. Phillips, EDITORS

PETER LANG
New York • Washington, D.C./Baltimore • Bern
Frankfurt am Main • Berlin • Brussels • Vienna • Oxford

Library of Congress Cataloging-in-Publication Data

Queer online: media technology and sexuality /
edited by Kate O'Riordan, David J. Phillips.
p. cm. — (Digital formations; v. 40)
Includes bibliographical references and index.
1. Gays. 2. Internet—Social aspects.
3. Interpersonal communication. 4. Computer networks—Social aspects.
5. Communication—Technological innovations.
I. O'Riordan, Kate. II. Phillips, David J.
HQ76.25.Q375   306.76'602854678—dc22   2006102418
ISBN 978-0-8204-8631-4 (hardcover)
ISBN 978-0-8204-8626-0 (paperback)
ISSN 1526-3169

Bibliographic information published by **Die Deutsche Bibliothek**.
Die Deutsche Bibliothek lists this publication in the "Deutsche
Nationalbibliografie"; detailed bibliographic data is available
on the Internet at http://dnb.ddb.de/.

Cover art by W. Gary Smith
Cover design by Lisa Barfield

© 2007 Peter Lang Publishing, Inc., New York
29 Broadway, 18th floor, New York, NY 10006
www.peterlang.com

Contents

Part III: Reformulating Identities and Practices

Part IV: Relocating Structures and Agencies

Foreword

LARRY GROSS, ANNENBERG SCHOOL FOR COMMUNICATION,
UNIVERSITY OF SOUTHERN CALIFORNIA

When twentieth-century Scottish geneticist J.B.S. Haldane famously remarked, "It is my supposition that the Universe is not only queerer than we imagine, but it is queerer than we can imagine," he was certainly not thinking of cyberspace, and he was certainly not using queer in its now-familiar sexual connotation. Still, there is something eerily prescient in this claim, if we apply it to the brave new World Wide Web in which we are now enmeshed. Why is that? What is there about the Internet that makes it somehow, queer?

Well, for one thing, there's the disembodied, performativity of cyberspace, the place where no one knows you're a dog, or whatever you choose to present yourself as. Queer folk are past masters at this game, as nearly every one of us went through the training program during childhood. Even if we weren't singled out for special (unwelcome) attention as sissies, tomboys or other gender nonconformists, most of us survived society's sexual bootcamp—highschool—either by masquerading and passing, or living on the margins.

Then there's the possibility offered via the Internet to locate others with shared interests and needs, however scattered geographically and distant socially they might be; to make the connections that are the ground out of which community can rise. In the past few decades social historians, initially working in community-based grassroots projects and later within the academy, have charted the submerged archipelago of queer life across the United States. In these narratives communication networks, initially informal and word-of-mouth, but increasingly embodied and extended via community-based media—first newsletters, then magazines and newspapers—are accorded a central role. Martin Meeker's *Contacts Desired: Gay and Lesbian Communication and Community, 1940s–1970s,* offers the most explicit account of what he calls the sexual communication network as an agent of change (Meeker, 2005).

Meeker begins his exploration of the role of communication networks in the emergence of gay male and lesbian communities in twentieth-century United States with a telling anecdote. The story is about a teenager named Harry Hay, who will later found the first modern homosexual liberation organization, the Mattachine Society. As recounted by Hay's biographer, Stuart Timmons, Hay's first sexual encounter with a young sailor included receiving the news that he was part of a "silent brotherhood" that existed across history and geography. Hay was assured that as he learned to identify other members of this invisible tribe, even in the midst of frightening and alien places, he would be home and safe (Timmons, 1990, p. 36). As Meeker says, this is the quintessential saga of homosexuality:

> The experience of this process is shared not by all but by an untold number of women and men who come to identify themselves as homosexual. Even more than coming out (the moment of revealing one's homosexuality to one's friends, family, and the world at large), connecting (the moment of emerging from the isolation and invisibility into which most who would later identify as gay or lesbian are born) is the point at which someone becomes homosexual—or, rather, gay male or lesbian. (Meeker, 2005, p. 6)

Today, it's likely that young people will know about homosexuality at an early age. Given the emergence of gay people onto society's public stage, the mass media, it seems unlikely that anyone grows up thinking that "they're the only one" or not having any label for the feelings of difference they are experiencing.

Today's stories start at a younger age. Nearly ten years ago Savin-Williams summarized a body of research on the stages of the coming out process conducted over more than two decades and concluded that the ages at which these "developmental milestones are reached . . . have been steadily declining from the 1970s to current cohorts of youths . . . awareness of same-sex attractions has dropped from the onset of junior high school to an average of third grade" (1998; p. 16). Savin-Williams attributed this reduction in the age of self-definition to the "recent visibility of homosexuality in the macro culture (such as in the media), the reality of a very vocal and extensive gay and lesbian culture, and the presence of homosexuality in their immediate social world" (1998; p. 122). That immediate social world, for many young people, now includes the Internet.

The largest online survey of GLBT youth, conducted in 2000 by Out-Proud, and Oasis Magazine, was completed by 6,872 respondents aged 25 or under. Two-thirds of the respondents said that being online helped them accept their sexual orientation, 35% that being online was crucial to this acceptance. Not surprisingly, therefore, many said they came out online before doing so in "real life"—this was much more the case for males— 57%—than for females—38%—and more for those who had spent more time online.

Connections online sometime lead to real-life meetings: about half of the respondents report such meetings, and 12% of the males (but only 4% of the females) said they met someone offline for the purpose of having sex. About a quarter of both males and females met someone "with the hope that we might become more than friends." In general, a quarter of the respondents said that they met the people they've dated online.

Queer youth often feel isolated and rarely have access to a supportive queer community in their vicinity. Sixty percent of the respondents said they did not feel as though they were part of the gay, lesbian, bisexual, and trans-gendered community; but 52% said they felt a sense of community with the people they've met online. While one of the clichés of computer-mediated communication is that one can hide one's true identity, so "that nobody knows you're 15 and live in Montana and are gay" (Gabriel, 1995), it is also true that going online offers many folks an opportunity to shed the mask they wear in their "real lives"—at home, at school, and at work.

New media create opportunities for the formation of new communities, and the Internet is no exception. In contrast to most other modern media the Internet offers opportunities for individual engagement both as senders and receivers, permitting the coalescing of interest-based networks spanning vast distances. The potential for friendship and group formation provided by the Internet is particularly valuable for members of self-identified minorities who are scattered and often besieged in their home surroundings.

Queers were among the first to realize the potential of this new technology. As an Associated Press story put it in the early days of the Web, "It's the unspoken secret of the online world that gay men and lesbians are among the most avid, loyal and plentiful commercial users of the Internet" (6/24/96). Not surprisingly, it wasn't long before entrepreneurs began to develop this promising tract of electronic real estate. As Tom Rielly, the founder of Planet Out, an electronic media company that began on the Microsoft Network in 1995, explained, "Traditional mass media is very cost-intensive. Gays and lesbians don't have a high level of ownership of mainstream media properties. The Internet is the first medium where we can have equal footing with the big players" (Lewis, 1995). For Rielly and his financial backers the attractions of marketing to a large and underserved group were obvious. But cyberspace also provides "a gathering point for millions of lesbians, gay men, bisexuals, transvestites and others who may be reluctant to associate in public" (ibid.). For those who are, with or without good reason, afraid to visit gay establishments or subscribe to gay publications, "gay online services bring the gay community into their homes, where they're shielded from their neighbors and coworkers" (AP, 6/24/96).

The Internet is not utopia, however, as I trust we all have learned, some through painful experience. It may offer us opportunities to escape into an alternate universe—often one peopled with folk who share one's special, possibly arcane interests—but we often discover that most travelers have brought along the biases and prejudices they carry in the rest of their lives. Virtual communities can be gated and restricted as well as open and playful. We've also learned, often the hard way, that online communities, like their material world counterparts, can be ghettos as well as liberated zones. They open us to new forms of surveillance and they expose us to new vulnerabilities. As the authors of the present volume realize, and as many of them demonstrate through examples and analysis, the border between the "online" and the "real world" has become increasingly blurred.

In 2005, according to the latest survey by the University of Southern California's Annenberg's Center for the Digital Future, 79% of Americans went online, spending an average of over thirteen hours per week. In 2000, the first year of the Center's ongoing survey, 47% reported home Internet access; in 2005 this had risen to 66%, and 48% have broadband access at home. As our social, economic, political and cultural lives are more and more lived in these increasingly interwoven realms we are all well advised to become navigators as well as surfers, savvy consumers rather than passive recipients of the bounty pouring from the digital cornucopia. And for those who are committed—as scholars, as citizens, or both—to the exploration of the contested territories of gender and sexuality, it is imperative to become engaged citizens of both realms. In that cause the present volume will serve us well as Baedeker, compass and phrasebook.

References

Associated Press (AP). 1996. "Gay and Lesbian Net Surfers: A Dream Market in the Online World." June 24.

Gabriel, Trip. 1995. "Some On-Line Discoveries Give Gay Youths a Path to Themselves." *The New York Times,* July 2, p.1.

Lewis, Peter. 1995. "Planet Out's Gay Services on Virtual Horizon." *The New York Times,* August 21, p. D3.

Meeker, Martin. 2005. *Contacts Desired: Gay and Lesbian Communications and Community, 1940s–1970s.* Chicago: University of Chicago Press.

Savin-Williams, Ritch. 1998. *". . . And Then I Became Gay."* New York: Routledge.

Timmons, Stuart. 1990. *The Trouble with Harry Hay: Founder of the Modern Gay Movement.* Boston: Alyson Publications.

Acknowledgments

Some of the initial ideas for this book came out of two events, the "Sexualities, Medias and New Technologies: Theorising Old and New Practices" conference at the University of Surrey, UK, 2001; and the "Critical Cybercultural Studies: Current Terrains Future Directions" symposium at the University of Washington in Seattle, USA, 2003. We would like to thank all of the participants of these events, and the organizers—Nina Wakeford, Nicola Green and the team at INCITE, and David Silver, Adrienne Massanari, and their colleagues at the University of Washington—for the inspiration.

The response to the call for papers for this collection was overwhelmingly enthusiastic and we would like to thank everyone who responded, and who shared their work and ideas in this process. In addition to their intellectual contributions, we would particularly like to thank those contributors who are included in this collection for all their hard work, and cheerful disposition throughout.

The diverse networks that make up the Association of Internet Researchers (AoIR) have been an influential source of encouragement and support, as well as providing networks for intellectual exchange and we would like to acknowledge the role of this organization, and particular individuals within it, especially Steve Jones and Nancy Baym. The AoIR conference at the University of Sussex in 2004 was also significant in shaping this project, and brought several of the contributors into closer conversation.

Much is owed also to our respective friends and colleagues including Maureen McNeil, Joan Haran, and Jenny Kitzinger at the Universities of Cardiff and Lancaster respectively (UK), and many colleagues at the Department of Media and Film Studies at the University of Sussex (UK), with particular thanks to Caroline Bassett and Sally Munt. At the University of Texas at Austin, Mary Kearney, Michael Kackman, Sharon Strover, Karin Wilkins, and Carolyn Cunningham offered great intellectual and personal support.

As ever, we are also indebted to our families and friends for their support and forbearance. Kate O'Riordan would particularly like to acknowledge Molly, Rachel, Josie, Ben, Carlotta, Lois, Ella, and Jenny. David Phillips would particularly like to acknowledge Gary Smith, Almarin Phillips, and Kate O'Riordan.

Introduction

KATE O'RIORDAN AND DAVID J. PHILLIPS

This collection draws together contemporary research into queer theory and practices, as they intersect with new media and communication technologies. In the operation of this drawing together we do not seek to provide a homogenous view of either queer theory or communication technologies but we aim to bring together a range of diverse positions, which can be read as multiple and sometimes contradictory points of engagement. As well as setting up these chapters in conversation and debate with each other, we also take this opportunity to discuss some of the key texts, which are part of the context of this work.

The Introduction offers a discussion of preceding and intersecting literature that foregrounds some of the material drawn out in the analyses provided in part I: Theoretical Landscapes. After which we set out some of the contexts of debates in the 1990s and 2000s, which relate to the themes drawn out in the chapters. Finally, we offer a general overview of this book. Parts II, III, and IV into which the contributions are organized are Rethinking Community and Spatiality; Reformulating Identities and Practices; and Relocating Structures and Agencies, respectively.

Preceding and Intersecting Literature

There is a wealth of literature dealing with queer theories and practices and even more dealing with media and communication technologies. However, there is a relative scarcity of literature and commentary that draws these elements together. Thus, rather than seeking to provide an overview of queer literatures and media and communication technology literatures, we highlight here a selection of those contributions that have brought these two areas into engagements with each other.

Critical engagements with queer and cyber in the 1990s included a range of isolated articles, which brought these two elements into an exchange, largely appearing in collections that focused either on queer or on media and communication technologies (e.g., Boone et al. 2000; Dery 1994). However, there were also some more sustained convergences in the form of monographs such as Allucquere Rosanne Stone's (1995) *The War of Desire and Technology at the Close of the Mechanical Age* and Sue Ellen Case's (1999) *The Domain Matrix: Performing Lesbian at the End of Print Culture*. Nina Wakeford's article, "Cyberqueer," appeared in 1997 in the *Lesbian and Gay Studies Reader: A Critical Introduction* (Munt and Medhurst 1997). Although Wakeford did not coin the term "cyberqueer" at this point, she developed and critiqued it. This article was reprinted in *The Cybercultures Reader* (Bell and Kennedy 2000) and the extent of its ongoing citation makes this worth foregrounding in this context. We return to this article later in this section.

Larger collections that brought queer and media and communication technologies together include the following: the section "Cybersexual" in *The Cybercultures Reader* (Bell and Kennedy 2000); the special edition of *The International Journal of Lesbian and Gay Studies* "Queer Webs" (Alexander 2002); *Mobile Cultures: New Media in Queer Asia* (Berry et al. 2003); and *Queer Theory and Communication: From Disciplining Queers to Queering the Disciplines* (Yep et al. 2004).

The work of other writers who we think are particularly relevant to the contexts of this collection includes analysis by Lauren Berlant, Judith Butler, Joshua Gamson, Judith Halberstam, Susan Stryker, and Michael Warner. This brief overview is not intended to be exhaustive but is intended to foreground work that deals with queer and cyber intersections, and on which this collection builds. It also highlights some of the writers on which we draw and whose work the writers in this collection also build on.

"Cyberqueer" and "Cybersexual"

Nina Wakeford's chapter on "cyberqueer" asked what the coupling of cyber and queer might produce, or more precisely, what cyber might add to queer. The implication in this argument is that sometimes this coupling is unhelpful and less productive than might have been expected in the 1990s. Wakeford anticipates that this coupling might be reductive in that it can produce readings of websites articulating partial interpretations of Judith Butler (1990) or Eve Sedgwick (1990). Wakeford does not directly answer the question of how productive the cyber/queer coupling might be; she does not fully evaluate work that she identifies as appropriating Butler and Sedgwick for a "queer" analysis of "cyber" texts. However, the overall tone of prognosis is not optimistic:

> In fact the impression is that cyberspace is the postmodern space *par* excellence
> [. . .]. Perhaps the closeness of fit is a bit too convincing? What is lost if
> cyberqueer research becomes merely a celebration of parody and performance,
> or the simplistic application of an author's reading of *Gender Trouble* or *The Epis-
> temology of the Closet?* (Wakeford 1997: 412)

However, as well as providing an indirect critique of the points at which
cyber/queer intersects for other authors, Wakeford also provides a further
typology of cyber/queer intersections in computer-mediated communication
(CMC) practices, and also points toward a research agenda that moves from
textual readings to a consideration of economic contexts. Thus, Wakeford's
article on the one hand warns against, and resists, cyber/queer couplings,
while also on the other hand provides an impetus to, and for, such couplings.

The "cybersexual" section of *The Cybercultures Reader* sets Wakeford's
article against some of the work that Wakeford is critiquing, including Ran-
dall Woodland's (2000) "Queer spaces, modem boys and pagan statues."
This section of the reader also includes work by Gareth Branwyn, Daniel
Tsang, Thomas Foster, and Sadie Plant. These articles were all published
between 1995 and 1998 in their original forms and were preoccupied with
performativity, sexuality, gender, virtuality, and embodiment. To some
degree, each of these articles attempts to examine a reformulation of
body/identity relationships and constitution, in relation to mediation. While
several of these articles develop a positive tone (Branwyn, Woodland, Tsang),
this is balanced against contributions that articulate a guarded pessimism and
reflection on the constraint and control implicated and produced through
media and communication technologies in the 1990s (Foster, Plant, Wakeford).

"Queer Webs" and "Mobile Cultures"

Despite Nina Wakeford's call for a critical attention to political economy and
production, the special edition of the *International Journal of Lesbian and
Gay Studies: Queer Webs,* focused on representation and the Web. In this collection however, representation was carefully contextualized as a set of political practices and cultural productions. The collection's editor, Jonathon
Alexander, set out to ask how representations "affect the socio-political landscapes we inhabit—and which inhabit us" (Alexander 2002: 81). In this context then the use of theoretical frameworks to help understand the formations
and reformulations of cyber/queer is set up as a political imperative with
potentially rich outcomes.

These accounts of cultural production and queer web use show that the "application of an author's reading of *Gender Trouble* or *The Epistemology of the Closet*" (Wakeford 1997: 412) need not inevitably be simplistic. In addition to examining the complexity of readings of the above texts, the *Queer Webs* collection also highlighted the variety of tools and methods deployed through queer theory and exemplified a developing and diverse field.

Parallel, linked, and alterior couplings to those in the United States and Europe also opened up across Asia in the mid-1990s (Berry et al. 2003). The *Mobile Cultures: New Media in Queer Asia* collection, like *Queer Webs,* also focused on representational practices. The book attempts to focus on the "globalisation of sexual cultures" and "the study of new media" (Berry et al. 2003: 2). However, it follows Arjun Appadurai (1996) in stressing a heterogeneous critique, instead of conceptualizing globalization as monolithic and homogenizing. While the collection critiques the terms "new media" and "queer Asia," it also uses them as devises for producing intricate and multiple intersections of local and global through tropes of mobility, and its' hidden other, immobility. *Mobile Cultures* and the *Queer Webs* collection highlight the ongoing importance of place, space, embodiment, and everyday life in the construction and production of queer techno-practices.

In this turn to place, space, and embodiment—indeed, in the questioning of the uses of the metaphors of "space" in engagements with new media—queer cyber studies have, implicitly and explicitly, called on recent work on queer geographies (Valentine 1993). These investigate the cultural and political economies of places, and the reflexive construction of places and identities. Chauncey (1994), for example, explores the communal practices of gay men involved in constructing and sharing gay "maps" of Manhattan. Rothenberg (1995) examines how lesbians have come to create Park Slope as a recognizable lesbian neighborhood. All of this can be seen as pursuing what Berlant and Warner (1998) refer to as "the queer project . . . [of supporting] forms of affective, erotic, and personal living that are public in the sense of accessible, available to memory, and sustained through collective activity" (562). Much of this queer geography, whether in the study of gay neighborhoods or gay tourism, strategically integrates global and local practices, economic and cultural structures, collective and individual agencies (Binnie 1995).

Scholars continue to pursue this strategy as "the queer project" embraces cyberspace, and the structuring contexts of community morph from zoning laws and residential real estate markets to media ownership and audience commodification. Here, too, researchers in "new" media can call upon traditions of work in "old" media. Genres (and tropes of identity) have been studied as reflections and articulations of corporate media structures (see, for example, Kearney 2004). Sender (2001) and Chasin (2000), among others, have explored how the construction by media organizations of gay men and lesbians, as audiences and markets, has perverted the queer project of radical imagination. On a more optimistic note, Gamson (1998) showed how the institutional imperatives of television producers made talk shows viable (albeit limited and contradictory) sites for the contestation and undermining of heteronormativity.

Although these researchers may be seen to be investigating certain media forms, they are in fact centrally concerned with the institutionalization of those forms. That is, Gamson and Kearney can reach contradictory conclusions because they are referencing, not television as such, but the historical configuration of institutions structuring television.

Likewise, as the focus of studies of online practice moves from the participants in multiuser domains (MUDs) or USENET to websurfers or online shoppers, we can expect different analytic approaches as well as different empirical insights. For example, with the advent of the World Wide Web in 1994, what had been primarily textual practices were reformulated and reproduced in more visual forms. Driven by both the intensification of the commodification of the image in the 1990s, and the use of infrastructures that facilitated visual communication; the emergence of the commercial web was both driven by and a driver for this reformulation of virtual visuality. The digital media production communities of the 1990s (e.g., Web design and dot.com) developed both on the fringes and in the center of the integration of the Web with global media ownership. The casual labor market engendered and exploited by these developments has been a significant element in this reformulation of "the internet" as "the Web" (Gill 2002).

Also through the 1990s, ownership and control of the infrastructure of the internet, including backbone carriers, ISPs, and Web portals, became increasingly the domain of fewer, larger, and more integrated media corporations. Gamson has noted that this has entailed a "transformation of gay and lesbian [internet] media from organizations answering at least partly to geographical and political communities into businesses answering primarily to advertisers and investors." He also notes an accompanying "tightening of relationships between mainstream political organizations, nongay corporations, and national gay and lesbian media" (Gamson 2003, quoted in Gamson and Moon 2004: 58). Campbell (2005), too, has pursued the political and cultural repercussions of this transformation, as "Janus-faced . . . online portals . . . present themselves as inclusive communities to gay and lesbian consumers while simultaneously presenting themselves as surveilling entities to corporate clients" (663).

However, the collapse of "the internet" into "the Web" is not total. That formulation is under stress as a multiplicity of formats, platforms, and uses arise to confront it. We would like to see more work that takes explicitly queer approaches to new structural trends including global struggles over the regulation of peer-to-peer networks, data retention practices, and intellectual property.

While attending to global economies it is also important to think about specificity, locality, and the micropolitics of everyday life. The broad sweep of queer theory as an intellectual construct is tremendously enriching, but we must also remember the everydayness of queer lives and the mundane reach of queer thinking. This collection returns, in part to the everyday mobilization, operation, assembling, and challenging of queer across situated bodies interacting in local and global contexts. In this juxtaposition of the theoretical and empirical, we hope to show that contemporary ideas and practices about queer subjects and the current intersections of queer and cyber formations are both radically different and have direct similarities to those fifteen years ago. In bringing together crucial examinations of the intersecting fields of sexuality, gender, nation, ethnicity, age, communication, and the internet, we provide an overarching contextualization and consolidation of cyber/queer practices and theories. In doing so, we reflect David Silver's (2004) conceptualization of cybercultural studies as a moving field and Eng, Halberstam and Munoz (2005) contention that queer is still a force to be reckoned with as we revisit contemporary intersubjectivities in the technopractices of everyday life.

Structure

Part I: Theoretical Landscapes

This collection does not attend to the macropolitics of capitalism but deals with the struggles of day-to-day life in situated, but globally connected spheres of intersubjectivity and interaction. Its reach is not grand but it is particular.

Kate O'Riordan, in chapter 1, traces the tropes of cyber and queer as they travel across theory and practices in the 1990s and beyond. In this chapter, a tracing of the movement of cyber and queer as metaphors, theoretical tools, and tropes, through visual and textual production, is used to suggest that how such tropes are deployed has important consequences for our understanding of both queer and media and communication technologies.

David Phillips and Carolyn Cunningham, in chapter 2, consider the implications of a queer sensibility for our meta-conceptualizations and uses of technologies, especially the information systems that underlie, and in fact significantly constitute, life online. This chapter brings together work on technologies of surveillance and queer theory and suggests the ways in which these frameworks could be brought into engagement with each other to think more productively about the laws, economics, and techniques structuring information and knowledge production.

In chapter 3, we draw on research (un)covering the gendered "everyday techno-practices" (Karl this volume) of life in the UK, in work by Irmi Karl, who writes in the frame of, but also takes issue with, Roger Silverstone's influential turn to "everyday life." In doing so Karl's chapter makes three important arguments. The first explores how examinations of the gendered consumption of information and communication technologies (ICTs) can benefit from queer theory, the second reinforces the case that online media must be contextualized by locating it relation to everyday life, and the third provides a perspective to the question of how intrinsic technology is to the study of sexual identity.

Thus the chapters in part I of the collection deal with a focus on the micro in relation to the macro. They examine practices in the context of theory and set out a beginning of some of the intellectual landscapes of queer techno-practices. In setting this diverse collection of contributions together we aim to provide an overdue contribution to media and communication studies from queer theory and to revisit queer theory through the examination of diverse communication and media practices. This collection aims to hold in tension a series of diverse and conflicting positions in the hope of contributing to a rich sense of the intersectionality which keeps open the possibility of queer as a productive force and provokes an understanding of the multiple and intersecting issues at risk in queer technologies, communication, and communicating queerly.

Part II: Rethinking Spatiality and Community

In this part, three authors explore the relation of online and offline spaces and identities. Nathan Rambukkana, in chapter 4, studies the changing relation of leathersex and sadomasochism, Marjo Laukkanen, in chapter 5, approaches the intersubjectivity of teenagers in Scandinavia, and Adi Kuntsman, in chapter 6, explores the integration of bar culture and online discourse in the queer diasporas of Russian-speaking Israelis. These three chapters are characterized by an attention to the construction and reformulation of space as it intersects with community formations and productions, foregrounding how spatiality and community can be rethought through each other in different ways.

Part III: Reformulating Identities and Practices

The affective lures of the screen are also considered by Shaka McGlotten in chapter 7, extending the trajectories set up by Stone (1995) which extend through the visual art work of Shu Lea Cheang and other (new)media artists. The work of race in the chat rooms of Toronto in chapter 8, and the interconnections of transvestitism and the digital image in chapter 9, which are explored by Andil Gosine, and Debra Ferreday and Simon Lock, respectively, bring together constellations of diverse subjects, practices, and discourses. Linking these three chapters is a focus on the reformulations of desire, affect, visibility, subjectivity, identity, and the screen.

Part IV: Relocating Structures and Agencies

Christy Carlson in chapter 10 on *Law and Order* provides serious consideration to intertextuality and the proliferation of intersecting mediascapes. In chapter 11, a corrective to a focus on alternatives and activism is provided by John Campbell's analysis of the production of citizenship through consumption. In chapter 12, Sharif Mowlabocus also considers the resources that online communication offers in the production of marginalized gay male subjectivities, that is, the communities of "barebacking." All three of the chapters take a specific structural economy as their framework (media, consumer, moral), and examine how these are both relocated and reproduced through contemporary practices.

References

Alexander, J. 2002. "Introduction to the Special Issue: Queer Webs: Representations of LGBT People and Communities on the World Wide Web." *International Journal of Sexuality and Gender Studies* 7(2/3), 77–84.

Appadurai, A. 1996. *Modernity at Large: Cultural Dimensions of Globalisation*. Minneapolis: University of Minnesota Press.

Bell, D., and Kennedy, B. M. (Eds.). 2000. *The Cybercultures Reader*. London: Routledge.

Berlant, L., and Warner, M. 1998. "Sex in Public." *Critical Inquiry* 24(Winter), 547–566.

Berry, C., Martin, F., and Yue, A. 2003. *Mobile Cultures: New Media in Queer Asia*. Durham, NC: Duke University Press.

Binnie, J. 1995. "Trading Places: Consumption, Sexuality, and the Production of Queer Space," in D. Bell and G. Valentine (Eds.), *Mapping Desire: Geographies of Sexualities* (pp. 182–199). London: Routledge.

Boone, J. A., Dupuis, M., Meeker, M., Quimby, K., Sarver, C., Silverman, D., et al. (Eds.). 2000. *Queer Frontiers: Millennial Geographies, Genders, and Generations*. Madison: University of Wisconsin Press.

Butler, J. 1990. *Gender Trouble*. New York: Routledge.

Campbell, J. E. 2005. "Outing PlanetOut: Surveillance, Gay Marketing and Internet Affinity Portal." *New Media and Society* 7(5), 663–683.

Case, S. E. 1999. *The Domain Matrix: Performing Lesbian at the End of Print Culture*. Bloomington: Indiana University Press.

Chasin, A. 2000. *Selling Out: The Gay and Lesbian Movement Goes to Market.* New York: Palgrave.

Chauncey, G. 1994. *Gay New York: Gender, Urban Culture, and the Making of the Gay Male World, 1890–1940.* New York: Basic Books.

Dery, M. (Ed.). 1994. *Flame Wars.* Durham, NC: Duke University Press.

Eng, D. L., Halberstam, J., and Munoz, J. E. 2005. "What's Queer about Queer Studies Now?" *Social Text 23*(1), 1–17.

Gamson, J. 1998. *Freaks Talk Back.* Chicago: University of Chicago Press.

Gamson, J. 2003. "Gay Media, Inc.: Media Structures, the New Gay Conglomerates, and Collective Sexual Identities," in M. McCaughey and M. Ayers (Eds.), *Cyberactivism: Critical Theories and Practices of Online Activism* (pp. 255–278). New York: Routledge.

Gamson, J., and Moon, D. 2004. "The Sociology of Sexualities: Queer and Beyond." *Annual Review of Sociology 30*, 47–64.

Gill, R. 2002. "Cool, Creative and Egalitarian? Exploring Gender in Project Based New Media Work in Europe." *Information, Communication and Society 5*(1), 70–89.

Kearney, M. C. 2004. "Recycling Judy and Corliss: Transmedia Exploitation and the First Teen-Girl Production Trend." *Feminist Media Studies 4*(3), 265–295.

Munt, S. R., and Medhurst, A. (Eds.). 1997. *Lesbian and Gay Studies: A Critical Introduction.* London: Cassell.

Rothenberg, T. 1995. "'And She Told Two Friends': Lesbians Creating Urban Social Space," in D. Bell and Gill Valentine (Eds.), *Mapping Desire: Geographies of Sexualities* (pp. 165–181). London: Routledge.

Sedgwick, E. K. 1990. *Epistemology of the Closet.* Berkeley: University of California Press.

Sender, K. 2001. "Gay Readers, Consumers, and a Dominant Gay Habitus: 25 Years of the Advocate Magazine." *Journal of Communication 51*(1), 73–99.

Silver, D. 2004. "Internet/cyberculture/digital culture/new media/fill-in-the-blank studies." *New Media & Society 6*(1), 55–64.

Stone, A. R. 1995. *The War of Desire and Technology at the Close of the Mechanical Age.* Cambridge, MA: MIT Press.

Valentine, G. 1993. "Negotiating and Managing Multiple Sexual Identities: Lesbian Time-Space Strategies." *Transactions of the Institute of British Geographers, NS 18*, 237–248.

Wakeford, N. 1997. "Cyberqueer," in S. R. Munt and A. Medhurst (Eds.), *The Lesbian and Gay Studies Reader: A Critical Introduction* (pp. 20–38). London: Cassell. (Reprinted in Bell, D. and Kennedy, B. M. (Eds.). 2000. *The Cybercultures Reader* (pp. 403–415). London: Routledge.)

Woodland, R. 2000. "Queer Spaces, Modem Boys and Pagan Statues," in D. Bell and B. M. Kennedy (Eds.), *The Cybercultures Reader* (pp. 416–431). London: Routledge.

Yep, G. A., Lovaas, K., and Elia, J. P. (Eds.). 2004. *Queer Theory and Communication: From Disciplining Queers to Queering the Disciplines.* Binghampton, NY: Harrington Park.

Part I
Theoretical Landscapes

1. *Queer Theories and Cybersubjects: Intersecting Figures*

Kate O'Riordan

Introduction

This chapter examines the terms "cyber" and "queer" as they have been put together in theoretical contexts, and areas of cultural production and practice. It traces this coupling of cyber and queer through academic texts, films, novels, and internet sites, drawing partly on Nina Wakeford's synthesis of how these terms relate to each other (Wakeford 1997). The chapter examines this coupling and provides an elucidation of the collisions and collusions of figures, theories, and practices. It examines cyber and queer as utopian metaphors, discursive formations, figurations, and practices that intersect across particular sites and looks at the points at which cyber and queer become conflated or mapped onto each other. It attempts not only to disaggregate some of these conflations and elisions, but also to outline the ways in which these couplings have been productive.

At the heart of this analysis is a bid to consider ways that cyber and queer discourses have offered/produced subjectivities, both as identities and as imagined positions; the chapter thus examines cyber/queer figures, outlining their appearance and disappearance, and foregrounding the points at which such subjects have got stuck, and produced points of closure. The argument that I wish to make is that the productive coupling of these two discourses, of the terms cyber and queer, may be as much a stumbling block as a facilitator in helping to investigate and theorize this nexus.

The first part of the chapter outlines the context of this work and introduces some of the ways that cyber and queer subjects have been figured in film, novels, CMC, and theory. This is followed by an introduction to some of the points at which these might be said to *get stuck* together, which is to say that I introduce points where this coupling begins to produce closure, rather than opening up new possibilities. Building on this, the main part of the chapter focuses on queer theory, and, in particular, how cybersubjects have played through cybercultures. The last part looks at the ways in which these discourses have sticking points, and then turns to the more productive legacies of these collisions and collusions.

Contexts, Figures, and Sticking Points

During the early to mid-1990s in Britain, the repercussions of queer theory were being constituted across academic feminism and lesbian and gay studies. At the same time the internet was emerging as an important area of study and a key structuring device for academic networks. Queer was simultaneously developed through activist allegiances where it has continued to have significance. This chapter provides an overview of some of the intersections of cyber and queer imaginaries, figures, and theories in this period. It examines their figurations across a range of sites including academic theory, cultural production, and subcultural practices. Throughout this overview attention is paid to the tensions produced in figuring the subjects of queer— a paradoxically "subjectless" (Butler 1998) critique—that also coheres around imagined and material bodies. The figuring of cybersubjects and their production across multiple sites also hinges on the tension of the simultaneously subjectless and embodied possibilities of such figures. Abstractions and distractions in the discourses of queer and cybersubjectivity are also worked through in this chapter to elucidate the different operations across these sites. This chapter attempts to avoid the reiteration or valorization of such abstractions and seeks to clarify the way that these terms (cyber and queer) have been figured across many sites and continue to haunt practices and analyses of technologies of communication and identity. There have been many permutations, some more symbolic and some more material, of queer and cyber. Cyber subjects, and queer subjects, have figured in a range of different sites including films, novels, newspaper and magazine articles, television documentaries and dramas, internet sites, and academic theory. These figurations occurred, in the 1990s, through visual production, textual production and performance and have operated across academic theory and niche and mass-market cultural production. Cybersubjects have been figured more predominantly in mass-market forms such as Hollywood film (*The Net, The Matrix*) while cyber/queer subjects have remained marginal figures more commonly found in niche market forms such as independent film (e.g., *Dandy Dust, Teknolust*) and academic theory (e.g., Morton 1995; Wakeford 1997).

In addition to being figured through multiple media forms, queer and cybersubjects can be understood as being produced through specific material practices. For example, cyber subjects have been produced through the practices of, representations, and identification with, hacking, computer programming, Web design, Web using, and browsing. They can also be understood to be produced through corporeal enrollment and consumption through prosthetics and wearables such as VR devices, prosthetic limbs, and Bluetooth headsets. Queer subjects can be understood as being produced through practices of, and identification with, sex acts, desires, activism, space, reading practices, and participation. Queers are also produced through corporeal and spatial enrolment (sex acts, bookshops, clubs, urban areas), the consumption of prosthetics such as sex toys, and practices of bodily modification such as sex reassignment. Cyber/queer operates at the intersections of these sets of practices.

These intersections and the layering of figurations, and of subjects constituted through material and corporeal practices, produce complex sociomaterial discourses through which queer/cyber subjects are mobilized. Queer/cyber subjects are figured through niche market media texts with limited circuits of production and consumption. Queer/cyber subjects have been understood as being produced through those practices where digital media and queer cultures intersect and are produced through each other. Cyber/queer subjects have been produced then through the interstices and intersections of figurations and embodied users.

Sites of cyber/queer production include academic and theoretical writing such as Donald Morton's (1995) "The Birth of the Cyberqueer" and Nina Wakeford's (1997) "Cyberqueer." The cyberqueer has been figured in films such as *Dandy Dust* (1998), *IKU* (2000), and *Teknolust* (2002). It is also figured through installation work such as "The Brandon Project" (Shu Lea Cheang). Novels such as *Nearly Roadkill, Trouble and Her Friends,* and *Prozac Highway* also provide figurations of cyber/queer subjects. Cyberfeminism and cyberpunk have provided their moments of intersection with this nexus through work by science fiction writers such as Melissa Scott. Kathy Acker and Sadie Plant's writings both operate across the boundaries of theory and fiction and produce points of identification with, and alienation from cyber/queer figures; the user metaphors of the 1990s like "webgrrl" and "razorgrrl" also invoke a cyber/queer subject and at such moments cyberfeminisms and cyber/queer directly intersect.

The temporal overlap in the 1990s and the co-participation in queer theory and cybercultures meant that individuals who were recognized as activists, advocates, and academics in relation to queer, were often also implicated in cybercultures. Such individuals include Kate Bornstein, Pat Califia, Shu Lea Cheang, Sandy Stone, Del La Grace Volcano, and Nina Wakeford. Academic activity in relation to feminism and studies of science and technology has also been figured as pertaining to queer ways of knowing (e.g., cyber and cyborg feminisms).

There has been a particular stickiness (Haraway 1997) to the intersection of cyber/queer in the mid-1990s, foregrounded by Nina Wakeford when she reflected on what—if anything—cyber and queer might add to each other (Wakeford 1997). This stickiness although productive in the sense in which Haraway (1997: 68) uses it, I would suggest, leads in places to both cyber and queer becoming elided in particular ways, that is to say it loses its stickiness in becoming stuck. If queer is to be thought of as a dynamic political force, I would suggest that it has also had its points of stutter and stasis. If the figuration of cybersubjects provided sticky ways of thinking through and reconfiguring confrontations with technology, then it also provided ways of becoming stuck in relation to communication technology.

The way in which this movement from stickiness, to stuck, occurs is in the mapping of one thing on to the other so that there is no room for further openings. Rather than see this as a "simplistic" (Wakeford 1997) operation, the mapping of cyber on to queer and vice versa can be seen as an elaborate detailing of the ways in which cyber/queer is performative, work that betrays an anxious desire to make performativity mean "expressive." To use the cybersubject to exemplify performativity, for example, is to create such a sticking point that requires suturing and closure to shut it down, where the subjectless valence of performativity will always be in excess of a subject. Taking a theoretical framework and using a set of practices or a specific formation to map out that framework provides, I would suggest, a circularity and a point of closure that doesn't allow for further opening up and blunts theoretical tools. The work of suturing two things together too closely and attempting to perform a kind of seamlessness in the coupling creates a stumbling block to movement. This kind of collusion occurs in relation to cyber and queer in a way analogous to the suturing of poststructuralism and hypertext (Landow 1992). The practices and forms of hypertext were used at points as evidence of the virtual materialization of poststructuralism. This mapping of one thing on to the other produces elision and conflation and refuses the nuances of dialectical play, where things refuse to correspond and have to be held in tension, thus refusing that which might be productive. The mapping of the cyber subject as and on to the queer subject has provided such a point of closure, as well as moments of productive slippage.

While the mid-1990s wasn't the beginning of cybercultural studies, internet research, or queer, it was a period of sustained attention and excitement in relation to identity and the Web, and equally deep skepticism as in the "birth of the cyberqueer" (Morton 1995). In this period, there were intense collisions and collaborations across queer theory and cyberculture, as the imagined ideal queer subject and the imagined ideal cybersubject were in some ways produced through each other and came to occupy the same ground. Paradoxically, the simultaneous disavowal of the very idea of the subject came from theorists of performativity and queer at the same time (Butler 1998). It is these figurings of the intersecting (ideal) queer and cyber subjects, and the encounters of queer bodies and internet communication that are central to thinking about the context of current cyber/queer formations and disruptions. These figures continue to haunt current formations in both productive and destructive ways.

Cyber/queer subjects can be thought of in terms of the historical production of utopias. As Maren Hartmann argues, all technologies come with attendant utopias (Hartmann 2004) and the intersection of queer and cyber can be seen as the intersection of two promissory discourses, which unfold through utopian thinking about technological futures. Cyber and queer can both be seen as terms that are metaphorical in origin, ways of imagining reconfigured futures that have become discursively diffuse, shaping and describing ways to think about identity and communication. However as Hartmann argues in relation to the user metaphors of cyberspace, at some point metaphors that emerge in relation to radical change become avenues for archaeology (Hartman 2004: 4). Like Hartmann's user types, cyber and queer are set of "possible ways of articulating and interpreting the *utopian dialectic* between the "what is" and "what could be" (Hartmann 2004: 5), although I interpret utopian as what cannot be, but what can be imagined as part of a hopeful politics. Queer and cyber emerged in the same time frames, as ways of thinking about the present through the future and as attempts at reconfiguring materiality. It is these emergences and the legacies of these moments that are examined here.

Queer Theory and Queer Subjects

Queer is a multivalent signifier and while I attempt to provide some disaggregation of this here it would be counterproductive to unpack queer into individual LGBTI categories. Queer is different from the sum of these and is ill-served by such reduction. Maintaining the tension of subject and subjectless is one of the challenges of working with queer framings. I understand queer to be a subjectless critique (Butler 1998) and a political and theoretical force, as well as an intersection of identities. Simultaneously, queer adheres to and is produced through bodies, experiences and practices. These two levels—critique and embodiment—also intersect.

CMC has provided one form in which queer bodies produce and are produced through queer texts and queer cultural production. Celebrated and visible instances of this occur in the work of Shu Lea Cheang and Sandy Stone, among others. Potentially more mundane or everyday instances of this intersection occur in the newsgroups, listservs, home pages, and blogs of queer identified individuals and groups of users.

Queer emerged in relation to CMC in the 1990s, and the mobility and materiality of both forms is important in this mutual production (Berry et al. 2003) but it is equally important to stress that this is not the only co-incidental site. In this analysis I am focusing on the intersections of queer and CMC (and other permutations of CMC including networked communication and digital media). This is however an artificial cut, which allows me to bring the intersection of queer and cyber into focus but leaves much unsaid, particularly around the development of queer in relation to feminism and lesbian and gay studies. While some of the chapters in this book help to address this erasure, this chapter remains a partial contribution to a set of much larger conversations.

Many assertions, promises, descriptions, and definitions have been produced in relation to queer theory. This chapter does not seek to expand these even further, however it does seek to revisit and examine how queer theory has intersected with cybercultural studies and what has been productive and destructive about those encounters. Thinking about queer and cyber theories, about fifteen years into their respective (re)formations, demands both an examination of how theory travels, and what it does in that traveling, and a consideration of how particular moments and formations have occurred within those changing contexts.

Queer theory has always been a deliberately slippery set of formations, strategically attempting to avoid closed signification and remaining "subjectless," although not "frictionless" (to appropriate and disavow Stablie's critique of poststructuralist feminism (Stabile 1994)). There is a material ethics to refusing fixity. The capacity for queer to be part of a dynamic force for critique and activism has been evidenced in the past and continues to be powerful (Eng et al. 2005). To cut out one moment, the role of queer activism in the mobilization against the G8 meeting in Scotland in 2005, for example, has a particular significance and specificity within anti-capitalist assemblages where heroic heterosexual masculinity has become a dominant frame. In the words of Jasbir K. Puar, "Queer times require even queerer modalities of thought" (2005: 121). In our current times when the "normalisation" of discrimination, torture, and war continue to be the business of global politics, an investment in queer resources seems ever more urgent. Queering the subject of the "war on terror," for example, can be used to illuminate "the production of normative patriot bodies that cohere against and through queer terrorist corporalities" (Puar 2005: 124). Thinking about the horror of these bodies with those of the bodies of murdered transpeople in the United States can produce a sense of the ways in which the world has radically changed in the last fifteen years, the ways in which it has remained almost entirely the same, and the ways in which there have been returns to politics once thought to be in the past. That these things can coexist—future, present, and past, fixed and unfixable, changed and unchanged—points toward the imperative for the dynamic possibilities of queer theories and queer methodologies to be developed as sharp tools.

Queer, like other modes of thought and action, has had its destructive potential, capacity to elide, silence and suppress, evoke false hopes; and facile and destructive operations have also occurred. The nihilism and disgust that can be read into *No Future* (Edelman 2005), for example, toward queer and straight bodies and the explicit misogyny produced through the horror of the reproductive body could support the speculation that queer has collapsed under the weight of its own vacuous narcissism. However, the simultaneous production of queer intersectionality with epistemology and methodology (Wakeford 2004; Phillips this volume) and the war on terror (Puar 2005) signals further the power of queer's capacity to be used to dynamically effect, and to sometimes escape, the closures of circularity.

Cyber Theories and Subjects

In the same way that it is problematic, but important to articulate the subjectless valence of queer, especially in relation to its historical specificity, there is a paradoxical and intensely fragile tension in attempting to excavate cybersubjects. Simultaneously more materially elusive and more discursively visible than queer subjects, the figuring of cybersubjects has nonetheless had productive and pervasive effects. Like the figuration of queer subjects, at moments the cybersubject has stood in for postmodernism and been figured as a particular kind of exemplar. Studies of self-identified cyber subjects (Terranova 1996) through subcultural groups such as hackers (Taylor 1999) and the cultural production around the technoculture of the 1990s reproduced versions of cybersubjectivity that were both valorized (hackers) and mythic (transhuman). Discourses of transhumanism (e.g., Pepperell 1997) pervaded the 1990s cultural productions of the technoculture such as *Wired,* and cyberpunk, and have found institutional approval today in the shape of such departments as the "Oxford Institute for the Future of Humanity."

The cybersubject has been figured through the fantastic imagery of the transhuman, the cyborg and cyberspace, and through the mundane imagery of the cyborg as humans as we already are (Haraway 1991). Thus, cybersubjects are multiple figures intersecting with discourses of transhumanism, informatics and code, and those of embodiment and intersectionality. An aspect of the cybersubject as figured through Stone—whose work provides many coincidental points in the collisions and collaborations of queer and cyber—is the insistence (against the enclosure of the subject (Stone 1996))

that identity is multiple and fluid—or at least is in process, and is simultaneously material and immaterial. An effect and source of cyber subject formations has been an aggregate attention to the idea of the self as inchoate, an
incontinent project in process, developed by Sigmund Freud, as opposed to
the legal liberal subject, required by regimes of governance, to be produced
through the mechanisms of nation states. In this sense cybersubjects have
been produced through a queer frame of subjectlessness. However, they have
often been dislocated from intersections with race, class, gender, and sexuality; and cybersubjects have often been figured as/through images of domination such as the masquerade of the universal transhuman (Moravec 1988;
Pepperrell 1997) and the disembodied "point of view" of knowledge producing masculinity (Hayles 1999).

The cybersubject has appeared as a productive force through moments of
material self-realization and through the operations of figuration. In the
cyberpunk novels of the 1980s and 1990s the unstable and changing cybersubject is the anti-hero mobilizing social change and resistance (Gibson
1984; Scott 1994). This imagined role has also played out in relation to
hacking and anti-capitalist subcultures, especially at the point of their convergence, and particularly in the media imaginary, these narratives of hacker
as hero perhaps reached their mass-market apex in *The Matrix* trilogy. While
the queer as hero has not had quite such mass-market appeal (arguably the
UK television drama "Queer as Folk" is an exception), and the cyberqueers
of texts such as *Trouble and Her Friends* (1994), *Nearly Road Kill* (1996),
and *Dandy Dust* (1998) have only ever reached small audience groups.

The full permutations and diversity of cybersubjects would be impossible
to map here but it is worth noting a little more of this diversity. McKenzie
Wark's "trans-individual" is another kind of cyber subject, and one that he
argues is beyond the understanding of "the cyber-lib. mind" (Stanley and
Wark 1997). This argument sets up an interesting juxtaposition between the
transhuman individual of "cyberlibertarianism" (e.g., Moravec 1988), which
intensifies individualism, and the potential trans-subjectivity invoked by
Wark, which intensifies intersectionality. Wark's version hopes for a trans-
subjectivity that moves beyond a model of individuals locked into endless dialogue to something closer to a productive coexistence of intersectionality
(Stanley and Wark 1997). Hartmann's vision of multiple "user metaphors"
elucidates the coexistence of cyberflaneuses, webgrrls, cyberpunks, netizens,
cybernauts, and surfers as coexisting potential cybersubjectivities. I draw on
these elucidations to attend to the multiple ways in which cybersubjects have
been imagined and experienced, and the ways in which these figures are
always connected to thinking about the future.

However, while the cybersubject has been an inspirational figure with
promise for some, it has also produced elision, silence, and suppression,

evoked false hopes, and facile and destructive operations. The representations of a particular U.S.-based, white, middle-class masculinity, in relation to this subject position and the reiteration of privileged and arrogant views from nowhere (Haraway 1997), have been destructive forces. As well as this reiteration there has also been an ongoing recycling of assertions, and repeated returns, such as the kind of identity tourism critiqued by Lisa Nakamura (2002). A significant point of getting stuck is the compulsive return to the idea that identity is more fluid and radically different online than off and that this can be voluntaristically "toured" through. This repeated return has been a significant stumbling block, and a point of getting stuck in the potential to claim the productive dynamism of these subjects and figures. One of the destructive forces in figurations of the cybersubject is this persistent circulation of tourist differentiation (on-/offline). Cybersubjects can promise a radical difference and disjuncture between new media forms and other forms, but it is at this point that they begin to be stretched beyond use and operate as an abstract distraction.

Sticky Intersections: Sticking Points

Susan Stryker's discussion of "the transsexual timebomb" (Stryker 1999) can be read as part of queer theory's production, and critique, of the trans figure as the ideal queer subject for this subjectless theoretical frame. While Turkle's (1997) narratives about the self and the screen can be perhaps read as exemplary of a particular kind of transpersonalism and identity play, Wark's conceptualization of transindividualism was also developed and circulated in the same period as a counter to the transhuman of "cyber libertarianism." Thus, in specific moments queer and cyber theory are constituted through each other in the production of a "trans" subject. This is possibly most clearly imagined in the work of Kate Bornstein, both in (1998) *My Gender Workbook* and also particularly in her fictional collaboration with Caitlin Sullivan (1996) *Nearly Roadkill: An Infobahn Erotic Adventure*. Another constituent literary moment includes Melissa Scott's (1994) *Trouble and Her Friends*. This literary, and later filmic constitution, and the simultaneous conflation of the queer and cyber subjects through a generalized trans subject can also be linked to the location of queer and cyber in the textual. Queer theory has been dominated by a disciplinary location in the humanities and although "cyberqueer" via Nina Wakeford is a sociological move, "the birth of the cyberqueer" (Morton 1995) has a specifically literary genealogy.

One of the intersections between queer/cyber occurred at the point of "trans" in its multiple significations, figurations, and subjects. In the case of queer theory this was around transgender and transsexuality (Stryker/Stone), and in the case of cybertheory transindividualism/transhumanism

(Wark/Moravec). While conceptual developments around theatre (Laurel 1993), identity play (Turkle 1997), identity workshops (Bruckman 1992) and transindividualism (Wark 1997) in relation to networked computing and digital production had some force in shaping how CMC and the internet were, and continue to be understood; transgender and transsexuality became the focal point for lines of development and dispute across feminisms and queer theories, especially around the figure of the transwomen. As Claire Hemmings (2002) points out, in using the transsexual subject as both the ideal center and the boundary marker for queer, a disaggregation of transgender and transsexual occurs where the former is reclaimed as queer and the latter is expunged from queer as too heterosexual. In Judith Halberstam's ftm (1998) construction, the moments where trans can be read as so plastic that it is almost applicable to anything, the collapsing point of cyber/and queer becomes apparent. It is at this point where all figures lose their specificity and all subjects become equally (empty) that specificity is collapsed, and the potential for meaning starts to be evacuated. When figures and subjects evoke such universality that they can be exported and imported across all sites without changing meaning, I would suggest that they start to be exhausted.

Although transgender and transsexuality have been significant in the cyber/queer intersection, both the cases of transgender (and that of lesbian feminism) expose the problematic tensions of the fluid identity paradigm. Although transgender is a theoretically fluid subject; the experience of transsexuality is often that of an essential identity. Lesbian feminism is also often expressed through a policing of the borders of the categories of women and lesbian. The capacity for either of these positions to be encapsulated in a queer formation is limited and contingent. Although the theoretical model of transgender is made to articulate the ideal queer subject (Hemmings 2002), trans experience is not only or always queer. It is possible to experience trans through a heterosexual narrative of desire and becoming, as it is possible to experience lesbian identity through an antagonistically anti-queer frame.

Although there have been assumptions about the freedom of the cyber-subject to perform an identity of choice online, there have simultaneously been continued anxieties about authenticity online. One of the archetypal cyber myths, which underscores this anxiety most clearly, is the oft cited tale of Joan the disabled woman whose experience of embodiment turns out to be that of an able bodied man (Stone 1996). Transsexual narratives (Johnson 2001; Prosser 1998) problematize the correlations made between embodied experience and authentic identity in this paradigm because it is often the case that a trans person experiences the body as the site of deceit (e.g., wrong body narratives) and identifies an articulated identity, separated from the morphology of the body, as the site of authenticity (Johnson 2001; Prosser 1998). The cyber-anxiety around reclaiming bodily morphology as the site of authentic identity, coupled with transsexual narratives about authentic identity being dislocated from the shape of the body effects a series of tensions between both the positioning of online media as a site of gender play, and the experience of transgender subjects such as transsexuals, for whom embodied experience is precisely the problem.

Coincidences

However, while these discourses and figures collide and collaborate, and figures proliferate and travel; communities of interest and practices have continued to form alongside and despite such oscillations. Thus communication through the internet has continued to sustain and produce queer community formations, despite the assumptions of gender-swapping and play which might have undermined such crucially embodied entities (Turkle 1997). The spectacular cyberqueer has been reconfigured through a diffuse set of everyday practices and networks, although still haunting these formations.

"Soc.motss" and the multiple formations that have both flourished and collapsed online since 1983 are evidence of these everyday practices. "Soc.motss," was first set up as net.motss in 1983, and then changed to soc.motss when the USENET hierarchies were reformed in the mid-1980s (1987). The history of soc.motss is well documented by the group and the archives preserve the first posting as well as birthday postings fifteen years on. While there has been other commentary on this formation (Wakeford 1997) it is worth returning to it in this context.

"Motss" is an instance of queering the online gay scene, with its' ambiguous title, thought to help keep the group gay-centered rather than attracting negative attention and heterosexual voyeurism (although this naming was not initially voluntary). However, the use of "non-heterosexual" and "Lesbian, Gay, Bisexual, Trans and Others (LGBTO)," the mixed genders of the group, and the ambiguous "motss" label, contribute toward a queer formation. This occurs through the appearance of queer as a space of possibility rather than another "gay" label. This relatively early example of queer online community seemed to vindicate the promises of new beginnings in cyberspace as it created a queer virtual arena that was more than the sum of lesbian and gay. This is important in terms of thinking about cyberqueer because it contributes toward a focus on what *is* produced through new social formations. CMC did not produce an ontological break but there was some epistemic production through such reformulations. One of those has been an increased capacity to produce, and question, queer formations through a global, or at least international, context.

The cybercultural studies of the late 1980s and early 1990s are often characterized as "cyberhype." Later "second generation" (Silver 2000) cyber discourses still retained the influences of this hyperbole and individualized essentialism (Plant 1998). Essentialist accounts of disembodiment such as those apparent in Turkle's narratives of gender experimentation in the 1990s (Turkle 1997) can be a destructive force in thinking about cyberqueer because they potentially evacuate power from accounts of identity. This occurs through a stress on identity as voluntary. This imbalance where agency appears primary, and the simultaneous over determination attributed to the technology characterized some of the cultural production of the 1990s. Although it is also noticeable that when cyberhype is attributed it becomes elusive to pin down and it is sometimes set up as a straw figure. Some critics whose work has been labeled as cyberhype or "technomaniac" (Stabile 1994) are much more careful in their analysis or mode of engagement than the accusation allows for. However, the consistent circulation of a disembodied figuration of voluntary cybersubjectivity simultaneously undermines the importance of embodied experience, which is central to identity politics, and queer as a political figure.

An additional assault was made upon the productive capacity of cyberqueer by the post-1994 commercialization of the Web, and with it, the capacity of late capitalism and its technologized infrastructures to further commodify identity politics through niche marketing. The development of online media monopolies, marketing their portals as "communities" is documented by Joshua Gamson (2003) through the emergence of PlanetOut and the mainstreaming of lesbian and gay as consumer groups. This account of the economic infrastructures of online queer media portals provides a way of tempering the utopian thinking that can go with cyber/queering and complimenting it with a sense of the economic and regulatory location, elements sometimes missing in accounts of queer digital media consumption and production. It importantly underscores the production of such subjects through technologized systems of capital.

However, as documented in Jonathan Alexander's (2002) "Queer Webs" and in several other studies since (e.g., Berry et al. 2003), including those in this book, there has been a proliferation of queer communication, community, and activism online since the emergence of the commercial Web. As with offline queer spaces the boys appear to have more of it. In the more mass-market sectors queer is used as a rhetorical strategy to expand the gay market. "Gaydar," which has become the premier meeting service in the UK, is very much a boy's toy, and has also branded itself at points as the "king of queer." The alternative—"Gaydar Girls"—although commercially viable, is a much less generic service in queer communities in the UK. As with offline communities, the problem of identity categories, sex segregation, and transgender have also come into conflict in the policing of community online. More flexible than the infamous Michigan Women's Music Festival's "women born women" only policy, several feminist discussion forums decided (after deliberation) to allow transwomen "in" to the women-only online "space." Thus, it appeared that more divergent and less hierarchical queer community formations might sometimes be facilitated by online communication and contribute to "rainbow" coalitions offline. Effectively, it seemed that internet based communication networks might get around the "sex wars" over pornography/SM on one hand, and trans/the category of women on the other. In other words it seemed possible at times that queer formations could be produced through and produce networks that might hold the possibility of dialectic tensions without always necessitating painful collapse.

The work of Shu Lea Cheang is also important in the proliferation of cyberqueer subjects and both the *Brandon Exhibition* and *IKU* are significant moments in the cultural productions of cyber/queer intersections. Jacobs argues of *IKU* that

> I.K.U. critiques the emergence of upwardly mobile transnational queer viewers who escape in electronically mediated transgressions of race, gender and nationality without becoming part of activist communities. (Jacobs 2003: 219)

Cheang's earlier work the Brandon Exhibition, the first online exhibition hosted by the Guggenheim, also marks a particular moment in the productive intersections of queer and cyber. This political project centered on the case of Brandon Teena, a transman who was raped and murdered in Nebraska in 1993. It is important to note that many of the explorations of cyber/queer relate to visual culture as well as being textually realized. Stone, Cheang, and Wark, for example, are dealing with a visual arts framework and all, in different ways, experiment with visual culture and production. The potential for the visual to supplement (or circumvent) the textual and provide different ways of knowing and communicating materiality, virtuality, and bodies is part of the contribution of this visual work, which has provided an alternative framework to the textual, and in some ways one less prone to closure. Although also celebratory and elitist, the attempts by visual artists to experiment with cyberqueer in the early and mid-1990s indicated moments where promise and critique worked together. In addition to the Brandon Exhibition already mentioned, the "Cyberqueer" event of 1994, in New York, part of the Gay and Lesbian Experimental Film Festival, promised "discussion and debate about digital queerness" and invited participants to "share a critique" as well as "ride (. . .) in a virtual landscape of desire" (Stryker 1994).

The theatres of MUDs and MOOs, and other multi-user domains (e.g., online gaming), both textual and graphic, have been explored as the sites where both online community and identity play can work in tandem (Bruckman 1992; Reid 1996; Schaap 2002). In these instances identity play is often the premise of the community, where character authoring is a skill. Alternatively, game playing may be the skill, while an assumed character is part of the play. While some of these environments have facilitated the expression of multiple or experimental genders (e.g., "per" as an alternative form of "his" or "her") or the anthropomorphism of other animals and objects, gender definition and sexuality remain important identifiers and players often narrate experiences of being continually asked to "reveal" their actual identity in this respect (Bassett 1997). What also emerges from studies of graphic avatar communities is that visually stereotypical sexed bodies are used as frequently and often more dominantly than experimental or avant-garde avatars (Taylor 2002).

Thus, although the ideal cybersubject as fluid and the ideal queer subject as fluid converge in fictions such as Sullivan and Bornstein's and critique's such as Turkle's, there is more evidence to suggest that online queer communities are stratified into fixed identity hierarchies (Munt et al. 2002), and anxiety about bodily identity is a strong determinant in online queer formations. To take the example of gaydar, which predominantly serves gay men, it is clear that embodied experience and online image correlations are the foundation of the gaydar process. An object of engaging with the "Gaydar" exercise is often to meet in person and to experience embodied sex. To this end the "Gaydar" profile is subject to a strict hierarchy of categorization and objectification and a photograph is an important factor in the process of self-constitution (Mowlabocus 2004). On "Gaydar Girls" the list of choices to self-select gender and sexuality categories are highly limited and prescriptive, and "queer" is not a designated category—thus even at this level, remaining a subjectless critique (Butler 1998).

There are several important tensions that run through cyber/queer politics, experience, and theory. The cybersubject, assumed as a fluid performative freed from embodied constraints (e.g., Wark's the trans-individual), intersects with the ideal queer subject as trans, bisexual (Hemmings 2002). This intersection is both a collision and collusion in that it produces a series of tensions with simultaneously utopian and dystopic network effects. The queer subject assumed as a fluid pansexual, bi- or trans subject appears to map on to the cybersubject assumed as free flowing and elective, in an illusion of virtual materialism. However, at the center of the ideal cybersubject runs an anxiety over authenticity, reproduced at the site of embodiment through which existence is "warranted in the body politic" (Stone 1996: 65). At the center of the ideal queer subject is a fluidity rarely experienced by queer subjects who are more likely to identify through one of the choices on the queer identity menu. The "queerest" identity in the hierarchy, trans, is embodied in transsexual subjects who are neither necessarily queer nor experience bodies that are the authentic site of their identity and who have been repudiated through some queer approaches (Hemmings 2002). These tensions continue to operate as hauntings and as explicit figures in contemporary engagements with what might be called queer technopractices (Karl this volume).

The successful formation of online queer communities has also fragmented into prescriptive identity menus, which serve commercial marketing purposes as much as they are expressive (Gamson 2003). In terms of numbers and commercial viability, the portals of PlantOut, Gaydar, and the Blue Room (Diva Online) with their select and click identity menus are the contemporary sites of online queer identity formation. However, Soc.motss, for example, is still around and operates in an independent parallel to these monopolies. Multiple sites such as newsgroups, home pages, e-mail lists, zines, activist and fetish sites, MUDS, MOOs, IRC, IM blogs, and journals also operate alongside commercial formations and beyond the frame of the fluid cybersubject, and the individual and community negotiation and constitution of identity operate in these multiple sites, intersecting with the ongoing politics of queer.

The collisions and collusions that I hope to have articulated here are those of the repeated openings and closures around queer and cyber, and the structuring residues of the intersection of cyber/queer in the mid-1990s. Where performativity unfolded across both the ideal cybersubject, and the ideal queer subject, subjecting identity and community to a legacy of productive and destructive forces that have made heavy assaults on what it means to be queer online. My argument here is that it is important to think about the legacies of cyber/queer when thinking about contemporary intersections of queer and communication technologies and networks. What can be drawn from these legacies are strategies to avoid circularity and closure. What I hope to produce from this is a set of reminders that too perfect a coupling between theories, practices, and cultural forms can end up in closures and stumbling points. It is in providing strategies for keeping the tensions and spaces required for dialectical intersections open, that one of the important aspects of queer lies.

References

Alexander, J. 2002. "Homo-Pages and Queer Sites: Studying the Construction and Representation of Queer Identities on the World Wide Web." *The International Journal of Sexuality and Gender Studies* 7(2/3), 85–106.

Bassett, C. 1997. "Virtually Gendered: Life in an Online World," in K. Gelder and S. Thornton (Eds.), *The Subcultures Reader* (pp. 537–556). London and New York: Routledge.

Berry, C., Martin, F., and Yue, A. 2003. *Mobile Culture: New Media in Queer Asia.* Durham, NC, and London: Duke University Press.

Bornstein, K. 1998. *My Gender Workbook: How to Become the Kind of Man or Woman You Always Thought You Could Be . . . or Something Else Entirely.* London and New York: Routledge.

Bornstein, K., and Sullivan, C. 1996. *Nearly Roadkill: An Infobahn Erotic Adventure.* London: Serpent's Tail.

Bruckman, A. 1992. "Identity Workshop: Emergent Social and Psychological Phenomena in Text-Based Virtual Reality." Retrieved June 23, 2006, from http://www.cc.gatech.edu/fac/Amy.Bruckman/papers/index.html

Butler, J. 1998. *Bodies That Matter: On the Discursive Limits of "Sex."* London and New York: Routledge.

Campbell, J. E. 2004. *Getting It On Online: Cyberspace, Gay Male Sexuality, and Embodied Identity.* New York: Harrington Park Press.

Edelman, L. 2005. *No Future: Queer Theory and the Death Drive.* Durham, NC: Duke University Press.

Eng, D. L., Halberstam, J., and Munoz, J. E. 2005. "What's Queer About Queer Studies Now?" *Social Text 23*(1), 1–17.

Gamson, J. 2003. "Gay Media Inc. Media Structures, the New Gay Conglomerates and Collective Sexual Identities," in M. McCaughey and M. D. Ayers (Eds.), *Cyberactivism: Online Activism in Theory and Practice* (pp. 255–278). London: Routledge

Gauntlett, D. 1999. "Digital Sexualities. A Guide to Internet Resources." *Sexualities 2*(3), 327–332.

Gibson, W. 1984. *Neuromancer.* New York: Ace Books.

Halberstam, J. 1998. *Female Masculinity.* Durham, NC: Duke University Press.

Haraway, D. 1991. *Simians, Cyborgs and Women: The Reinvention of Nature.* London: Free Association Books.

Haraway, D. 1997. *Modest Witness: Feminism and Technoscience.* London and New York: Routledge.

Hartmann, M. 2004. *Technologies and Utopias: The Cyberflâneur and the Experience of Being Online.* Munich, Germany: Reinhard Fischer Verlag.

Hayles, K. N. 1999. *How We Became Posthuman: Virtual Bodies in Informatics, Literature and Cybernetics.* Chicago and London: University of Chicago Press.

Hemmings, C. 2002. *Bisexual Spaces: A Geography of Sexuality and Gender.* London and New York: Routledge.

Jacobs, K. 2003. "Queer Voyeurism and the Pussy-Matrix in Shu Lea Cheang's Japanese Pornography" in C. Berry, F. Martin, and A. Yue (Eds.), *Mobile Culture: New Media in Queer Asia* (pp 201–221). Durham, NC and London: Duke University Press.

Johnson, K. 2001. "Studying Transsexual Identity: A Discursive Approach," in F. Haynes and T. McKenna (Eds.), *Unseen Genders: Beyond the Binaries* (pp. 143–156). New York: Peter Lang.

Kibby, M., and Costello, B. 2001. "Between the Image and the Act: Interactive Sex Entertainment on the Internet." *Sexualities 4*(3), 353–369.

Landow, G. 1992. *Hypertext: Convergence of: Convergence of Contemporary Critical Theory and Technology.* Baltimore, MD: Johns Hopkins University Press.

Laurel, B. 1993. *Computers as Theatre.* New York: Addison Wesley.

McGlotten, S. 2001. "QueerSpace Is the Space of the Screen." *Text, Practice, Performance III 64,* 89.

Moravec, H. 1988. *Mind Children: Future of Robot and Human Intelligence.* Cambridge, MA: Harvard University Press.

Morton, D. 1995. "Birth of the Cyberqueer" *PLMA,* 110, New York: MLAA of America.

Mowlabocus, S. 2004. "Being Seen to Be Gay: User Profiles and the Construction of Gay Male Identity in Cyberspace." Paper delivered at Ubiquity? The Fifth Annual Conference of the Association of Internet Researchers, University of Sussex, Brighton, UK.

Munt, S., Bassett, E. H., and O'Riordan, K. 2002. "Virtually Belonging: Lesbian Identity and Coming Out Online." *The International Journal of Sexuality and Gender Studies* 7(2/3), 125–137.

Nakamura, L. 2002. *Cybertypes: Race, Ethnicity and Identity on the Internet.* London and New York: Routledge.

Pepperell, R. 1997. *The Posthuman Condition.* London: Intellect Books.

Plant, S. 1998. *Zeroes and Ones: Digital Women and the New Technoculture.* London: Fourth Estate.

Prosser, J. 1998. *Second Skins: Body Narratives of Transsexuality.* New York: Columbia University Press.

Puar, J. K. 2005. "Queer Times, Queer Assemblages." *Social Text 23*(1), 121–139.

Reid, E. 1996. "Text-Based Virtual Realities: Identity and the Cyborg Body," in P. Ludlow (Ed.), *High Noon on the Electronic Frontier: Conceptual Issues in Cyberspace* (pp. 327–346). Cambridge: MIT Press.

Schaap, F. 2002. *The Words That Took Us There: Ethnography in a Virtual Reality.* Amsterdam: Aksant Academic Publishers.

Scott, M. 1994. *Trouble and Her Friends.* New York: Tor Books.

Silver, D. 2000. "Looking Backwards, Looking Forwards Cyberculture Studies 1990–2000," in D. Gauntlett (Ed.), *Web.studies: Rewiring Media Studies for the Digital Age* (pp. 19–30). Oxford: Oxford University Press.

Stabile, C. 1994. *Feminism and the Technological Fix.* Manchester, UK and New York: Manchester University Press.

Stanley, C., and Wark, M. 1997. "Nettalk: An Interview with McKenzie Wark." Retrieved March 22, 1997, http://www.ljudmila.org/nettime

Stone, S. 1996. *The War of Desire and Technology at the Close of the Mechanical Age.* Cambridge, MA: MIT Press.

Stryker, B. 1994. Advertisement for "Cyberqueer" mix 94: Gay and Lesbian Experimental Film Festival, November 10–20, 1994, Anthology Film Archives, New York.

Stryker, S. 1999. "Christine Jorgensen's Atom Bomb: Transsexuality and the Emergence of Postmodernity," in E. Kaplan and S. Squiers (Eds.), *Playing Dolly: Technocultural Formations, Fantasies, and Fictions of Assisted Reproduction* (pp. 157–171). New Brunswick, NJ: Rutgers University Press.

Taylor, P. 1999. *Hackers: Crime in the Digital Sublime.* London and New York: Routledge.

Taylor, T. L. 2002. "Living Digitally: Embodiment in Virtual Worlds," in R. Schroeder (Ed.), *The Social Life of Avatars: Presence and Interaction in Shared Virtual Environments* (pp. 40–62). London: Springer-Verlag.

Turkle, S. 1997. *Life on the Screen: Identity in the Age of the Internet.* New York: Simon and Schuster.

Terranova, T. 1996. "Posthuman Unbounded," in G. Robertson (Ed.), *Future Natural* (pp. 165–180). New York: Routledge.

Wakeford, N. 1997. "Cyberqueer," in S. R. Munt and A. Medhurst (Eds.), *The Lesbian and Gay Studies Reader: A Critical Introduction* (pp. 20–38). London: Cassell.

Wakeford, N. 2004. *Queer Theory and Internet Research Keynote Session.* Paper delivered at Ubiquity? The Fifth Annual Conference of the Association of Internet Researchers, University of Sussex, Brighton, UK.

Films

Cheang, Shu Lea. (2000). *IKU*, Japan.

Hershman-Leeson, Lynn. (2002). *Teknolust*, USA/Germany/UK.

Scheirl, Hans. (1998). *Dandy Dust*, UK/Austria.

Wachowski, Andy, and Wachowski, Larry. (1999). *The Matrix*, USA.

Winkler, Irvin. (1995). *The Net*, USA.

2. Queering Surveillance Research

DAVID J. PHILLIPS AND CAROLYN CUNNINGHAM

In 2002, the *Wall Street Journal* published an article entitled "If TIVo thinks you are gay, here's how to set it straight." At the center of the story was the dilemma faced by Basil Iwanyk, a straight film studio executive who believed that his TIVo[1] thought he was gay, because it kept automatically recording gay-themed TV shows. Thinking he could outsmart his machine, Iwanyk overcompensated by obsessively recording hyper-masculine programs, such as history and war shows. Unfortunately, this convinced his TIVo that he was a neo-Nazi (Zaslow 2002).

This event had significant cultural salience, sparking, in addition to the *Wall Street Journal* article, subplots for at least two sitcom episodes and lots of blog commentary. In a sense, it can be seen as the closing bracket for one of the first popular comments on identity and the internet—the cartoon by Peter Steiner of a dog in front of a monitor, commenting to another dog "On the internet, no one knows you're a dog" (Steiner 1993). Together, these two cultural moments prompt a fascinating set of questions, including "Am I a dog?", "Who knows I'm a dog?", and "How did I get to be a dog?" Finally, one wonders, with Art McGee, "What's wrong with being a dog?" (McGee 1995).

In this chapter, we provide a political, theoretical, and methodological framework for approaching these questions. In particular, we argue for increased collaboration and conversation between scholars of queer theory, technology studies, and surveillance studies. Queer studies provide insights into how, with what resources, and to what effect social identities are performed. Surveillance studies lay the groundwork for understanding how information environments work and how they distribute resources for identity performance. Technology studies examine the material and cultural conditions under which infrastructures (that is, interlocking and interdependent systems of law, technique, economics, and culture) are developed and maintained. Together, they provide a framework both for understanding new modes of identity management and for intervening in those processes.

What's at Stake?

For decades, corporations have been using communication and computing technologies to track, represent, and analyze individual and group behavior. In 1978, the Claritas Corporation introduced PRIZM. This service gathered the census data for each postal (ZIP) code, then performed analyses to create statistical "clusters" of ZIP codes with similar demographics. Each of the sixty-six clusters was given a name, like "Bohemian Mix," "Blue Blood Estates," or "Shotguns and Pickups" (Claritas Corp. 2006; Larson 1992). Direct marketers could then be assured of the statistical likelihood that residents of a certain ZIP code would share certain demographic characteristics. They could decide which type of person they wanted to reach, and send mail only to the residents of the ZIP codes within clusters of that type. The PRIZM system is in some senses an archetype of surveillance, as this chapter understands the term. According to this understanding, surveillance is a process of knowledge production in which entities are uniquely identified, their activities tracked and recorded, those records analyzed for patterns and norms, and those norms applied back to individuals in the population. Through the census system, PRIZM gathers data on individuals. From that data, it creates norms and identities. Using the postal system, it can address individuals, guided and informed by the individuals" relation to the norms it has produced.

All of these subsystems—the unique identification of individuals, the gathering of data, the statistical analysis, and the response to individuals—have been refined over the years as communication and computing systems develop. Biometrics, driver's licenses, and cell phone numbers are used as unique identifiers. Monitoring has grown more pervasive, as location is tracked with mobile phones, and purchases are monitored through loyalty cards and electronic payment systems. Pattern analysis has grown more nuanced and sophisticated. Databases can be merged and scanned for links between individuals through Non-Obvious Relation Analysis (NORA) software. Statistical methods such as pattern discovery have extended and replaced cluster analysis. Opportunities for response are more finely tuned as well. The five-digit ZIP code has been replaced by the ZIP+4 system, which permits identification down to the level of several households. Mobile phones are addressed to a single person, rather than a household. It has even been suggested that the individual TV screens in airplanes could be programmed to deliver messages personally tailored to the expected viewer (Garfinkel 2000).

By incorporating cookies, the designers of the World Wide Web have made it a surveillance system par excellence. Users (or their machines, which are often effectively identical) can be uniquely identified and their Web traversals tracked and analyzed. They can then be served "personalized" messages based on their stated preferences, or the relation of their records to some set of constructed norms and expectations.

Not only is surveillance technique growing more sophisticated, it is more pervasive. In particular, it is migrating from the commercial to the government sector. The pattern analysis techniques originally designed to detect credit card fraud are now being used to monitor the welfare system (Gilliom 2001). In the wake of the attacks on September 11, 2001, countless monitoring and analysis projects have been proposed or implemented, including MATRIX, Total Information Awareness (TIA), Computer Assisted Passenger Profiling (CAPPS II), and the recently disclosed analysis of tens of millions of telephone call records. Many of these are direct descendents of commercial data mining practices (O'Harrow 2005).

The practices used by marketers to create and sell new products in new markets, and target the right sort of message to the right sort of person at the right sort of moment, are now used by border, intelligence, and police agencies to detect deviancy and normalcy. At some level, all of these—commercial and governmental applications alike—do the same thing. They distribute risks, opportunities, and suspicion among individuals according to that individual's perceived membership in socially constructed categories.

Activists, policy makers, and scholars have turned to a body of sociological and legal literature on privacy as they have approached and addressed these new configurations of surveillance. However, for numerous reasons, privacy has proved an insufficient response, intellectually, rhetorically, and legally (see critiques by Gilliom (2001), Phillips (2003), Nissenbaum (2004), and Pateman (1983), among others). For the purposes of this chapter, though, we will focus only on one shortcoming of the privacy approach. That is, privacy protects the autonomous individual, but the processes described above are fundamentally about the creation of social knowledge, social position, and social order. In the rest of this chapter, we suggest that queer theory can have a lot to say about this new landscape of knowledge production, especially as queer theory is integrated with surveillance studies and technology studies.

Why Queer Theory?

There are at least three strands of queer theory that can help us get a handle on surveillance. Speaking entirely too broadly, these are the studies of discourse, of performativity, and of publics.

Surveillance is a discourse. That is, the various techniques of surveillance—identification, monitoring, analysis and response—are routinized, regulated, and institutionalized practices that produce and circulate knowledge. Surveillance, like all discursive structures, brings into being of objects of analysis, objects of power, and objects of knowledge. One of the foundational works in queer theory, *History of Sexuality* (Foucault 1978) chronicles on how sexuality became an object of study and regulation, through institutionalized techniques of confession and analysis. Discourse, as a constructive technique, is recursive. As people are made to speak about sexuality, as institutions are created to regulate and prompt talk about sexuality, sexuality itself becomes reified as a field of knowledge, as an object of knowledge, as a malleable and articulate entity. The ideals thus created—of the pederast, the homosexual, the sadomasochist—are acted upon as though they were real. Thus through discourse—an institutionalized and historically contingent process—types of persons are granted practical reality. Queer theory studies this discursive construction and maintenance of identity positions.

Queer theory is also overtly political. It studies the constructed and contingent nature of identity in order to expose, subvert and queer the processes of their construction. It reveals the workings of knowledge production in order to create some, perhaps interstitial, room for alternative identities and alternative knowledges. This potential productivity is essential to the queer theoretic approach. Queer theory aspires toward "changed possibilities of identity, intelligibility, publics, culture, and sex" (Berlant and Warner 1998: 548). It asks what opportunities a discursive formation creates for discursive counterpractices (Halperin 1995).

The notion of performativity is central to another strand of queer theory. As Erving Goffman put it, well before the advent of anything called "queer theory," life itself is "dramatically enacted"

> to *be* a given kind of person . . . is not merely to possess the required attributes, but also to sustain the standards of conduct and appearance that one's social grouping attaches thereto. A status, a position, a social place is not a material thing, to be possessed and then displayed; it is a pattern of appropriate conduct, coherent, embellished, and well-articulated. . . . It is something that must be enacted and portrayed, something that must be realized. (Goffman 1959: 75)

Yet these identities, these "kind[s] of person[s]" are not invented out of whole cloth with each social interaction. Instead, we negotiate and improvise on common cultural ideals of identity, propriety, and context. According to Goffman, social performance is a "command of idiom" in which we call upon culturally established roles (man, woman, wife, waiter, lawyer, etc.) and contexts (the office, the home, a street in New York or a street in Peoria).

Gay and lesbian cultural studies have produced a significant body of work exploring just how the idioms of appropriate or deviant sexual identities and practices are propagated. Much of this work has been performed by media scholars, examining how sexual identities were coded in certain eras and in certain media (Faderman 1991; Gross 2001; Russo 1981). Still others have examined the political economy of sexual identities, analyzing how gay identities are commodified as audiences and markets in the television, print, and film industries (Binnie 1995; Chasin 2000; Sender 2001). All of these probe the creation of ideal identities, the discursive maintenance of status and position. The performative strand of queer theory explores the ways in which the discourse can be used upon itself to address and subvert the ideals it creates, to show the contingent and constructed nature of (especially) gendered and sexualized identities, through conscious, ironic, and strategic performances; that is, through drag (Butler 1998). Stone (1995) and Haraway (1991), among others, have celebrated new online communication technologies for their potential to mediate this sort of performative play, through what may be seen as cyberdrag.

Performances are public; they are directed at the other; they are inherently social. The production of a performance's meaning, the transformation of a gesture to a signal, requires an audience, a listener, a responder. Queer, subversive, or playful performances of common ideals are only effective if someone is there to get the joke. Therefore queer scholars study the imagination, reification, and address of this other. Berlant and Warner are particularly insightful in this regard. In "Publics and Counterpublics," Warner offers an excursion into the role of publics and counterpublics in the fashioning of the social world, exploring how and to what effect one imagines oneself addressed by public speech, and how one imagines the audiences of one's speech, whether that audience be "posterity," "humanity," or "right-thinking people everywhere" (Warner 2002: 73). He (with Lauren Berlant) also links this creation of the public with the political and economic structures of media organizations and urban spaces (Berlant and Warner 1998; Warner 2002). Throughout, the ideal is of queer world-making—"world-making . . . dispersed through incommensurate registers, by definition unrealizable as community or identity" (Warner 2002: 198).

This unrealizability is part of the queer ideal. Identity positions are always to be contingent, adaptable, strategic. Indeed, the apparent ahistoricity of online performance and play made it seem, in the 1980s and early 1990s, infinitely and invitingly queer. The bloom is now off that particular rose, and scholars, many of them represented in this collection, have shown how very historical the online world is, how every Web user sits in sedimented physical and social space while online, how racism and sexism follow one's disembodied online presence. But, with few exceptions (notably Campbell 2005), writers have not taken into account the ways in which surveillance and monitoring pervade online interactions.

As we mentioned earlier, online media, especially those accessed through the World Wide Web, are potentially the most finely integrated and pervasive surveillance system the world has yet known. It is also one of the most invisible and poorly understood. Online, one is never sure who is watching us, never mind with what purpose or according to what ontology they are making sense of our performance. One is never really sure if, or to whom, or to what end, one is a dog.

We have found that, in queer theory, we have an intellectual approach which at least begins to ask the right kinds of questions of online surveillance practice. Whether we are dealing with our TIVo, our online auction site, or our social networking site, we might ask the following:

▼ To what degree do, can, or should, the systems permit individuals to claim a particular social identity in a particular social context? How do they allow subjects to mirror and hone their own performances, and to be aware of the reactions of the audience for whom they perform?

▼ To what degree do, or should, surveillance systems enable the subcultural generation of knowledge and publics? How do they permit the formation of in-groups who are able to share insights and produce knowledge with each other, while excluding out-group members? How do they permit one to hail others?

▼ How do they access and reference common contexts, public spaces, from which to produce subcultural knowledge? To what degree do they permit the public claiming of their resources? To what degree do they, or should they, make their own workings visible and facilitate the public visibility of the various knowledges produced by their members?

Once queer theorists have helped us form questions, we can turn to others to explore approaches to their answers.

Why Surveillance Studies?

As mentioned earlier, queer studies, and gay and lesbian cultural studies, have done a fine job of examining these questions in traditional media and in public spaces (Bell and Valentine 1995; Califia 2000; Capsuto 2000; Chauncey 1994; Faderman 1991; Gross 2001; Ingram et al. 1997; Knopp and Brown 2003; Leap 1999; Rothenberg 1995; Russo 1981; Walters 2001). As scholars such as Campbell explore the commodification of subcultural identity new online media, they might look to a substantive body of work in the overlapping literatures of surveillance and privacy.

One strand of surveillance studies specifically concerns itself with the categorization, typification, and valuation of individuals, generally for the purposes of increased market efficiency. Gandy's *The Panoptic Sort* was one of the first scholarly works to lay out both the motives and the techniques of large corporations in their use of personal information (Gandy 1993). Turow (1997) has followed up this work in his study of the effects of increased fracturing of audiences, both through increasingly sophisticated demographic techniques and through more precise targeting of individuals for persuasive messages. Lyon is coordinating major research projects on the ethics of this sort of social discrimination (see, for example, Lyon 2003a).

Others have researched the state's interest in surveillance in the production of security, predictability, and normalcy. Norris and Armstrong's (1999) study of closed circuit TV systems in England offers great insight into the processes, both micro and macro, by which norms of gender, race, and class are policed in public spaces, mostly in the service of consumer capital. A host of studies have been published since 2001 chronicling the efforts of various nations, but particularly the United States, to identify, track, and analyze the activities of ever more people in greater detail (Lyon 2003b; O'Harrow 2005; Rosen 2004; Schneier 2003).

Together, these do a great job of placing surveillance and data exchange in historical, economic, and political context. They explicate how, by what historical processes, norms are produced, entities and identities reified, regulated, and placed in stable configurations.

Very few are concerned specifically "online" interactions, though almost all directly address the collection, storage, and transfer of digital information—data records. None is explicitly queer, though almost all pay homage to Foucault, especially *Discipline and Punish* and his metaphor of the panopticon (Foucault 1977). This metaphor is an extrapolation of a prison designed by Jeremy Bentham in the eighteenth century. This prison consisted of an outer circle of individual cells. These cells were illuminated and visible to an observer in a darkened central tower. This invisible observer could watch the actions of each individual, compare and analyze the prisoners as a group, and respond specifically to each individual, with punishment or reward, thus efficiently managing the prison population as a whole. Foucault posits the panopticon as a discourse—a means of knowledge production—that was increasingly institutionalized in various settings, including armies, factories, hospitals, work houses, and schools.

However much surveillance scholars embrace the notion of surveillance as discourse, there is generally little affection for a queer embrace of the discourse, of exploring its productive possibilities, of subverting it, rather than resisting it. There is often an air of fatalism or despair in surveillance scholarship. In part, this has come because of the perceived failure of privacy as a principle guiding viable responses to surveillance practice.

Lyon, for example, is wary of the discursive entrenchment of surveillance through privacy talk, noting that "the quest for privacy *produces* surveillance, because privacy is also looked to as protection *against* surveillance" (Lyon 2002: 2). Gilliom (2001) observes that those subject to intense surveillance, specifically Appalachian welfare recipients, do not resist with talk of privacy rights. Instead, they shape and justify their resistance through concepts of care, especially maternal care.

Solove (2004), too, rejects an all-knowing and personally invasive Big Brother as a metaphor for the dangers of surveillance. Instead, he offers Kafka's *Trial* as a more apt and useful analogy. The problem is not, he suggests, that a single, overarching, despotic and repressive regime tracks and responds to our every move. Instead, the problem is that we have no idea how the world we live in is created and maintained. The rules, the rulers, the structures and entities through which we move are invisible and nonsensical to us. Not to strain the earlier image, but we don't know if, how, or to whom we are a dog, or even what a dog is supposed to be.

These feelers away from privacy, toward other metaphors, other frames, other institutions of meaning suggest that the soil is well prepared for a blossoming of queer theoretical insights. Grafting the political economic expertise of surveillance studies with the social perspective and political project of queer theory seems like a great idea to me. Gay, lesbian, and queer studies can offer surveillance studies a new historical and theoretical perspective on the social consequences of surveillance practices, leading, at least, to better questions, and avoiding the typical dead ends and faux-paradoxes of the privacy policy discourse: "rights of individual" vs. "needs of society," or "privacy" vs. "safety and security." Conversely, surveillance studies can offer queer studies an understanding of the legal, technical, and economic infrastructures mediating new forms of identity practices. Together, they offer a framework for the political analysis of infrastructures of identity and visibility.

Technology Studies

Other responses to surveillance have come from engineers, entrepreneurs, and technology developers. In the 1990s, as the surveillant capacity of the internet became clear to some activists, hackers and cryptographers produced many techniques designed to intervene in the surveillance process. These included techniques for anonymity, such as digital cash (Chaum 1985) and pseudonymous e-mail and Web surfing (Goldberg and Shostack 1999). They also included methods for disguising the activities taking place, for example, via encrypted e-mail or phone calls. Some suggested interface designs that could make the surveillance activities themselves more visible, or offer users options of when and how to reveal information (Bellotti 1997; Cranor 2002). In general, these proffered solutions suffered from the same plight as early surveillance research. They fell back on privacy as the social ideal to be nurtured. That is, they believed that what was to be protected was the fully formed and isolate individual. Few, if any, gave much thought to the ideal of promoting or protecting community. Those that did understood community, very narrowly, as a collection of individuals. Few considered identity as a fluid, contested, and social product. Thus, few designs attempted to provide the kind of visibility, trust, and contingency necessary for identity management (Phillips 2002).

This is much less the case today. More and more work, both technical and critical, is being done on the design of social software. These include systems for finding or offering expertise in a crowd (Markoff 2006), recommender systems that allow users to choose the population with whom they will be grouped in statistical analysis (Canny 2002), techniques for determining in-group membership (Boyd 2002), and social networking software that allows users to construct their identities by explicitly noting and making visible their relations to others. Others are working on the emergent nature of identities and contexts by studying "how and why, in the course of their interactions, . . . people achieve and maintain a mutual understanding of the context for their actions" and designing systems to "support the processes by which context is continually manifest, defined, negotiated, and shared" (Dourish 2004: 22, 26).

The designers of these systems need queer theoretical insights. Queer theory needs familiarity with the discursive structures these systems facilitate. All—systems designers, surveillance scholars, and queer activists—need a grasp of the processes by which infrastructures of surveillance are developed.

By "infrastructure" we refer to overlapping and intertwined technical systems, laws, institutional configurations, and cultural understandings (Star and Bowker 2002). Infrastructures are never total or stable, but are constantly restructured by interested actors working within specific configurations of resources and constraints. The "infrastructure" of surveillance creates patterns of access to the resources of knowledge production and social visibility. The usefulness of the infrastructure, then—the political and social work that it does—is the product of myriad technical, ideological, and regulatory activities.

Activist surveillance scholarship must ask by what processes desired infrastructures can be realized. This is an exceedingly complex question, since infrastructural change occurs at many levels, through many modes, in many locales. Small changes in one locale have reverberations throughout the infrastructure in ways that may be invisible to observers and analysts trained in specific fields. For example, federal laws require that communication networks be designed and implemented in order to facilitate certain types of data collection. These laws are in part justified by reference to standard industry practices of data collection. Those industry practices, however, are themselves shaped by technical innovations, public safety mandates, and new markets for data which make data interception and collection more feasible and more profitable. Thus, references in one milieu to standards in another milieu result in a spiral of "normal" surveillance (Phillips 2003). Neither economics, nor public safety, nor law enforcement, nor telecommunications network design can explain the entire process. As another example, new techniques of personal data handling intended to promote autonomy in personal information exchange may fail, for complex reasons, to be successfully integrated into common practice. Countless protocols for anonymous cash, pseudonymous web browsing, or infomediaries have been proffered in the marketplace, yet very few have been commonly adopted (Phillips 2002, 2004).

Surveillance can organize national security interests as well as grassroots opposition. It can facilitate the deployment of emergency response teams as well as the deployment of culturally stultifying entertainment products. It can be used not only to recognize, reify, and serve new identity groups, but also to extract and commodify local or subcultural knowledge. These uses are best thought of not as trade-offs or balances among competing interests, but as necessary conflicts that will be mediated by the surveillance infrastructure. The infrastructure becomes the playing field for those contests. The goal of queer surveillance research is to discover possible configurations of practices of identification, tracking, monitoring, and response that might produce knowledges that are not domineering or oppressive, but instead may be deployed by the known population itself, in order to make sense of the world from an alternative perspective, to maintain subcultural identity and to articulate that identity with the larger social order. This chapter hopes to help generate such research by fostering dialogues among theorists and practitioners "about the ways in which radical cultural agendas and contemporary critical cultural theory can be part of [the design] process" (Wakeford 2003: 240).

Note

1. TIVo is a service that makes digital recordings of cable or broadcast television shows for later viewing. In addition to storing the programs on a home digital video recorder, the service also monitors the selections made by the user, suggesting, and occasionally recording automatically, "similar" content for the user's enjoyment.

References

Bell, D., and Valentine, G. (Eds.). 1995. *Mapping Desire: Geographies of Sexualities.* London: Routledge.

Bellotti, V. 1997. "Design for Privacy in Multimedia Computing and Communication Environments," in P. Agre and M. Rotenberg (Eds.), *Technology and Privacy: The New Landscape* (pp. 63–98). Cambridge, MA: MIT Press.

Berlant, L., and Warner, M. 1998. "Sex in Public." *Critical Inquiry 24*(Winter), 547–566.

Binnie, J. 1995. "Trading Places: Consumption, Sexuality, and the Production of Queer Space," in D. Bell and G. Valentine (Eds.), *Mapping Desire: Geographies of Sexualities* (pp. 182–199). London: Routledge.

Boyd, D. 2002. "Faceted Id/Entity: Managing Representation in a Digital World." Unpublished Master's Thesis, Media Arts and Sciences, Massachusetts Institute of Technology.

Butler, J. 1998. "Imitation and Gender Insubordination," in D. H. Richter (Ed.), *The Critical Tradition: Classic Texts and Contemporary Trends* (pp. 1514–1525). New York: Bedford-St Martin's.

Califia, P. 2000. *Public Sex: The Culture of Radical Sex.* San Francisco: Cleis Press.

Campbell, J. E. 2005. "Outing PlanetOut: Surveillance, Gay Marketing and Internet Affinity Portal." *New Media and Society 7*(5), 663–683.

Canny, J. 2002. "Collaborative Filtering with Privacy via Factor Analysis," in mediumbtext> Proceedings of the 25th annual international ACM SIGIR conference on Research and Development in Information Retrieval (pp. 238–245). New York: ACM Press.

Capsuto, S. 2000. *Alternate Channels: The Uncensored Story of Gay and Lesbian Images on Radio and Television.* New York: Ballantine Books.

Chasin, A. 2000. *Selling Out: The Gay and Lesbian Movement Goes to Market.* New York: Palgrave.

Chaum, D. 1985. "Security Without Identification: Transaction Systems to Make Big Brother Obsolete." *Communications of the ACM 28*(10), 1030–1044.

Chauncey, G. 1994. *Gay New York: Gender, Urban Culture, and the Making of the Gay Male World, 1890–1940.* New York: Basic Books.

Claritas Corporation. 2006. "Frequently Asked Questions About 'You Are Where You Live.'" Retrieved May 31, 2006, http://www.claritas.com/MyBestSegments/Default.jsp?ID=51

Cranor, L. 2002. *Web Privacy with P3P.* Sebastapol, CA: O'Reilly.

Dourish, P. 2004. "What We Talk About When We Talk About Context." *Personal and Ubiquitous Computing 8*(1), 19–30.

Faderman, L. 1991. *Odd Girls and Twilight Lovers: A History of Lesbian Life in Twentieth-Century America.* New York: Columbia University Press.

Foucault, M. 1977. *Discipline and Punish: The Birth of the Prison.* Trans. A. Sheridan. New York : Pantheon Books.

Foucault, M. 1978. *History of Sexuality: Volume I.* New York: Pantheon.

Gandy, O. H. 1993. *The Panoptic Sort.* Boulder, CO: Westview.

Garfinkel, S. 2000. *Database Nation.* Sebastapol, CA: O'Reilly.

Gilliom, J. 2001. *Overseers of the Poor: Surveillance, Resistance, and the Limits of Privacy.* Chicago: University of Chicago Press.

Goffman, E. 1959. *The Presentation of Self in Everyday Life.* New York: Doubleday.

Goldberg, I., and Shostack, A. 1999. "Freedom 1.0 architecture and protocols." Retrieved January 12, 2000, http://www.freedom.net/info/freedompapers/ Freedom_ Architecture_protocols.pdf

Gross, L. 2001. *Up from Invisibility: Lesbians, Gay Men, and the Media in America*. New York: Columbia University Press.

Halperin, D. M. 1995. *Saint Foucault: Towards a Gay Hagiography*. New York: Oxford University Press.

Haraway, D. J. 1991. *Simians, Cyborgs, and Women*. New York: Routledge.

Ingram, G. B., Bouthillette, A.-M., and Retter, Y. (Eds.). 1997. *Queers in Space: Communities/Public Spaces/Sites of Resistance*. Seattle, WA: Bay Press.

Knopp, L., and Brown, M. 2003. "Queer Diffusions." *Environment and Planning D: Society and Space 21*(4), 409–424.

Larson, E. 1992. *The Naked Consumer*. New York: Penguin.

Leap, W. (Ed.). 1999. *Public Sex/Gay Space*. New York: Columbia University Press.

Lyon, D. 2002. "Editorial. Surveillance Studies: Understanding Visibility, Mobility and the Phenetic Fix." *Surveillance & Society 1*(1), 1–7.

Lyon, D. (Ed.). 2003a. *Surveillance as Social Sorting: Privacy, Risk, and Automated Discrimination*. London: Routledge.

Lyon, D. 2003b. *Surveillance Since September 11*. Cambridge, UK: Polity.

Markoff, J. (2006, May 29). "Software to Look for Experts Among Your Friends." *The New York Times*, C5.

McGee, A. 1995. Untitled paper delivered at Computers, Freedom and Privacy Conference, March 1995. Quoted in Cranor, Lorrie, "CFP Conference Report," http://lorrie.cranor.org/pubs/cfp95.html

Nissenbaum, H. 2004. "Technology, Values, and the Justice System: Privacy and Contextual Integrity." *Washington Law Review 79*, 119–157.

Norris, C., and Armstrong, G. 1999. *The Maximum Surveillance Society*. Oxford: Berg.

O'Harrow, R. 2005. *No Place to Hide*. New York: Free Press.

Pateman, C. 1983. "Feminist Critiques of the Public/Private Dichotomy," in S. I. Benn and G. F. Gaus (Eds.), *Public and Private in Social Life* (pp. 281–303). London: Croom Helm.

Phillips, D. J. 2002. "Negotiating the Digital Closet: Online Pseudonyms and the Politics of Sexual Identity." *Information, Communication, and Society 5*(3), 406–424.

Phillips, D. J. 2003. "Beyond Privacy: Confronting Locational Surveillance in Wireless Communication." *Communication Law and Policy 8*(1), 1–23.

Phillips, D. J. 2004. "Privacy Policy and PETs: The Influence of Policy Regimes on the Development and Social Implications of Privacy Enhancing Technologies." *New Media & Society 6*(6), 691–706.

Rosen, J. 2004. *The Naked Crowd*. New York: Random House.

Rothenberg, T. 1995. "'And She Told Two Friends': Lesbians Creating Urban Social Space," in D. Bell and G. Valentine (Eds.), *Mapping Desire: Geographies of Sexualities* (pp. 165–181). London: Routledge.

Russo, V. 1981. *The Celluloid Closet*. New York: Harper & Row.

Schneier, B. 2003. *Beyond Fear*. New York: Copernicus.

Sender, K. 2001. "Gay Readers, Consumers, and a Dominant Gay Habitus: 25 Years of the Advocate Magazine." *Journal of Communication 51*(1), 73–99.

Solove, D. 2004. *The Digital Person: Technology and Privacy in the Information Age*. New York: New York University.

Star, S. L., and Bowker, G. 2002. "How to Infrastructure," in L. Lievrouw and S. Livingstone (Eds.), *Handbook of New Media* (pp. 151–162). Thousand Oaks, CA: Sage.

Steiner, P. (July 1993). "On the Internet, No One Knows You're a Dog." *New Yorker Magazine,* 61.

Stone, A. R. 1995. *The War of Desire and Technology at the Close of the Mechanical Age.* Cambridge, MA: MIT Press.

Turow, J. 1997. *Breaking Up America.* Chicago: University of Chicago Press.

Wakeford, N. 2003. "Research Note: Working with New Media's Cultural Intermediaries: The Development of Collaborative Projects at INCITE." *Information, Communication, and Society* 6(2), 229–245.

Walters, S. D. 2001. *All the Rage: The Story of Gay Visibility in America.* Chicago: University of Chicago Press.

Warner, M. 2002. *Publics and Counterpublics.* New York: Zone Books.

Zaslow, J. (November 26, 2002). "If TIVo Thinks You Are Gay, Here's How to Set It Straight." *The Wall Street Journal,* A1.

3. On-/Offline: Gender, Sexuality, and the Techno-Politics of Everyday Life

IRMI KARL

Making Connections—An Introduction

Queer theory proper is often abstracted from the quotidian realities of lesbian and gay male life (Halperin 2003: 343).

> [T]he literature on media users is that the press, radio, television and the Internet are each examined in what are almost separate paradigms, with little consideration of how various media are interleaved, and with little cross-fertilisation of ideas in the study of various mass media. (Mackay and Ivey 2004: 1)

For the past decade or so, online media and more specifically the Internet have received a substantial amount of attention from feminist and queer theory writers alike. Fueled by hopes and fears around the possibilities of new *virtual* gender and sexual politics, what seems to have emerged is a body of work that could be described as predominantly favoring approaches, which tend to focus primarily on online media technologies and forms of textual analysis. However, with a "dialogue between Queer theory and sociology" (Seidman 1996: 13) well on its way and an emerging interest in "the social, political and economic importance of cyberqueer spaces" (Wakeford 2000: 408), the opportunity to let queer cyber studies farther out of the textual and virtual closet seems promising.

In the spirit of seeking to overcome abstraction and separation and to forge further dialogue, this chapter sets out to explore and examine connections: connections between gender and sexuality, between feminist and queer perspectives on gender and sexuality, between identity and technological practices, new and old media as well as on-/offline experiences of everyday life. One of the main intentions of making these connections is to draw together still somewhat disparate literatures and situated knowledges that can further inform our understanding of the relationship between information and communication technologies (ICTs), practices of consumption and identity formation. By emphasizing some of the theoretical linkages already achieved in the field of (new) media and ICT consumption, gender and queer theory as well as by highlighting possible future connections, this contribution seeks to encourage further empirical research in these areas.

What follows aims to contribute to contemporary debates on gender, (queer) sexualities, and technology in three ways: first, it will be argued that the study of the gendered consumption of ICTs can benefit greatly from queer theory and its insistence on sexuality as a worthy analytical category, rather than to subsume it under gender as an area of study. As Clare Hemmings has pointed out, it seems problematic and undesirable to prioritize sexuality over gender or vice versa (Hemmings 2002: 39). In this sense, it can be argued that the production and intersections of gender and sexual identities need to be addressed more overtly across the field of ICT consumption research in order to avoid the reproduction of assumptions about continuities between anatomical sex and gendered practices when discussing gendered uses of ICTs.

Second, it will be argued that in order to re-evaluate questions of gender and sexual identities produced by an engagement with online media, it is important to recognize that online media themselves are not consumed in isolation. Rather, they constitute part of a broader set of everyday technopractices and information and communication technologies. With reference to my own ethnographic research into women-centered households,[1] it will be illustrated how perceptions and use of new media technologies are intrinsically linked and bound up with the everyday politics of space and time, public and private, and as such, are gendered and sexed in particular ways.

Third, if we are to take Elia's observation that "[v]irtually anything can be queered" (Elia et al. 2003: 336) into account, the question of how intrinsic technology is, and more specifically new ICTs, to the study of (queer) sexual identity also needs to be asked. In this sense queer theory's "textual or discursive idealism" (Seidman 1997: 16) may be empirically re-examined.

Setting the Agenda for a Queer Informed Future

If queer theory is going to have the sort of future worth cherishing, we will have to find ways of renewing its radical potential—and by that I mean not devising some new and more avant-garde theoretical formulation of it but, quite concretely, reinventing its capacity to startle, to surprise, to help us think what has not been thought. (Halperin 2003: 343)

In his personal as much as scholarly reflections on the history and future of queer theory and activism, David M. Halperin muses about just how and at what cost "such a simple, unassuming little word" has, coupled with the word "theory,"[2] achieved not only to question "lesbian and gay studies" and inspire new forms of political activism, but also managed to become thoroughly "absorbed into our (largely heterosexual) institutions of knowledge" (2003: 339, 341) and allowed itself to be canonized by the academy. The notion of absorption in this context refers not only to the loss of queer theory's radical, transgressive potential to shake up current sexual and gender politics and theory, but also highlights its tendencies to remarginalize individuals and groups of people by subsuming, for example, racial, ethnic, and other cultural interests and practices under the umbrella of "Queer Studies" (Alexander 2003: 350). Halperin is by no means alone in questioning the future project of queer theory and queer political action in the new millennium. Indeed, after nearly fifteen or so years of laboring under the banner of queer theory and politics, the emphasis now seems to be on amending and extending its reach in order to "make it more useful for communication of political issues and programs" and to infuse it with "greater concern with the material world and with a politics that entails real causes and risks" (Smith 2003: 347). Amendments to what has long been criticized as queer theory's over-emphasis on textual and discursive interpretations and poststructuralist "hyper"-theorization may then include a more noticeable shift toward embracing empirical methods and a greater focus on everyday social practices and interactions in future work.

One of Halperin's concerns is that queer theory has been too easily absorbed into established disciplines and subsequently applied to already established topics and fields of enquiry, losing its critical edge in the process (2003: 242). However, I would like to argue that there is still plenty of scope to bring some of the theoretical tenets of queer theory to, for example, the critical study of gender, sexuality, and consumption of (new) media technologies, particularly on a more sociological level. As I will illustrate below, studies of the gendered consumption of (new) media and ICTs, often drawing on poststructuralist feminist theory, can subsume sexuality within the category of gender and thereby render the role of sexuality in the constitution of gender identities somewhat invisible as an analytical category. At the same time as the interest in empirical explorations of the relationship between on-/offline experiences of media users is growing (Bakardjieva 2005; Lally 2002; Livingstone 2002; Livingstone and Bovill 2001; Ward 2005,) there is still a distinct lack in new media studies to engage with non-normative identities. As Nina Wakeford has pointed out, it is still very difficult "to find any body of work which worked through the epistemological and methodological implications of the multiplicities, incongruities and partialities of knowledge outside mainstream social groups and cultural locations [. . .]" (2004: 130). Discussions of gender and technology are too often still marginalized in mainstream studies engaging with the processes of ICT consumption and/or hinge on an evaluation of what women and men, girls and boys do with ICTs. The remaining questions in this context are what kinds of gender identities are being forged in the process and how do sexual identities intersect with gender identities through an engagement with the technological.

I would argue that queer theory has its work cut out by trying to push further into the mainstream of new media research despite some of its shortcomings, and that it should do so in dialogue with feminist perspectives on gender. The next section will therefore take the first steps by discussing the importance of sexuality in relation to gender, the problems and possibilities arising from queer theory's emphasis on the textual, as well as the move toward the queering of sociology.

Gendered Consumption of ICTs and the Question of Sexuality

Since the early 1970s, some two decades before queer theory established itself to signify a wide range of scholarly activity dedicated to the study of sexuality, feminist thinkers have concerned themselves with the relation of gender and media consumption. One of the major points of critique at the time was that they saw the mass media as a major cause of the general reproduction of patriarchal sexual relationships (Ang and Hermes 1991: 308–309). Over the years more sophisticated textual and reception analyses made it clear that textually inscribed feminine subject positions are not uniformly and mechanistically adopted by socially situated women viewers and readers. Feminists have not only investigated the gendered character of textual practices and audience reception (Ang 1991; Gray 1992; Hobson 1980; Seiter 1999) but also questioned and informed mainstream sociological understanding of technology. Insights stemming from their "unconditional focus on analyzing gender as a mechanism that structures material and symbolic worlds and our experience of them" (van Zoonen 1994: 33) have contributed substantially to our growing understanding of the relationship between gender and technology. Cynthia Cockburn's assertion that "social relations of technology are gendered relations, that technology enters into gender identity, and [. . .] that technology itself cannot be fully understood without reference to gender" (Cockburn 1992: 32) is still salient although perhaps not far-reaching enough.

One of the striking features of much research produced on the gender-technology relationship is that there is still so little consideration of the connection between gender and sexuality. Even cyberfeminism remains committed to the analysis of gender, while cyberqueer approaches mostly locate their emphasis in the non-normative with regard to identities, social groups, and cultural locations. Furthermore, this is where the impact of change may be felt most, much of the mainstream literature on technology and everyday life, although in parts inclusive in terms of its focus on how people use and interact with a whole range of (new) media technologies (Mackay and Ivey 2004; Moores 1993, 2000; Silverstone et al. 1992; Morley 1992) still relates what constitutes the feminine and the masculine too tightly to concretely sexed bodies—male and female. In this context, sexuality is almost always assumed to be heterosexuality, remaining unquestioned and unexamined. As Gust A. Yep writes in his essay "The Violence of Heteronormativity in Communication Studies," "[a]lthough we are living in times of declaration and affirmation of diversity and difference, heterosexuality is still generally treated as a monolithic and unitary concept," its complexity therefore being disregarded (Yep 2003: 29).

Looking at the history of the study of gender and technology as well as the emergence of cyber/culture/queer studies, we can find clear resonances of the underlying and far-reaching debates about the viability and status of gender and/or sexuality as separate analytical categories and the tensions between them. Elizabeth Weed points out in her introduction to the edited collection *Feminism Meets Queer Theory* that despite the fact that queer theory and lesbian and gay studies have acknowledged their intellectual debt to feminist theory and women's studies and vice versa, and despite the fact that for "many in the academy, feminism and queer theory are most easily understood as two branches of the same family tree of knowledge and politics" (Weed 1997: vii) their relationship remains an uneasy one. The problem, as Weed puts it, rests not with what queer theory stands for, but rather with queer theory's representation of feminism which renders it unrecognizable— "[n]o matter how reluctant queer theory has been to pin itself down as a coherent set of theorizations, it has been consistent about one aspect of its project: considerations of sex and sexuality cannot be contained by the category of gender" (Weed 1997: viii). But should the price of moving sexuality so firmly on to the agenda of lesbian and gay studies as well as queer theory come at the expense of gender studies and material or sociological analyses? Feminists as well as queer feminist theorists have been making inroads since the mid- to late 1990s to readdress what could effectively be seen as a categorical split, designating gender as a concern of feminists and feminism and sexuality to the field of lesbian and gay studies and queer theory. Judith Butler recalls the writing of *Gender Trouble* (1990) in part as a response to her growing unease with the fact that "countless feminist frameworks seemed either to elide or pathologize the challenge to gender normativity posed by queer practices" (Butler 1997: 2). Importantly, several years on, Butler comments that it would be a misrepresentation of recent feminist history to characterize feminism as an exclusive focus on gender and, among other things, erase the "significant differences between feminists who make use of the category of gender and those who work within the framework of sexual difference" (Butler 1997: 19; Braidotti 1994; Grosz 1995). The conceptual and methodological crux seems that, as Butler puts it:

> The analysis of gender, on the one hand, tends toward a sociologism, neglecting the symbolic or psychoanalytic account by which masculine and feminine are established in language prior to any given social configuration. Recourse to sexual difference, then tends to be concerned with the status of the asymmetrical relation to, in Lacanian terms, "non-relation" between the sexes as well as the separability of the symbolic and social domains whereby the symbolic is understood to precede and orchestrate the parameters of the social. (1997: 21)

The tension between the symbolic and the social is being exercised across a range of feminist and feminist queer literatures (Jackson and Scott 1996; Richardson 1996). Stevi Jackson, for example, in her critical evaluation of heterosexual desire and practice from a position as a materialist feminist and sociologist views Queer with "sceptical interest." For her, "queer theory is simply a reinvention of the sociological wheel" and, by focusing on the cultural and discursive, limited in that it is "paying little attention to social structures and material social practices" (Jackson 1999: 161). Nevertheless, she summarizes the communalities of queer theory and feminist approaches as follows:

> they call into question the inevitability and naturalness of heterosexuality, its normative status. Furthermore, feminist and queer theorists, to a greater or lesser extent, link the heterosexual/homosexual divide with gender. Whatever theoretical differences exist within and between these two diverse and overlapping constituencies, the common assumption is that neither gender boundaries nor the boundary between heterosexuality and homosexuality/lesbianism are fixed by nature. Queers and feminists both take an oppositional relationship to a social and cultural order which enshrines male dominated heterosexuality as a largely unquestioned norm. (Jackson 1999: 161)

Seeking communalities and connections between feminist and queer feminist perspectives can only be seen as a project in progress. Indeed, as Annamarie Jagose and Don Kulick point out, "[i]f LGBTQ[3] studies initially insisted on a clear distinction between gender and sexuality, that cleavage was subsequently contested by many who objected to the normalizing capacity of any neat quarantining of the cultural work of sexuality and gender" (Jagose and Kulick 2004: 211). Although we may never be able to establish the exact relationship between sexuality and gender, Jagose and Kulick see this as one of the underlying motivations of LGBTQ and feminist work—to ceaselessly imagine it in new ways. Critical of her own analytic splitting of gender and sexuality in the past, Arlene Stein now resorts to "gender sexuality and sexualize gender while being self-conscious about when I am lumping and when I am splitting them" (Stein 2004: 256). I would like to suggest that this perspective on gender and sexuality is useful in that it allows empirical, sociological as well textual and discursive approaches to the study of the inter-relationship of gender and sexuality as well as gender and sexuality without one perspective taking precedence over the other.

As Nina Wakeford has noted, "[t]here has been a persistent silence on matters of sexuality in critical cultural studies of technology" (2000: 410). If the term and the practice of cyberqueer can then be taken to signify itself "an act of resistance in the face of such suppression" (2000: 410), we should also ask to what extent and how the insights gained from cyberqueer studies with its focus on computer-mediated communication can be translated to inform the mainstream literature on gendered technology consumption and transform itself in the process. As I will suggest below, the relationship between ICT consumption and (queer) sexual and gender identities should not be contained by our focus on cyberspace(s), but rather more holistically attempt to evaluate how on-/offline experiences and old and new media practices intersect in everyday life encounters. The outcome of such a holistic approach is set to put a further dampener on utopian visions of cyberspaces and new electronically mediated sexualities and genders. At the same time, it will allow us to critically revisit and rearticulate the possibilities envisaged by poststructuralist/postmodern queer feminist thinkers with regard to the performativity and fluidity of gender and sexuality and evaluate the role technology plays in this context. I concur with Claire Hemmings who, in search of the "situated experience of bisexual subjects" insists on "the importance of poststructuralist feminist and/or queer epistemologies in providing a framework to make sense of the everyday" (Hemmings 2002: 37). What emerges from poststructuralist feminist/queer epistemological perspectives are certain methodological implications regarding enquiries into sexual and gendered subjectivities:

> The questions we ask must necessarily be other than 'What is the woman's or lesbian's experience in this context?' or even 'What is the feminist or queer reading of this context?' Such questions assume that there is a single experience or a single reading that will be identifiable and knowable. Instead, the task is to examine the knowledges that emerge from interactions among and between sexual and gendered subjects, and to assess the political and ethical value of such knowledges. (2002: 41)

In order to address knowledges that emerge from interaction among and between sexual and gendered subjects, I would argue that in situ qualitative sociological approaches in general and ethnographic approaches to everyday life in particular can be productive. This means that we have to re-evaluate the relationship between queer theory and sociology since it has not always been acknowledged nor is the outcome of this relationship necessarily being practiced as widely as it could be. Queer theory has originally come under fire, partly from within its own ranks, for being too textual in its focus (Epstein 2002; Namaste 1996; Seidman 1996, 1997). As Epstein puts it, "[i]n subject matter, queer studies emphasize literary works, text, and artistic and cultural forms; in analytical technique, deconstructionist and psychoanalytic approaches loom large" (2002: 51). In a move to address this issue and by wanting to avoid a reinvention of the sociological wheel, queer theorists and sociologists like Seidman and Epstein have illustrated how sociological work from the 1960s to the 1980s has indeed informed early work in the gay and lesbian arena (such as the "social constructionist" perspective, which itself draws from symbolic interactionism and labeling theory). However, since the late 1980s, aspects of the constructionist perspective have been challenged by queer theory's attempt to shift the debate from explaining the modern homosexual to questions of the workings of the hetero-/homosexual binary (Seidman 1997: 82). Importantly, as Ki Namaste points out, poststructuralist queer theory, rather than focusing too narrowly on homosexuality and homosexual subject positions, brought the study of heterosexuality itself to the sociological project:

> Rather than designating gays, lesbians, and/or bisexuals as the only subjects or communities worthy of investigation, a poststructuralist sociology would make sense of the manner in which heterosexuality is itself a social construct. (Namaste 1996: 203)

In this context, and as much as the inside/outside trope (Fuss 1991) has then been useful in terms of looking at the development of homosexual communities as well as the reproduction of heterosexuality hegemony, Namaste identified the need to further deepen a poststructuralist sociological approach to sexuality in order "to take into account the range of non-heterosexual identifications available" (1996: 205). This should serve us as an important reminder of the dangers of exclusively addressing hetero- and homosexuality at the cost of considering the availability of more diverse sexual and gender positions.

I find it encouraging that, on the basis of the insights gained during a lecture series and discussion forum entitled *Queer Today . . . ?*,[4] raising concerns such as "the queer emphasis on transgression for its own sake" (Hemmings and Grace 1999: 391) and narrowly defined queer subjects (e.g., lesbians and gays) as well as objects (sexuality or sexual communities), Claire Hemmings and Felicity Grace saw it as productive to broaden the focus of enquiry. Subsequently, the second lecture series *Queer Too . . . ?*[5] started to engage with "the everyday practices and experiences that form our, for the most part, mundane queer lives" (Hemmings and Grace 1999: 392). Taking the queer lens to everyday life allows us to make connections between the intersections of gender and sexual identities. This enables us to probe those intersections and identities with regard to a whole range of mundane "acts and processes," including our relationships with ICTs. In this sense the results of (queer) ethnography as a means of examining the everyday should therefore be of interest to anyone.

Everyday Techno-Practices On-/Offline

It is within the sphere of everyday life that individuals and groups can be agents, able insofar as their resources and the constraints upon them allow, to create and sustain their own life-worlds, their own cultures and values. It is within the sphere of everyday life that the ordinariness of the world is displayed, where minor and often taken-for-granted activities emerge as significant and defining characteristics. [. . .] And it is in the conduct of everyday life that we can begin to observe and try to understand the salience of information and technologies in humanity's general project of making sense of the world, both private and public. (Silverstone 1995: 2)

Some fifteen years ago, Roger Silverstone, Eric Hirsch, and David Morley embarked on an ethnographic study of actual practices of ICTs in nuclear family households. Crucially, their efforts came at a time when "[t]he study of television audience had broken down precisely at the point at which it was to be confronted in its social and cultural complexity" (Silverstone et al. 1991: 205). At a point, perhaps, textual interpretations and audience reception studies as well as the singling out of specific media/texts seemed somewhat exhausted. On the one hand, this study allowed them to reflect on methodological issues evolving from an engagement with everyday practices, for example, questions regarding the possibilities and limitations of qualitative interviewing, participant observation, objectifications, and reflexivity produced by research participants and researchers alike. On the other, it subsequently contributed toward an understanding of the household and the domestic sphere as a "moral economy" where a wide range of old and new ICTs and their consumption as texts as well as technologies interrelate with a larger "transactional system of economic and social relations within the formal or more objective economy and society of the public sphere" (Silverstone et al. 1992: 16). As such, it also highlighted the active and indeed gendered engagement of the households or the family in order "to create and sustain its autonomy and identity (and for individual members to do so the same) as an economic, social and cultural unit" (19). Eileen Green has since pointed out that it may be more productive to actually talk about "different and at times conflicting moral economies," rather than a household economy (Green 2001: 182). Calling on Silva's (2000) ethnographic research on family life, she highlights that "[s]uch moral economies will influence both the purchase of ICTs and their use" (Green 2001: 182).

The home as a specific site of everyday life, albeit itself conceptually complex (Bakardjieva 2005), has proven to be a fruitful anchor for a diverse range of inquiries into the adoption, appropriation, and consumption of (new) media and as such continues to be sought after. In this context, we must be careful not to conflate the concepts of family, household, and home in that they carry particular historical, cultural, and ideological meanings and are as such not interchangeable. Over the years, the attention given to the interplay among and between individuals, households, and families and the use of domestic media technologies has produced a considerable body of work, emphasizing either the position that we "must consider the media environment as a whole rather than ask about the use of each domestic medium separately" (Livingstone 2002: 167; Mackay and Ivey 2004) or drawing out the politics of everyday life with regard to more specific encounters with particular technologies and technological practices (e.g., the home computer and Internet use) (Lally 2002; Bakardjieva 2005). What is evident from these studies is that all media constitute a part in our life world and that, although specific media may play a role in different ways at different times, new media do not simply replace old media but find their place in the home through complex processes of renegotiation of consumption practices as well as technological convergence.

Significantly, some of the literature that addresses so successfully the processes of domestication of ICTs and the changing techno-politics of everyday life in the light of the appropriation of new media tends to emphasize approaches to the examination of gender in terms of what women and men (or girls and boys) do with technologies. This perspective allows us, for example, to chart how (new) domestic technologies can indeed challenge presumably existing gendered relationships with regard to the domestic division of labor as well as "gender-specific household technologies, gendered access to the economic resources of the household, and gendered differences in the right to spare time within the routines of the household" (Lally 2002: 157). However, I would like to argue that this perspective tells us rather less about what kinds of masculinities and femininities are being produced by women and men in the context of everyday techno-practices and/or neglects to acknowledge that these gender identities cannot be taken for granted or easily attributed to sexed bodies. Furthermore, it can be argued that studies of this kind still foreground nuclear family households with some variation in terms of the inclusion of single parent/persons households. The point here is not to question the relevance of these settings and household/family types for critical inquiry as such. Rather, I wish to highlight a blind spot with regard to questions of sexuality and sexual identities, which have so far remained mostly unexamined and therefore seem to operate on a kind of commonly agreed on or understood notion of (hetero)sexuality. This in turn may leave our understanding of how gender and sexual identities intersect, are negotiated and discursively produced through our engagement with ICTs truncated. A theorization of the gender-technology relationship ought to at least consider the extent and the ways in which this relationship may also be sexed, thereby questioning not only the impact of non-normative sexualities in relation to gender, but also to deconstruct perceived heterosexual gender identities. The moral economies of households, the relationship between private and public spheres and spaces, our experiences at work and during leisure time constitute a tightly knit web where gender identities inform sexual identities and vice versa. New ICTs, by way of their articulation as texts and technologies, offer means of expressing, rearticulating, and reinscribing these identities and are being reconfigured themselves during these processes. In this context we may then not only ask what becomes of the computer and computing practices on-/offline with regard to mothers, wives, husbands, children, etc., but also how these individuals, families, and households draw from gendered and sexed technological repertoires to make sense of their doings, and what kinds of constraints and possibilities may thereby be experienced. ICTs, it can be argued, not only signify certain gendered economic and cultural values but can also be said to be part of a (hetero)sexual economy where they, in their materiality as well as textual significance, become markers of sexual difference that constitute part of everyday techno-politics.

Queer ethnographic approaches should and can blur the boundaries between social scientific and humanities approaches to the study of the everyday, gender and sexuality, by making use of, for example, Butler's theory of gender performativity (1990) and by probing it in the light of empirical inquiry. Making this connection across disciplinary boundaries enables us to question those analytical assumptions that insist on continuities between anatomical sex and gendered practices on one hand, without falling into poststructural relativism on the other. Furthermore, as I will argue below, queer ethnographic approaches enable us to seek locations, spaces, living conditions, and forms of cohabitation for enquiry that, although potentially of great value to a general understanding of techno-practices of everyday life, still escape mainstream sociological interest and attention (McKie et al. 1999; Weeks et al. 2001).

Holistic Approaches to the Study of ICT Consumption

In her critical engagement with the topic of cyberqueer studies, Nina Wakeford highlights a number of problems regarding the research primarily under-taken in this area. The problems range from a reluctance to move beyond the dominant paradigm of queer theory, in which sexuality becomes the prime mover, and race and gender remain "relatively stable" (Wakeford 2000: 412) to uncritical postmodern celebrations of identity as fluid and performative and the lack of attention to what happens to the "real" body when the computer is turned on or indeed switched off. I would like to suggest that at least some of the challenges faced by cyberqueer inquiries stem from the main-stream literature on the Internet and virtual spaces, in that some of the ten-sions and problems that have emerged were and are partly due to the tendency to separate on- and offline experiences altogether, or by prioritizing the former at the expense of the latter. As Maria Bakardjieva (2005) notes in her discussion of virtual communities, few studies relate online experiences to the everyday life experiences of users, including empirically grounded anthro-pological ones. With reference to Wellman and Gulia (1999), she stresses that

> all these analyses are premised on a false dichotomy between virtual communities and real life communities. This split is unjustifiable. (Bakardjieva 2005: 167)

A number of authors have commented on the different phases Internet research has gone through since the early 1990s (Wellmann 2004; Feenberg and Bakardjieva 2004; Ward 2005). Katie Ward, for example, illustrates how initial debates focused on the kind of reality emerging online, often taking an overly optimistic and utopian interpretative stance and thereby "contribut-ing to, and perpetuating, a notion that the 'virtual' and 'physical' occupy opposite positions in a dichotomous relationship" (2005: 108). We can find this hopeful enthusiasm as well as some critical amendments to debates throughout the mainstream literature as well as in feminist and queer contri-butions (Jones 1995, 1997, 1998; Plant 1997; Smith and Kollock 1999). Still, microscale, social constructivist approaches as well as ethnographic methodologies have, as Leah A. Lievrouw points out, from the mid-1990s onward informed the debates and furthered our understanding of "the *inte-riority* of new media uses and meanings" (2004: 12). She attributes this shift to the growing influence of American cultural studies and British media stud-ies, challenging technological determinist accounts by writers such as John Naisbitt, Alvin Toffler, and Howard Rheingold. I would like to suggest that beyond the efforts made to further highlight the continuity between on- and offline experiences thus far (see, for example, Hine (2000) for an insightful and reflexive account of the possibilities of an ethnographic approach to the Internet and everyday uses as well as Jordan (1999) and Markham (1998)), there is still plenty of scope to broaden the horizon of empirical research based on ethnographic fieldwork.

The study of sexuality and sexual identities has clearly found a "love object" in new media and the Internet more specifically. The influences of queer theory's longstanding tradition of textualism can therefore be traced in some of the queer work on online interactions and spaces. While critical interpretations of this kind can indeed help us to get a sense of what types of interactions take place and how they are organized and expressed (i.e., compu- or virtual sex, online dating and gender-swapping, etc.), studies of this kind leave us at a guess with regard to the broader cultural and political implications of queer and indeed straight daily life. As inroads have been made in parts of the mainstream literature on the Internet to acknowledge virtual life's embeddedness in the real, so are queer net studies more and more interested in locating and relating, for example, "real" gay communities and cultures to online activities, demonstrating their interconnectedness as well as their points of divergence (McLelland 2002; Berry and Martin 2000). By using the Internet to study gay culture in Japan, Mark J. McLelland soon realized that virtual scripts (e.g., personal adverts on the Internet) can quickly turn into real-life sex. He therefore critically reflects on the shifts in his understanding of the Internet, "from a conduit for information about homo-sexuality in Japan to a social space in its own right that can tell us something about how sex between men is negotiated online and the implications that this may have for face-to-face interaction" (McLelland 2002: 402). Impor-tantly, he notes that it was the fact that he followed up virtual relationships with face-to-face meetings that allowed him to examine "the relationship between 'virtual' and 'actual' expectation" (2002: 402). Subsequently, online encounters became "real" life sex experiences, his dating partners became informants and his endeavor of virtual ethnography turned into a more holis-tic on-/offline project. Chris Berry and Fran Martin in their study of the role of cyberspace in queer Taiwan and Korea make a similarly strong case for the need to emphasize the connectedness between online and offline activities. In the context of their research they found that "these online discursive com-munities are not only integrated with existing offline activities but often also stimulate new offline connections" as well as stimulating queer activism, where meetings take place online as well as off the net (2000: 78).

I would like to bring this part to a close by offering a number of obser-vations and comments based on the literature considered with reference to my own ethnographic research into women-centered households and their techno-practices in Brighton, UK. First, it can be argued that by focusing the study of (queer) sexualities so primarily on net and related activities and expe-riences, we may be somewhat losing sight of the implications other media technologies and daily private and public practices have on the constitution of gender and sexual identities. As I have pointed out above, there is still a great need to introduce concerns of gender and sexuality into the mainstream literature on ICTs and everyday life, as much as there may be a further need for (cyber)queer studies to embrace, for example, the quotidian realities of lesbian and gay life which Halperin refers to at the beginning of this chapter. In this context, possible alternative locations and starting points for critical inquiry into ICT consumption, gender, and sexuality can fruitfully be sought in households and/or family settings that are, unlike nuclear family households, still under-researched. To choose, as in my case, women-centered households, where the women identify as lesbian, bisexual as well as straight (or in fact neither) as the center stage and starting point for empirical inquiry, is one possible option that allows us to redirect the focus of study onto a diverse field of living conditions and forms of cohabitation, which so far have been marginalized or tokenized in sociological and media studies traditions alike. These settings lend themselves to critically re-evaluate the practice of simply collapsing gendering processes onto concretely sexed bodies as they disturb the masculine/feminine as well as hetero/homo binaries. They also allow for a holistic and inclusive perspective on how, for example, techno-practices are entwined with domestic labor, leisure practices, and other work commitments. In addition, insights gained in these contexts can help us to shed critical light onto gendered practices in presumed (hetero)normative settings and encounters with technology.

Second, there still appears a relative readiness in the (cyber)queer literature to seek out clearly identified and identifiable lesbian, gay, bisexual, and transgender subject positions and sites, using queer as a kind of short-hand to denote all that which can be considered non-normative. This, it could be argued, may set up oppositions between queer and heterosexual identities by playing down the complexities and challenges of the construction of any kind of subject position as well as leaving normative ones under-examined. The decision not to pre-label or restrict my sample of households to lesbian or queer identified women, but to focus on how they rearticulated, expressed, and produced their sexual and gender identities over long periods of time, provided some insights into the tentative nature and instability of any kind of sexual subject position, as some of the women did indeed renegotiate and redefine their sexual identities over the years.

Third, it can be argued that to subsume gender under sexuality or vice versa in any kind of analysis will hinder us in evaluating the tensions at work at points of intersection. The way in which gender identities seem to be articulated, the understanding of certain kinds of femininities and masculinities, can more fully be explored when seen in the context of sexual identities. There are, for example, qualitative power differences between the performance of lesbian femme, lesbian femininity, or perceived *straight* femininities (although at times perhaps performed by lesbian-identified women or indeed rejected by straight-identified women). All of the women in my study did have a sense of having to express themselves within and through (hetero)sexual and gender normative frameworks. Their strategic interventions and transgressions as well as lapses with regard to avoiding or breaching perceived gender and sexual stereotypes were highlighted in their interview contributions. It could be argued that the interview process itself encouraged them to take a more conscious and reflective position than they perhaps would take up in their everyday lives. In this sense it may be noted that my findings based on participant observation and more informal conversations revealed the discursive persuasiveness of traditional gender positions, inviting their conscious as well as unconscious reproduction.

The politics of everyday life extend, of course, beyond the home and the domestic sphere. ICTs play a key role in rearticulating and blurring the gendered boundaries between the public and private. The trend toward technological mobilization and global virtual reach does, if anything, further the need to conceptualize the consumption practices of ICTs in a holistic manner. With regard to computer, e-mail, and Internet use in particular, the women in my study felt especially challenged to establish more manageable boundaries around work and leisure practices as well as to rearticulate their gender identities as women, mothers, professionals, and partners in sexual relationships in the light of their techno-practices. In this context the consumption of old media and ICTs such as radio, television, and the fixed phone was also affected in that they at times were re-engendered and seen as having a grounding and as such "normalizing" effect on everyday practices in terms of their temporal and spatial characteristics.

Technology and Gender/Sexual Identities

> The relationship between technology and sexuality is a symbiotic one. (Tsang 2000: 432)

This chapter set out to make connections between gender and sexuality, and feminist and queer theory, in order to suggest and to possibly inspire alternative modes and locations of inquiry with regard to the study of (new) ICTs. It has been argued that although feminist as well as some mainstream scholars have critically examined the ways in which the consumption of ICTs and media texts can be seen as gendered, so far little or no emphasis has been placed on examining the ways in which gender identities may intersect with sexual identities, and the role media technologies play in this process of identity formation. Arguably, this lack of attention fosters the (re)production of rather one-dimensional analyses of the gender-technology relationship. It suppresses not only the evaluation of the performative differences between certain kinds of femininities and masculinities which emerge in tandem with

the experience of varying and shifting experiences of sexuality/sexual identity, but ultimately hinders our understanding of the situated knowledges of
sexual and gendered subjects (Hemmings 2002) that emerge from the
engagement with the technological.

Queer theory, on the other hand, having convincingly established a case
for the acknowledgment of sexuality as an analytical category, still suffers to a
certain extent from gender blindness, the tendency of "hyper"-theorization
and from a favoring of textual and discursive approaches over sociologically
inspired enquiries. In this context it is being suggested that as part of the
ongoing project of queer theory/practice, a number of theoretical and
methodological avenues can be explored further. First, although the usefulness of sexuality as an analytical category cannot be overestimated, it should
not be applied in isolation and it should not only result in the selection of and
focus on "non-normative" sexualities, but also more overtly question and
examine perceived heterosexualities as well. As I consider it as part of a queer
project to try and gain more of the attention of (and reflexive absorption
into) mainstream (new media) research, one way of entering this field can be
through informing and enhancing theories of gender by including questions
regarding sexuality and sexual identities. This task cannot be left to (queer)
feminist theorists alone.

Second, how intrinsic the study of ICTs and media (texts) is to our
understanding of gender and sexual identities is beginning to establish itself
in research focused on cyber/online environments and practices as well as in
work undertaken in the longer standing tradition of examinations of popular
cultural texts. The argument in this context is that there remains a lot of
scope for types of critical inquiry, which emphasize and analyze the relational
character between on- and offline, old and new media practices and experiences. The focus on textual interpretations may tell us only part of a story by
neglecting, for example, those aspects which contribute toward textual formations and the circumstances of their consumption in the first place. What
is being suggested here is to shift queer theory's lens more firmly on to examining techno-practices as part of *ordinary* everyday life. Therefore, queer
identities, practices, and politics need to be recognized as constituted by as
well as constitutive of everyday (techno) cultures, rather than being treated as
extra-ordinary subject positions or forms of agency and (political) activism.
In this context I would like to, finally, suggest that we can expand our findings and understanding of (queer) techno-practices by applying a (queer)
ethnographic lens to domestic and work environments, private and public
spaces to establish their implication in the gendered and sexual meaning making of everyday live. By doing so, we not only learn about the eroticization of
new technology and the "sexual underground" of cyberspace as Tsang puts
it, but also start to question people's engagement with technological artifacts

themselves. We can then probe their symbolic meanings and textualities as well as their capacity to reproduce and challenge versions of heteronormativity. We may, as one of the women in my study did, for example, use a string of tinsel to re-appropriate the television set as a piece of "queer-technology" and therefore change the power dynamics in a mixed queer/straight household. Or we can position the television set to become center part of a perceived traditional living room set up to signal "normativity," as in the case of lesbian single mother. Old and new technologies are shaped by and are shaping our gendered and sexual identities. On- and offline (queer) experiences and their negotiations signal then, in many ways, continuity as well as change, rather than rupture in our everyday techno-cultures and practices.

Notes

1. Based on a longitudinal ethnographic study of women's ICT consumption in Brighton, UK. The premise of this ethnographic research project is to inquire into everyday techno-practices and the ways in which sexuality intersects with gender identities during these processes. In order to critically reassess research that has been undertaken in the area of nuclear families and domestic settings, alternative locations and living arrangements have been deliberately chosen, in my case by way of their women-centeredness: for example, mixed queer/straight women households, two lesbian households, and a single person household. In terms of ICT consumption, the focus is not centered around new media technologies as such, rather the aim is to illustrate the relationships and convergences between the old and the new ICTs. Furthermore, the connection between the private and the public sphere is being highlighted by considering the politics of the domestic as well as work and leisure practices.
2. Halperin credits Teresa de Lauretis as having "coined" the term "queer theory" by choosing it as a conference title in 1990 in order to provoke disruptions in "lesbian and gay studies" (see Halperin, 2003: 339–340).
3. Lesbian, gay, bisexual, transgender, and queer studies.
4. Lecture series organized by Clare Hemmings during the academic year 1997/98: *Queer Today . . . ? Contemporary Issues in Sexuality and Gender,* sponsored by the School of Literary and Media Studies, University of North London (UNL).
5. *Queer Too . . . ?* second lecture series organized by Clare Hemmings with Felicity Grace, co-sponsored by Literary and Media Studies at the University of North London (UNL) and the Department of Sociology at Goldsmiths College, London.

References

Alexander, B. 2003. "Querying Queer Theory Again (or Queer Theory as Drag Performance)," in J. P. Elia, K.E. Lovaas, and G.A. Yep (Eds.), *Queer Theory and Communication: From Disciplining Queers to Queering the Discipline(s)* (pp. 349–352). New York: Harrington Park Press.
Ang, I. 1991. *Desperately Seeking the Audience.* London: Routledge.

Ang, I., and Hermes, J. 1991. "Gender and/in Media Consumption," in J. Curran and M. Gurevitch (Eds.), *Mass Media and Society* (pp. 307–328). London: Edward Arnold.

Bakardjieva, M. 2005. *Internet Society—The Internet in Everyday Life.* London: Sage Publications.

Berry, C., and Martin, F. 2000. "Queer 'n' Asian on-and-off the Net: The Role of Cyberspace in Queer Taiwan and Korea," in D. Gauntlett (Ed.), *Web.studies* (pp. 74–81). London: Arnold.

Braidotti, R. 1994. *Nomadic Subjects: Embodiment and Sexual Difference in Contemporary Feminist Theory.* New York: Columbia University Press.

Butler, J. 1990. *Gender Trouble—Feminism and the Subversion of Identity.* London and New York: Routledge.

Butler, J. 1997. "Against Proper Objects," in E.Weed and N. Schor (Eds.), *Feminism Meets Queer Theory* (pp. 1–30). Bloomington and Indianapolis: Indiana University Press.

Cockburn, C. 1992. "The Circuit of Technology: Gender, Identity and Power," in R. Silverstone and E. Hirsch (Eds.), *Consuming Technologies—Media and Information in Domestic Spaces* (pp. 32–47). London and New York: Routledge.

Elia, J. P., Lovaas, K. E., and Yep, G. A. 2003. "Reflections on Queer Theory: Disparate Points of View," in J. P. Elia, K.E. Lovaas, and G.A. Yep (Eds.), *Queer Theory and Communication: From Disciplining Queers to Queering the Discipline(s)* (pp. 335–338). New York: Harrington Park Press.

Epstein, S. 2002. "A Queer Encounter: Sociology and the Study of Sexuality," in C. L. Williams and A. Stein (Eds.), *Sexuality and Gender* (pp. 145–167). Oxford: Blackwell Publishers.

Feenberg, A., and Bakardjieva, M. 2004. "Virtual Community: No 'killer application.'" *New Media and Society* 6(1), 37–43.

Fuss, D. 1991. *Inside/Out: Lesbian Theories, Gay Theories.* New York: Routledge.

Gray, A. 1992. *Video Playtime: The Gendering of a Leisure Technology.* London and New York: Routledge.

Green, E. 2001. "Technology, Leisure and Everyday Practices," in E. Green and A. Adam (Eds.), *Virtual Gender—Technology, Consumption and Identity* (pp. 173–188). London and New York: Routledge.

Grosz, E. 1995. *Space, Time and Perversion: Essays on the Politics of Bodies.* New York: Routledge.

Halperin, D. M. 2003. "The Normalization of Queer Theory," in G. A. Yep, K. E. Lovaas, and J. P. Elia (Eds.), *Queer Theory and Communication—From Disciplining Queers to Queering the Discipline(s)* (pp. 339–343). New York: Harrington Park Press.

Hemmings, C. 2002. *Bisexual Spaces—A Geography of Sexuality and Gender.* London: Routledge.

Hemmings, C., and Grace, F. 1999. "Stretching Queer Boundaries: An Introduction." *Sexualities* 2(4), 387–396.

Hine, C. 2000. *Virtual Ethnography.* London: Sage Publications.

Hobson, D. 1980. "Housewives and the Mass Media," in S. Hall, D. Hobson, A. Lowe, and P. Willis (Eds.), *Culture, Media, Language* (pp. 105–114). London: Hutchinson.

Jackson, S. 1999. *Heterosexuality in Question.* London: Sage Publications.

Jackson, S., and Scott, S. (Eds). 1996. *Feminism and Sexuality*. Edinburgh, UK: Edinburgh University Press.

Jagose, A., and Kulick, D. 2004. "Thinking Sex/Thinking Gender." *Journal of Lesbian and Gay Studies 10*(2), 211–313.

Jones, S. G. (Ed.). 1995. *Cybersociety: Computer-Mediated Communication and Community*. Thousand Oaks, CA: Sage Publications.

Jones, S. G. (Ed.). 1997. *Virtual Culture: Identity and Communication in Cybersociety*. London: Sage Publications.

Jones, S. G. (Ed.) 1998. *Cybersociety 2.0—Revisiting Computer-Mediated Communication and Community*. London: Sage Publications.

Jordan, T. 1999. *Cyberpower—The Culture and Politics of Cyberspace and the Internet*. London and New York: Routledge.

Lally, E. 2002. *At Home with Computers*. Oxford and New York: Berg.

Lievrouw, L. A. 2004. "What's Changed about New Media?" *New Media & Society 6*(1), 9–15.

Livingstone, S. 2002. *Young People and New Media*. London: Sage Publications.

Livingstone, S., and Bovill, M. (Eds.). 2001. *Children and their Changing Media Environment*. Mahwah, NJ, and London: Lawrence Erlbaum.

Mackay, H., and Ivey, D. 2004. *Modern Media in the Home: An Ethnographic Study*. Rome: John Libbey Publishing.

Markham, A. N. 1998. *Life Online—Researching Real Experience in Virtual Space*. Walnut Creek, CA: AltaMira Press.

McKie, L., Bowlby, S., and Gregory, S. (Eds.). 1999. *Gender, Power and the Household*. Basingstoke and London: Macmillan Press.

McLelland, M. J. 2002. "Virtual Ethnography: Using the Internet to Study Gay Culture in Japan." *Sexualities 5*(4), 387–406.

Moores, S. 1993. *Interpreting Audiences—The Ethnography of Media Consumption*. London: Sage Publications.

Moores, S. 2000. *Media and Everyday Life in Modern Society*. Edinburgh, UK: Edinburgh University Press.

Morley, D. 1992. *Television Audiences & Cultural Studies*. London and New York: Routledge.

Namaste, K. 1996. "The Politics of Inside/Out: Queer Theory, Poststructuralism, and a Sociological Approach to Sexuality," in S. Seidman (Ed.), *Queer Theory/Sociology* (pp. 194–212). Oxford: Blackwell Publishers Ltd.

Plant, S. 1997. *Zeroes and Ones: Digital Women and the New Techno-Culture*. London: Fourth Estate.

Richardson, D. (Ed.). 1996. *Theorizing Heterosexuality*. Buckingham, UK: Open University Press.

Seidman, S. (Ed.). 1996. *Queer Theory/Sociology*. Oxford: Blackwell Publishers.

Seidman, S. 1997. *Difference Troubles—Queering Social Theory and Sexual Politics*. Cambridge, UK: Cambridge University Press.

Seiter, E. 1999. *Television and New Media Audiences*. Oxford: Clarendon Press.

Silva, E. B. 2000. "The Politics of Domestic Consumption @ Home: Practices and Dispositions in the Uses of Technology," *Pavis Papers* No. 1. Faculty of Social Sciences: The Open University, Buckingham, UK.

Silverstone, R., Hirsch, E., and Morley, D. 1991. "Listening to a Long Conversation: An Ethnographic Approach to the Study of Information and Communication Technology in the Home." *Cultural Studies* 5(2), 104–127.

Silverstone, R., Hirsch, E., and Morley, D. 1992. "Information and Communication Technologies and the Moral Economy of the Household," in R. Silverstone and E. Hirsch (Eds.), *Consuming Technologies—Media and Information in Domestic Spaces* (pp. 15–31). London and New York: Routledge.

Smith, M. A., and Kollock, P. (Eds.). 1999. *Communities in Cyberspace*. London and New York: Routledge.

Smith, R. R. 2003. "Queer Theory, Gay Movements, and Political Communication," in G. A. Yep, K. E. Lovaas, and J. P.Elia (Eds.), *Queer Theory and Communication: From Disciplining Queers to Queering the Discipline(s)* (pp.235–348). New York: Harrington Park Press.

Stein, A. 2004. "From Gender to Sexuality and Back Again: Notes on the Politics of Sexual Knowledge." *Journal of Lesbian and Gay Studies* 10(2), 254–257.

Tsang, D. 2000. "Notes on Queer 'n' Asian Virtual Sex," in D. Bell and B. Kennedy (Eds.), *The Cybercultures Reader* (pp. 432–438). London and New York: Routledge.

Van Zoonen, L. 1994. *Feminist Media Studies*. London: Sage Publications.

Wakeford, N. 2000. "Cyberqueer," in D. Bell and B. Kennedy (Eds.), *The Cybercultures Reader* (pp. 403–415). London: Routledge.

Wakeford, N. 2004. "Pushing at the Boundaries of New Media Studies," in *New Media & Society* 6(1), 130–136.

Ward, K. 2005. "Internet Consumption in Ireland—Towards a 'Connected' Domestic Life," in R. Silverstone (Ed.), *Media, Technology and Everyday Life in Europe* (pp. 107–123). Aldershot, UK: Ashgate.

Weed, E. 1997. "Introduction," in E. Weed and N. Schor (Eds.), *Feminism Meets Queer Theory* (pp. vii–xiii). Bloomington and Indianapolis: Indiana University Press.

Weeks, J., Heaphy, B., and Donovan, C. 2001. *Same Sex Intimacies. Families of Choice and Other Life Experiments*. London and New York: Routledge.

Weeks, J. 1977. *Coming Out: Homosexual Politics in Britain from the Nineteenth Century to the Present*. London: Quartet.

Wellman, B. 2004. "The Three Ages of Internet Studies: Ten, Five and Zero Years Ago." *New Media & Society* 6(1), 123–129.

Wellman, B., and Gulia, M. 1999. "Net-Surfers Don't Ride Alone: Virtual Communities as Communities," in B. Wellman (Ed.), *Networks in the Global Village: Life in Contemporary Communities* (pp. 331–366). Boulder, CO: Westview Press.

Yep, G. A. 2003. "The Violence of Heteronormativity in Communication Studies: Notes on Inquiry, Healing, and Queer World-Making," in G. A. Yep, K. E. Lovaas, and J. P. Elia (Eds.), *Queer Theory and Communication—From Disciplining Queers to Queering the Discipline(s)* (pp. 11–59). New York: Harrington Park Press.

Part II
Rethinking Community and Spatiality

In this part of the book, the three writers are concerned with developing, challenging, and rethinking the intersections of community and spatiality. Community and space have both been central concerns in media and communication studies research, and questions about how they produce each other have been key issues in digital and networked communication practices. Such debates have revolved around the intersection of material and discursive spaces and places in the construction and performance of community, and the affordances of spatial metaphors to structure ways of thinking about communities.

Discourses of digitization and network cultures have been preoccupied with questions about the kinds of communities constituted through media and communications. From "homestead" and "frontier" metaphors, to debates about the dislocation of space, spatiality and community have been intimately entwined. These chapters are linked through an engagement with these issues and they revisit debates about space and community that continue to be central preoccupations. The intersections of nation, sexuality, violence, belonging, publics and communications, with spatiality and community are examined here in critical ways.

Nathan Rambukkana argues that the internet reconfigures subcultural public spheres, and in doing so his work demands a rethinking of notions of publics and subcultures. The specific uses of space in the development of subcultural capital are shown to be transformed and reformulated through the deployment of spatial metaphors in online communication practices. The intersections between different kinds of communication spaces, and the different kinds of im/materialities and embodiments that are articulated and practiced, illuminate the complex relationships that operate in the rearticulation of space, identity, and relations.

In the title to chapter 4, "Taking the Leather Out of Leathersex: The Internet, Identity, and the Sadomasochistic Public Sphere," Rambukkana indicates the active operations occurring through the re-spatialization of communication. This chapter argues that the production of different ways of communicating has key transformative implications for of the way subjectivities are produced and offered.

From a different angle entirely Marjo Laukkanen also argues that spatiality and community can be rethought by examining queer self-expression (and its limits). Drawing on the deployment of the metaphor of the closet, by those using CMC, to create an their own affirmative communication space, absent from other forums, these communication practices are seen to be transformative and transformed through context. Looking at the relocated closet in the multi-genre sites of magazine readership in Finland, chapter 5 examines discursive and material rethinkings of sexuality, sex, and gender; not only showing points of transformation but also examining the limitations and constraint within which these occur.

A key element in all of these chapters is the issue of belonging and how this is spatiality constructed, and how this construction both produces affiliation and demarcation. Adi Kuntsman's examination of Russian-speaking Israeli queer belongings in chapter 6 ("Belonging through Violence: Flaming, Erasure, and Performativity in Queer Migrant Community") illuminates the cooperation of violent mediated speech acts in the constitution of community practices. This chapter deals with issues of migration and diaspora; and the interaction of space and community building. It argues that the performance of difference, within groups, produces strong ties through the contestation of knowledge claims, which act to ritualize and reiterate group norms and experiences.

In all of these chapters spatiality is examined as a process which interacts with the dynamics of community. These sets of intersecting dynamics constitute spaces and communities, which reconfigure geopolitical loss or marginalization. These practices also foreground the different kinds of marginalizations that operate in the reformulated communication structures of the Web.

4. Taking the Leather Out of Leathersex: The Internet, Identity, and the Sadomasochistic Public Sphere[1]

Nathan Rambukkana

Introduction

The rise of Internet-mediated BDSM[2] communities and resources is slowly transforming the perceived need for engaging in the leather bar scene as a precursor to finding the "real" SM scene. The implications for this in terms of BDSM/leather identities are discussed in this chapter. This new sphere of participation can be at once more involved than previous forms of BDSM public sphere discourse, and at the same time allows for people to engage with it with fewer commitments with regard to sexual identity (in that it does not require special equipment or dress to participate). Using the language of the public sphere and of counterpublics, I suggest that this change has parsed the leather and BDSM communities, so that a leather identity is less often seen as a prerequisite for participating in organized BDSM culture.

The discourse of sadomasochism (SM) as a named subculture can be traced back to sociographic work of the 1970s, though as a lived subculture it most certainly preceded that date (Weinberg 1987: 51). Previous to that, much of the writing on the subject tended to see it as a perversion, if an oft positively regarded and eroticized one. This chapter will examine the influence of an Internet-mediated public sphere presence of sadomasochistic—or as it is now more commonly called, BDSM—culture on the nature of sadomasochistic community and identity formation. As the Internet has been referred to as "by far the single greatest point of entry for new players into BDSM" (Easton and Hardy 2001: 52), it is worth exploring what this new point of entry enables, mutates, or makes possible.[3]

Terms are a tricky issue in this chapter due to its diachronic focus. Though a "BDSM" culture is sometimes referred to as preexisting this particular coinage (being a later-developed, but more precise term for the not-necessarily-pain-centered activities that occur in the subcultural groups most often referred to as "sadomasochist"), I am referring to specific discourses that, using the Foucauldian sense of the word, have a discernible beginning, points of change, and sometimes endings (Foucault 1991: 54). These terms refer to distinct discourses, and as such the cultures that accrue to them can be seen as discourse-cultures, with written as well as lived ideologies. With this in mind, I will make reference an earlier visual discourse-culture of sado-masochism as Leathersex, the informational discourse-culture of sado-masochism as BDSM culture, and use "sadomasochism" in its broad sense: that of referring to sexual practices that involve some explicit element of pain and/or control between consenting partners, ethically and consensually articulated for the mutual benefit of both parties.

Subaltern Counterpublics and Subcultural Identity

In "Rethinking the Public Sphere: A Contribution to the Critique of Actually Existing Democracy," Nancy Fraser (1992) draws a strong link between what she calls subaltern counterpublics and subcultural identity. In a landmark reinterpretation of Jürgen Habermas's "The Structural Transformation of the Public Sphere" (1962), Fraser uses recent historiographic and revisionist historical work to question Habermas's idealization of the bourgeois public sphere as the ideal political counterweight to the governmental sphere. A public sphere, in Habermas's sense, can be understood as "a theatre in modern societies in which political participation is enacted through the medium of talk" and which is distinct from both the state and commerce (Fraser 1992: 110). In a critique and extension of this concept, Fraser proposes a "multiple publics" model of public sphere debate in which subaltern counterpublics (smaller spheres of public debate centered around the proliferation of specific discourses in society) interact in an inter-cultural way, working from within their own discourses to bridge the cultural gaps between discourse-cultures that must be properly traversed if authentic public sphere communication is to occur (1992: 126). Fraser's departure is in the suggestion that the functioning of these subaltern spheres (and their both intra- and inter-cultural communication) is significant for more than just the valid expression of culture-specific opinion. She identifies that publics are also important conduits for the enculturation of people into subcultural communities, as well as for the development of cultural identity for those who are already part of a cultural group.

Fraser writes "public spheres are not only arenas for the formation of discursive opinion; in addition they are the arenas for the formation and enactment of social identities" (1992: 125). She stops short, however, of attributing the status of "community" to these publics, as communities suggest "bounded and fairly homogeneous group[s]," while publics "emphasize discursive interaction that is in principle open-ended [between] a plurality of perspectives" (1992: 141, note 28). This distinction raises the question of the nature of micropolitical debate within subcultural groupings. By micropolitical, I mean specifically the intra-group debates and discussions that revolve around a group's constituent features, ideology, actions, and relations with other groups, as well as other self-referential matters. As discursive debate is an essential component of any healthy community, modern forms of communication, which can be seen as media that subtend public sphere interaction, have the potential to change the way such debate occurs—sometimes radically altering the nature of subcultural enculturation and experience. By exploring the relationship between sadomasochistic community formation and the media that support the BDSM subaltern public sphere,[4] I wish to demonstrate this alteration—one that here can be seen as a form of inversion.

BDSM in the Public Sphere

Serious sadomasochistic subculture is a fairly recent discourse-culture in our society. It is traceable as a distinct subculture back to Leopold von Sacher-Masoch's *Venus in Furs* (1870) and its subsequent, almost cultish, popularity (Glassco 1997). When the sexologist Richard von Kraft-Ebing coined and paired the terms "sadism" and "masochism" as appellations for common perversions in 1886, the discursive groundwork was laid for a reverse discourse, with subjects claiming these diagnostic titles as identities (Linden 1982; Foucault 1976). While one doesn't, of course, need to be part of a subcultural SM scene to take part in sadomasochistic activities, many have found these identities and communities positive and ethical additions to their lives and personalities. There have been people practicing SM under that name, other names, or no name throughout recorded history, and it is likely that as long as dominance and submission has been part of sexuality, so has its eroticization (Gebhard 1995). Private participation in SM requires only minimal access to its discourse: a book, a movie, or just a healthy imagination and a length of rope. Becoming part of a sadomasochistic subcultural group, however, is an involved process requiring access to spaces, knowledge about appropriate and especially inappropriate scene etiquette and practices, and (perhaps most importantly), having others believe that you belong as a part of that community.

It is very difficult to track the early history of sadomasochistic subcultural groups, which consisted of small circles of private practitioners and the occasional very private club, most of which didn't know of each other's existence (Stein 1991). From the early 1970s, however, the emergence of SM clubs and writing by sadomasochists for sadomasochists has enabled a semi-public community to be assembled (Houlberg 1995)—though it suffered in the 1980s from a crackdown in the United States on SM pornography (Califia 1988: 9–27). In the beginning, these subcultural groups comprised mostly gay men, and specifically "Leathermen," gay males who were discursively into leather apparel, SM, and often motorbikes (Houlberg 1995; Kamel 1995). The discourse of SM circulated within this subaltern counterpublic of leather clubs and specific books and magazines targeted toward Leathermen. A gradual diversification, however, began to creep into Leatherculture throughout the 1980s, with straight men as well as both gay and straight women joining existing SM clubs, or forming their own (Houlberg 1995). However, the SM community remained intimately linked with Leatherculture as the information that circulated within the sadomasochistic public sphere, while not exclusively available to those in Leatherculture, was certainly more available to, and keyed for, this audience. More importantly, that is where people went to look for it, often donning leathers and affecting/developing a leather identity to do so (Stein 1991).

Access to these semi-public spheres was essential for anyone who wanted to become part of the sadomasochistic community. As it is the nature of sadomasochistic activities to demand a highly stylized and specific re-keying of behavior which, outside an SM context is violent, hurtful, and dangerous (and indeed can be legally prosecutable (Weinberg 1995)), access to the discursive sphere of BDSM was the only way to become a part of its discourse-culture. The limited reach of the sadomasochistic public sphere and the identity co-requisites of participating in it therefore dictated who could easily participate in sadomasochistic subcultures. This dependence in sadomasochistic culture on the circulation and distribution of various media that enable a sadomasochistic discourse, therefore, deserves greater consideration.

Interlude: Media, Subcultural Capital, and the Internet

Before the issue of sadomasochistic discourse over the Internet can be addressed, however, the relationship between public sphere discourses and "the media" must be clarified. Habermas identifies a bourgeois "free-press" as a potential medium for public sphere debate, but laments the fact that, as he sees it, media institutions are quickly corrupted by private, state and/or commercial interests (Calhoun 1992). The media, then, is seen as circulating "manufactured opinion" and ceases to become the voice of an independent public sphere; it is rather a tool or branch of governmental or economic forces (Calhoun 1992: 23). By this reckoning, media functions as an antithetical force to public sphere relations. The Birmingham School[5] holds a similar position; in relation to subcultures, its various thinkers interpret expressions originating from within subcultural discourses as "authentic," while contributions to the same discourses from media and commerce are seen as "inauthentic" (Thornton 1995: 9). Going even further, Eric Clark (2000) posits that public sphere visibility is predicated on an imposed homogenization that threatens to render members of (especially marginalized) subaltern counterpublics functionally invisible with regard to their own discourses within the public sphere. He contends that if the bar that must be passed to participate in public sphere discourse is the assumption of a "publicly acceptable social aspect" it is begging the question of representation, making certain identities and practices, like those of drag queens and sex radicals, non-representable as such (Clark 2000: 41). He is particularly critical of mass media representation, which he seems to conflate with television, as many media theorists tend to (Thornton 1995).

All of these opinions, however, flow from the limited and singular conception that there is one monolithic public sphere. If we apply Nancy Fraser's revised "multiple publics" model, subcultural differences become the fuel for productive debate, rather than the silent irresolvable tragedy at the heart of shallow interaction. Homogeneity, of the type discussed by Clark, remains an important problematic, but one that is nuanced by other modalities of (counter) public sphere visibility.[6]

In *Club Cultures: Music, Media, and Subcultural Capital* (1995), Sarah Thornton develops a three-streamed rendering of media that can be much more useful than monolithic models when dissecting media/subculture relationships. She takes as a general premise the idea that the Birmingham cultural studies conception of subcultures—that they are authentic and pure entities that pre-exist corrupting media (and commercial) influences—is an oversimplification that ignores the fundamental ways that various forms of media work to circulate the discourses of these subcultures. She draws on the work of Pierre Bourdieu, extending his concept of cultural capital[7] to subcultures and defining *sub*cultural capital as "subspecies of capital operating within [...] less privileged domains" (Thornton 1995: 11). With this move she stakes her departure from the Birmingham tradition by theorizing that subcultural groups are not horizontally organized entities that exist in opposition to a vertically organized, stratified mainstream, but rather that they are discursive entities in their own right with an internal organization structured by a movement of subcultural capital.

Thornton theorizes that the possession of subculture-specific capital tracks one's potential status in that subculture. Since many elements that make up subcultural capital are informational, their circulation via various media are important determinants of the relations of members within those subcultures. By this conception, instead of an outside corrupting influence (as the Birmingham scholars would have it), or a homogenizing system (as Eric Clark would contend), media becomes "a network crucial to the definition and distribution of cultural knowledge" (Thornton 1995: 14). Thornton goes on to identify two forms of media that play significant roles in circulating subcultural discourse. The first, *niche media,* are ostensibly mass-media forms, but ones that have such a highly specialized target audience that they are—even in their advertising—firmly rooted in specific subcultures. *Micromedia,* on the other hand, are highly targeted and specific media such as flyers, posters, pirate radio, zines, and the Internet. The access to these forms can be seen as the social co-requisite to participation in many subaltern counterpublics. However, many of these forms of media are only available to people who have already become members of a specific subculture. Their limited circulation can make them difficult to get, and their use of subculture-specific jargon or slang can often make them difficult to interpret.

I would argue that the Internet, however, is a fundamentally different form of media. Its versatile nature renders it focused yet at the same time quite public. It has the specificity of niche and other micromedia sources, with the resultant ability to focus on, and cater to, quite specific subcultures, while at the same time making the fruits of those discourses available to people in general. It contains specific jargon and slang—the language of subcultures—but with the informational tools to decrypt it. In fact it is the informational nature of the Internet that gives it this versatility. It is a medium that contains and circulates subcultural capital, but unlike its more traditional counterparts, its access restrictions are organized along different lines than ones of sexual or stylistic identity.[8]

SM Enculturation and the Circulation of Subcultural Capital

Traditionally, there were several ways of getting enculturated into the world of Leatherculture and then into SM, but they all seemed to follow a similar pattern. In his article "The Leather Career: On Becoming a Sadomasochist," Kamel (1995) sketches out a typical pattern of SM enculturation as observed among gay men. Curiosity about SM would lead gay men to seek access to the sadomasochistic public sphere:

> Avenues of such information may include perusals through both pornographic and non-pornographic periodicals; questioning friends; weighing hearsay, myths, and rumors; and visiting leather-oriented establishments [which] may include out-of-town visits to S&M bath houses. (Kamel 1995: 55)

All of these actions have implications for identities. Purchasing or borrowing SM materials, revealing your interest to friends, and especially donning some leathers and becoming a patron of SM clubs or bathhouses have serious implications for the way others see you, and the way you see yourself. Indeed, Kamel goes on to say that if SM practices are indeed found to be pleasurable experiences, then an increase in commitment to Leatherculture is often the result, producing "a second coming out phase when leather bars, baths and perhaps bike organizations become a focal point of attention" (Kamel 1995: 56).

Cruising these, or similar, scenes to discover potential partners that will be willing to "train" a novice in the fine art of SM is a commonly referenced part of SM enculturation and appears often in fictional (e.g., Califia 1988: 28) and non-fictional (e.g., Stein 1991) SM narratives. These trainings can take place during public sex, individual sexual flings or (and quite often) through relationships. Knowledge of (and skill in) the art of SM is the most prominent form of subcultural capital in the SM community, with those in the know often able to use that cachet to social advantage. This can refer to everything from the knowledge of SM protocol; skill with ropes, floggers, and other toys; expertise with obscure or potentially dangerous forms such a piercing, cutting, and flame play; or just to sheer scene experience. In addition to finding partners, spaces and resources, membership in an SM community allows one to participate in micropolitical debate about SM identity. The media of these debates were often micromedia attached to a specific SM scene, like, for example, the newsletter or magazine of a particular SM club.[9]

In "The Magazine of a Sadomasochism Club: The Tie That Binds," Rick Houlberg (1995) investigates one such magazine. The monthly magazine of the club he studies was, at the time of study, sent out to over 800 members in the United States and abroad and contained everything from photos, poetry, and personal messages from members, to how-to articles, scene descriptions, short stories, and debates about how the club should be run and about SM in general. Though this medium for public sphere interaction was broader in scope, as the club in question had, by the late 1980s, started to represent people other than gay Leathermen, it was still an enclaved public sphere, as to receive the magazine you had to already be a club member (Houlberg 1995). In addition, to join many—though not all—of these clubs one needed to have the sponsorship of an existing member (Stein 1991). In general then, the typical SM career, which is predicated on a gradual accumulation of sadomasochistic subcultural capital, would involve taking part in some actions to come in contact with the SM community; forming an SM identity; and then potentially joining an extended SM subculture through a mediated sadomasochistic subaltern public sphere. This is also in line with view of how a public (or counterpublic) is formed by the auto-organizing fact of discourse

(Warner 2002). The micromedia SM discourse over the Internet, however, has the ability to support a different progression. Although still a micro-mediated form, due to its structure and more open points of access the type of counterpublic it organizes offers different constraints, opportunities, and flows. Thus, while not *causing* a difference in the process of BDSM encul-turation, it has the potential to *enable* different modes and approaches to subcultural participation.

The Internet-Mediated Sadomasochistic Public Sphere

Internet publics typify the subcultural ideal of being idea-driven. Unlike Fou-cault's reverse discourses that claim discursive space already marked out for certain people by a marginalizing discourse and work with it, the informa-tional aspect of cyberculture enables a direct relationship with notional aspects of people's personalities. In other words, it can act as a direct space of representation, one created from the bottom up as opposed to trying to reclaim spaces of representation in others' discourses. In *Virtual Spaces: Sex and the Cybercitizen*, Cleo Odzer writes "[a]11 social interaction combines our inner and outer worlds but cyberspace provides an especially versatile medium for expressing the internal" (1997: 6). Given Thornton's notion of subcultural capital as being the prime determinant of status in a subculture, Internet communities allow the free circulation of much of this information. The existence of a publicly accessible BDSM counterpublic allows people to become enculturated into an SM community through mere participation in the discourse-culture of BDSM over the Internet. And since there is no spe-cific SM-oriented investment entailed in computer-ownership, or Internet-access, this enculturation can occur outside and apart from the enactment of other social identities. Compared to the leather bar scene where "no one talked to anyone unless they were already friends or cruising each other" and where "sight and then touch seemed to be the main senses one communi-cated with" (Stein 1991: 143–144), the Internet allows for a more funda-mentally intellectual connection with the discourse of sadomasochistic sexuality.

This discourse can take many forms. There are websites devoted to the dissemination of BDSM information such as *bdsm-list.com,* and more interac-tive entities such as the newsgroup *soc.subculture.bondage-bdsm (s.s.b-b.)* where ongoing conversations on various topics occur. A content analysis of these sites shows that pictures and didactic diagrams, short stories and descriptions of scenes, and sometimes even video clips[10] are all available for public access. Beyond being a wealth of information in their own right, these sites usually reference other media sources such as books and magazines, with information on where they are available, and often links to allow you to purchase them privately, over the Internet.[11] A further level of involvement is the SM online group. Online groups such as *dssg.org* in Toronto provide much the same information as the magazines of specific SM clubs, but, unlike many of these predecessors, are available to anyone who sends an e-mail request to join. They are venues for ongoing debate on various issues within the SM world, book reviews, calendars of real-world events, scene summaries, and the like. It is through e-mail or newsgroup messages between and among different members of the same online group that this counterpublic can begin to foster a sense of community. A final Internet medium for BDSM interaction is the role-playing world of Internet chat sites such as MUDs and MOOs, and graphical online spaces such as MMOGs and MMOSs.[12] Cybersexual[13] encounters can be a powerful way to role-play certain sexual situations that one might be reticent to attempt in real life (Odzer 1997). In fact, some online virtual environments have "rooms" specifically designed for virtual sadomasochistic encounters, and indeed one MOO named *Strangebrew* was completely devoted to SM interactions (Odzer 1997). With new technology comes new possibilities for the extension of sexual discursivity. The MMOS *Second Life*, for example, contains many "mature" areas where BDSM sexuality is explored by avatars who don pixilated fetish gear and wield virtual floggers and canes. In fact at least one entire virtual neighborhood on *The Sims Online*, Rose Thorn Gardens, is entirely devoted to BDSM lifestyling and play, and in 2003 was inhabited by over 100 denizens (Urizenus, 2003).

Watching, participating in, or reading about the activities in these environments is a form of access to the sadomasochistic public sphere, analogous to being present at an SM scene, but more covert and with more freedom of identity. Indeed the ease with which one could participate in the online sexual SM discourse-culture led an unprecedented number of people who engaged in cybersex to try it, often using the anonymity of the Internet to try different subject positions (dom/sub; male/female; gay/straight) (Odzer 1997). Through this route, many people who might not ever feel comfortable in a leather bar find themselves able to engage with this counterpublic, some going farther and taking part in the online sexual SM discourse-culture, and some going as far as to make BDSM and/or BDSM culture a part of their offline sexual lives.

Conclusion: The Expansion of BDSM
or Taking the Leather Out of Leathersex

It is, therefore, now much easier to join a sadomasochistic counterpublic without first developing an SM identity. Through participation in an Internet-mediated public, one can first form an idea of the types of BDSM behaviors in which one may be interested. This can then lead to the adoption of an SM identity second, and subsequently to real-world actions. This may be compared to the previous model in which a person would need to develop a leather image (and often identity) first and then would "drift" through the leather community until bad experiences would set the "limit" of what he or she was interested in doing (Kamel 1995: 58). Furthermore, this form of subaltern sphere has the following qualities:

▼ SM practitioners in widespread areas can be part of a unified community with much more ease and regularity.

▼ Non-practitioners of SM can learn about SM and contribute to its discourse.

▼ People can experiment with the psychological and methodological aspects of SM interaction in safer virtual spaces.

▼ The subcultural capital of the sadomasochistic discourse-culture can be freely and widely distributed.

The results of this more open formation of subcultural capital distribution are widespread and not always positive,[14] but one of the most interesting is the parsing of Leatherculture and BDSM culture. Leatherculture—which incidentally also has a thriving Internet public sphere[15]—is no longer the "host" discourse for BDSM culture. While there were always non-sadomasochistic Leatherfolk and non-leather sadomasochists, until the proliferation of a more open sadomasochistic public presence, those who wanted to be part of a sadomasochistic community would generally think they had to adopt a leather identity to do so. This is ironic, as the majority of those in Leatherculture, while assumed to be SM-oriented, were, in fact, into vanilla sex; and while the majority of leather bars were full of gay men in search of the SM scene, few who actually had access to that scene chose to frequent leather bars too often, preferring private parties (Stein 1991). Now, in fetish clubs and at play parties, while many people are still adorned in leather and spikes, there are also people in jeans and T-shirts, comfortable in their subcultural identities due to their informational and experiential endowments of subcultural capital partially gleaned from their participation in an Internet-mediated sadomasochistic public sphere.

For BDSM practitioners, the Internet appears to enable the beginning of an apparently new style of BDSM discourse-culture, with many roots in Leatherculture, but certainly moving beyond it. And finally, since the subcultural capital of BDSM is centered around how one can appropriate coercion, sexual violence, restraint, domination, humiliation, and the like and rearticulate them in a safe, sane, and consensual way, and since these are the aspects of SM that most trouble its critics (Linden 1982), it seems as though having this information available beyond the purview of those within the sub-altern counterpublic proper would be beneficial to inter-cultural communication between this public sphere and others.

Notes

1. An earlier version of this chapter appeared under the title "Taking the Leather Out of Leathersex: The Implications of an Internet-mediated Sadomasochistic Public Sphere for Subcultural Identity Formation," in *GR—Journal for the Arts, Sciences, and Technology 2.2* (2004): 39–44.
2. A shortened acronym, the full form of which is BD DS SM (Bondage and Discipline; Domination and Submission; Sadism and Masochism.
3. Let me, from right off the bat (and as has become customary) defuse this chapter of the specter of technological determinism. That this chapter argues that the Internet (*qua* technology) enables, in interaction with human culture, some distinct qualities is clear. And yet, to simply mount a counterargument based on an accusation of technological determinism is overly facile. Technology, like other technical forms (such as language, market capitalism, the limerick) does have the ability, to a certain extent, to determine human affairs; but, it is a soft determination—like that of the stick that guides the growth of the tomato plant. It does not determine every aspect of the usage of the thing, but it influences things *in as much as they are tied to it*. It is also not alone in the field of determination. It, therefore, is as much to worry about as gravitational determination and nutritional determination—it is at play whenever technology is at play, and is worth considering for that reason. Any given technology offers constraints, possibilities, flows, lines of flight—some of which are unique to that form. But it is in the already-social (or socio-technical) where these forces come into play.
4. That the sadomasochistic public sphere can be said to be a public (or counterpublic) is evident in its constituent features. According to Michael Warner, a public "comes into being [. . .] in relation to texts and their circulation" (66) and has the following constituent features:

    1. It is self-organized.
    2. It is a relation among strangers.
    3. Its form of address is both personal and impersonal.
    4. It is constituted through mere attention.
    5. It is the social space created by the reflexive circulation of discourse.
    6. It acts historically according the temporality of its circulation.
    7. It is a poetic world making.

    In all these manners, the circulation of BDSM discourse, through its presentation and reception, forms both a public and a discourse-culture, and as well *enables* community (as opposed to creating or ensuring it, which are very different things).
5. Referring to thought coming out of the Centre for Contemporary Cultural Studies, University of Birmingham, England.
6. These other modalities often present commentary and critique on the more homogenous public sphere representations, extending, and complementing, their dis-

courses. As a result, these problematically narrow discourses, framed and reframed in these more productive arenas, have additional space to develop and differentiate from mainstream matter.

7. "[K]nowledge that is accumulated through upbringing and education which confers social status [. . .] the linchpin of a system of distinction in which cultural hierarchies correspond to social ones and people's tastes are predominantly a marker of class" (Thornton 1995: 10).

8. Such as the class-implicated ones of computer/Internet access, access to private computer-viewing environments, geographic access to the Internet, local obscenity laws, etc.

9. Though other micro-mediated forms such as handouts at SM clubs that outline rules and protocols and flyers promoting the dates and locations of future events were (and are) equally important.

10. An issue and influence that I don't address fully is that of sadomasochistic and BDSM pornography. I make such a distinction in the same way as I would make a distinction between "lesbian porn" and porn made by and for lesbians. While sadomasochistic pornography certainly has a strong influence on the shape and texture of the sadomasochistic public sphere, the sheer amount of porn made simply using the trope of SM, but without, for example, the ethics of consent and safety upheld within the BDSM discourse-culture proper, makes its discussion both problematic and beyond the scope of this essay. Suffice it to say that (1) It is an influence; (2) That influence is one of the internal problematics within the sadomasochistic public sphere; and (3) It cannot be taken as representative of the BDSM community as the intersection between pornography and SM often brings out the worst aspects of both beasts (e.g., sexist scenes with people who look like models in potentially unsafe conditions while the BDSM community at it best strives for the opposite on all of those counts).

11. Though there are some who would condemn this targeted marketing as an effect of the market segmentation of subcultures (e.g., Clark 2000: 50), many of the publications and/or equipment so-advertised is made by people within the SM community for the benefit of its members, making commerce—and even advertising—at this level subculturally authentic.

12. MUD (Multi-User Domain/Dungeon): A program that creates a text-based virtual environment with which multiple users can interact. Much like a text-based computer role-playing game, these versatile environments (which were very popular in the 1990s) can be programmed to emulate any sort of environment, from a forest glade to a fully equipped SM dungeon.

    MOO (MUD, Object Oriented): A slightly more complex chat system, involving programmable virtual objects.

    MMOG/MMORPG (Massively Multi-player Online [Role-Playing] Game): The descendant of the MUD, these immersive graphical environments are entered by millions of people and used for online gaming.

    MMOS (Massively Multi-User Online Space): Similar to MMOGs in technology, these new online spaces are becoming a new and popular venue for online social interaction.

13. Computer-based intellectual sexual encounters. These interactions can be as simple as "hot-chat" which involves simple talking and is usually accompanied by masturbation (and which is analogous to phone-sex), to fully narrative or graphical

encounters in which people's virtual avatars interact sexually in a cyberspacial environment. This latter form is often seen as so satisfying in itself that isn't always accompanied by masturbation, and is more analogous to role-playing (Odzer 1997: 12, 42).

14. For example, the issue of trust becomes an object of contention. Due to the nature of the BDSM community (that it is potentially both emotionally and physically dangerous; that there is a sometimes need for anonymity and secrecy; that there is the specter of legal issues, etc.) trust is essential. The fact of more open BDSM discourse means that the experience of trust no longer maps on to reputation or simple possession of subcultural capital—that X member has been part of a certain club for years or knows all the right lingo might now mean little or nothing in terms of real world experience. In this new world of BDSM, practitioners sometimes claim to have a lot of experience (with, for example, caning), when what they mean is they have lots of *virtual* experience of role-played caning (Easton and Hardy 2001: 62). There is also sometimes less care taken with safety and an inflation (or deflation, as the case may be) of personas and egos that are not calibrated by reality checks, etc. (Easton and Hardy 2001: 54). This and similar other issues are seen by some simply as an unfortunate consequence of the type of space cyberspace is, and by others as a "pollution" of a purer, more closed world of private BDSM discourse.

15. For an example and links, visit *The Leatherman's Discussion Group* at www.sfldg.org.

References

bdsm-list.com. Retrieved November 4, 2005, from http://bdsm-list.com/

Calhoun, C. 1992. "Introduction: Habermas and the Public Sphere," in Craig Calhoun (Ed.), *Habermas and the Public Sphere* (pp. 1–48). Cambridge, MA, and London: MIT Press.

Califia, P. 1988. *Macho Sluts*. Los Angeles and New York: Alyson.

Clark, E. O. 2000. *Virtuous Vice: Homoeroticism and the Public Sphere*. Durham, NC, and London: Duke University Press.

Easton, D., and Hardy, J. W. 2001. *The New Bottoming Book*. Emeryville, CA: Greenery.

Foucault, M. 1991. "Politics and the Study of Discourse," in G. Burchell, C. Gordon, and P. Miller (Eds.), *The Foucault Effect: Studies in Governmentality* (pp. 53–72), Chicago: University of Chicago Press.

Foucault, M. 1976. *The History of Sexuality: An Introduction*. Trans. R. Hurley. New York: Vintage.

Fraser, N. 1992. "Rethinking the Public Sphere: A Contribution to the Critique of Actually Existing Democracy," in C. Calhoun (Ed.), *Habermas and the Public Sphere* (pp. 109–142). Cambridge, MA, and London: MIT Press.

Gebhard, P. H. 1995. "Sadomasochism," in T. S. Weinberg (Ed.), *S&M: Studies in Dominance and Submission* (pp. 41–45). New York: Prometheus.

Glassco, J. 1977. "Introduction," in L. von Sacher-Masoch (Ed.), *Venus in Furs* (pp. i–xi). Trans. J. Glassco. Burnaby, BC, Canada: Blackfish.

Habermas, J. 1962. *The Structural Transformation of the Public Sphere: An Inquiry into a Category of Bourgeois Society*. 1989. Trans. T. Burger and F. Lawrence. Cambridge, MA: MIT Press.

Highleyman, L. 1996. "Kinky Bisexuals: Ultimate Switches or Ultimate Outcasts?" *Cuir Underground*. 2.4. (February). Retrieved June 3, 2003, from http://www.black-rose.com/cuiru/archive/2-4/bi-sm.html

Houlberg, R. 1995. "The Magazine of a Sadomasochistic Club: The Tie That Binds," in T. S. Weinberg (Ed.), *S&M: Studies in Dominance and Submission* (pp. 269–286). New York: Prometheus.

Kamel, G. W. L. 1995. "The Leather Career: On Becoming a Sadomasochist," in T. S. Weinberg (Ed.), *S&M: Studies in Dominance and Submission* (pp. 51–60). New York: Prometheus.

Leatherman's Discussion Group. Retrieved November 3, 2005, from http://www.sfldg.org/

Linden, R. R. 1982. "Introduction: Against Sadomasochism," in R. R. Linden, D. R. Pagano, D. E. H. Russell, and S.L. Star (Eds.), *Against Sadomasochism: A Radical Feminist Analysis* (pp. 1–15). East Palo Alto, CA: Frog in the Wall.

Odzer, C. 1997. *Virtual Spaces: Sex and the Cyber Citizen*. New York: Berkley.

soc.subculture.bondage-bdsm. s.s.b-b. Retrieved June 3, 2003, from news:soc.subculture.bondage-bdsm

Stein, D. 1991. "S/M's Copernican Revolution: From a Closed World to the Infinite Universe," in M. Thompson (Ed.), *Leatherfolk: Radical Sex, People, Politics, and Practice* (pp. 142–156). Boston: Alyson.

Thompson, M. 1991. "Introduction," in M. Thompson (Ed.), *Leatherfolk: Radical Sex, People, Politics, and Practice* (pp. xi–xx). Boston: Alyson.

Thornton, S. 1995. *Club Cultures: Music, Media and Subcultural Capitol*. Cambridge, UK: Polity.

Urizenus. 2003. "Interview with Anonymous, On Alphaville's Bondage, Discipline & Sadomasochism Community." *The Second Life Herald*. Retrieved August 28, 2006, from http://www.dragonscoveherald.com/blog/index.php?p=60

Warner, M. 2002. *Publics and Counterpublics*. New York: Zone Books.

Weinberg, T. S. 1987. "Sadomasochism in the United States: A Review of Recent Sociological Literature." *Journal of Sex Research 23*(1), 50–69.

Weinberg, T. S. 1995. "Sadism and Masochism: Sociological Perspectives," in T. S. Weinberg (Ed.), *S&M: Studies in Dominance and Submission* (pp. 119–137). New York: Prometheus.

5. Young Queers Online: The Limits and Possibilities of Non-Heterosexual Self-Representation in Online Conversations

MARJO LAUKKANEN

Even though the internet is widely described as a place of freedom (see Paasonen 2002: 8–11), many websites demand users to fill in a registration form before using or even entering the site. Quite often one is asked to mark one's sex, and almost always there are two choices: Male (M) or Female (F). Teresa de Lauretis points out that the moment we choose to mark F, we officially enter the sex-gender system. She emphasizes that after this, not only do others consider us female but also we are representing ourselves as woman. De Lauretis discusses this apparently small act by asking, "[I]sn't that the same as saying that the *F* next to the little box, which we marked in filling out the form, has stuck to us like a wet silk dress? Or that while we thought that we were marking the *F* on the form, in fact the *F* was marking itself on us?" (de Lauretis 1989: 11–12).

The internet has carried our hopes to be a media where sex and gender can lose their meaning or where they can vary from the male/female dichotomy (see O'Brien 1999: 77–79; Seidler 1998: 20). The online discussion world *LambdaMOO*, for example, offers a choice of additional gender designations like neuter, either, or plural (Roberts and Parks 2001: 269). Despite these possibilities, the words of de Lauretis come to my mind when I view the registration form on the *Demi* website.[1] It is the site of the most popular Finnish girls' magazine, and it is aimed at twelve- to nineteen-year-old girls. To fill in the registration form is the first step toward becoming a participating user and member of a group that is addressed as an online-community (see Gustafson 2002). Registered users of *Demi* can talk with each other on different discussion forums, write and read online-diaries, and look for pen pals. According to the users' self-representations in these different sections, *Demi* is not used only by teenage girls but also by teenage boys and slightly older women and men. Even though the site is primarily aimed at teenage girls, the default option for user in the registration form is "Male." If the user wants to represent herself as woman, she needs to press the arrow of a pull-down menu and choose "Female." If the user forgets to do this or does not want to mark her or his sex, the user is represented as a male.

The main focus of this chapter is to explore the limits and possibilities of non-heterosexual self-representation in online conversations. The emphasis is on the links and dynamics between self-representation of sex, gender, and sexual orientation. For example, what kinds of sexual self-representations are possible in the site where users are immediately divided into males and females? This is examined through the study of a group of non-heterosexual Finnish teenagers. The group started to form in 2002 on *Demi*'s forum *Relations,* where a discussion began under the title *closet.* In 2003 the group founded their own online space, an internet Relay Chat (IRC) room called the *#closet.* According to the group's homepage, the *closet* was originally meant for girls and young women who belong to sexual minorities. Later the group has welcomed all young people, who belong to gender and sexual minorities.

As a researcher, I have followed the group for over two years using an ethnographic approach. Internet researcher Christine Hine defines virtual ethnography as ethnography in, of and through the virtual. It requires a sustained presence of a researcher in the field setting, and an intensive and visible real-time engagement with mediated interaction with informants. (Hine 2000: 23–27, 64–65). My study did not start as a piece of ethnographic research, but in time it developed to be one. First I planned only to gather and copy conversations, and use critical discourse analysis (Fairclough 1995) to analyze them. Eventually, I did this, but I ended up using other methods too. The final empirical material consists of numerous online-observation hours, hundreds of copied conversations, tens of online interviews and e-mails with fourteen informants,[2] photographs, and one face-to-face meeting with a key-informant. The theoretical framework is based on Teresa de Lauretis' writings of sex, gender, and sexual orientation as social representations and self-representations. The research frame enables an analysis of the self-representations of the same group of users in different discursive spaces and in different interaction situations.

Online discussion forums and rooms are spaces where social reality and social representations are produced usually in text-based interaction (see Fairclough 1995: 6; O'Brien 1999). In online interaction the user's material body is often invisible to the others, but the user's body nevertheless has three social dimensions: material, represented, and imagined. The material body refers to an operating and feeling subject at the screen (see Campbell 2004: 1–4). The represented body refers to a body that is textually or visually represented on the internet. Self-representation is considered "true" if it "matches" with the material body. The imagined body refers to the user's image produced in the minds of other users. The imagined body is influenced by the user's self-representation, writings, and opinions.

This chapter begins with an interpretation of why and how the *closet* was founded on *Demi*. It is based on a critical discourse analysis of conversations inside and outside the *closet*. This is followed by a detailed analysis of how non-heterosexual informants define themselves in a group interview in the *#closet*. What kinds of definitions and representations are possible for them in online conversations and in online photographs? The limits and possibilities of self-representation are explicit especially in the accounts of two teenagers, drop_out and Erzbischof,[3] who have difficulties in defining and representing themselves in the dichotomized sex-gender system. Social representations, self-representations, and self-definitions intertwine in the online conversations and in the accounts of the interviewees. The last section of the chapter suggests that the ways users experience sex, gender, and sexuality crucially constrain the ways in which they can represent themselves on the supposedly "free" internet.

Becoming Closeted

In the Finnish language there is only one word for both sex and gender, and that is "sukupuoli." It consists of two words: "suku" can be translated as "family" or "gender," and "puoli" as "half" or "side." The compound refers to both reproduction and division into two, as theorist Tuija Pulkkinen (1996: 165) points out. So the Finnish word for sex/gender represents and produces a power system of sexuality which has been theorized as the heterosexual contract by Monique Wittig (1980/1992), as compulsory heterosexuality by Adrianne Rich (1980/1996), and as the heterosexual matrix by Judith Butler (1990: 151 note 6) in her early work. It reveals the inseparable link between binary sex/gender and heterosexuality in our culture.

The same power system that produces heterosexuality produces homosexuality since one cannot exist without the other. This becomes visible in the metaphor "closet." According to queer-theorist Eve Kosofsky Sedgwick (1990: 68–70) the closet is an essential metaphor that defines homosexuality and its oppression in Western cultures. It describes both the absence and presence of homosexuality in heteronormative society (Brown 2000: 1). "Being in the closet" means hiding one's sexual orientation, and "coming out" or "being out" refers to being open and public about it. Cultural researcher Affrica Taylor argues that in our culture the closet has a dual function: it is a protection and a prison. The act of coming out can make one vulnerable in a hostile environment, but it also offers the promise of liberating one's true self (Taylor 1997: 14). It is a personal as well as political act, due to its meaning for the modern gay rights movement (Phillips 2002: 408–409).

Some earlier studies suggest that coming out or being out is easier online than offline (see Brown et al. 2005; Shaw 1997; Wakeford 1997). The same idea is used in an advertisement that got social scientist Jodi O'Brien's attention. In the advertisement gay men were persuaded to use certain online conversation spaces by promising that "there are no closets in cyberspace." The advertisement argues that through the freedom of the internet one can be what ever he is or wants to be (O'Brien 1999: 82–83). The first time I came across the *closet* was in early spring 2003 during non-participant observation on *Demi*. At that time the site was visited by 50,000–60,000 different users monthly.[4] The asynchronous conversations took place on different forums, and participants used pseudonyms which they called "nicks." The conversations had their own rules and supervisors. Illegality, obscenity, and abusiveness were forbidden, but they were nevertheless quite common.

At that time the conversations on the forum *Relations* could be divided into three types according to the expression of sexual orientation. The first and clearly major part of the conversations consists of those in which sexual orientation is not the explicit topic; instead, participants talk about dating, love, and sex under titles like "Do you have a boyfriend?" or "About virginity." In these conversations romantic and sexual relations happen only between a boy and a girl. In other words, sexuality is constructed heteronormatively (Butler 1993; see also Yep 2003: 12–14). The second part consists of conversations where sexual orientation is the main topic and it is constructed explicitly. For example, the participants may ask, "What do you think about bi girls?" and some appeal to others to help them define their sexual orientation. The third part consists of conversations which all have the title *closet* and in which non-heterosexual girls talk with each other. The first and second types of conversation belong to the public space of *Demi*, while the *closet* is a space for a small subgroup of people inside the public forum.

To understand why the *closet* was founded I analyze and compare the construction of sexuality in the *closet* and in conversations where the sexual orientation is constructed explicitly. What makes this comparison meaningful is the link between these conversations. The former begun from the latter, more accurately, the *closet* group started to form in 2002 in a conversation that was titled "LeSBianS." The first message of this conversation consisted of two questions: "Are there any lesbians or bisexual women here? It would be nice to know am I the only one . . . ?" Empirical material for analysis was gathered about a year after this first message, in spring 2003.[5] During the gathering and the time of analysis I acted as an invisible and silent observer.

On the *Relations* forum, public conversations about sexual orientation are often polarized. Many participants either defend or oppose homosexuality. One of the most common defensive discourses is the *humane discourse* which emphasizes the similarity and equality of all people: "They are humans the same as straight!" Homosexuals are seen as normal and ordinary as heterosexuals. This discourse is also used by the Finnish gay and lesbian movement, which demands equal rights for non-heterosexuals and heterosexuals (Stålström and Nieminen 2000). The humane discourse questions heterosexuality as a norm. On the other hand, it is regarded as frustrating by many participants, because if the humanity of non-heterosexuals needs to be explicitly and constantly repeated, then it is not self-evident. Another defensive discourse is the *idealizing discourse,* in which homosexuals and bisexuals are regarded as better or more interesting people than heterosexuals.

In Finland homosexuality was decriminalized in 1971, and removed from the national classification of diseases in 1981 (Stålström and Nieminen 2000: 119, 128). In *Demi,* the majority of nicks defend homosexuality, but at the same time it is fiercely expressed as objectionable by some nicks. They often use the *pathologicalizing discourse,* in which everything else but heterosexuality is regarded as sick, abnormal, and filthy. Nicks who use this discourse often refer to throwing up and feeling sick if they see homosexuals or even think about them: "UGH! Gross and you think they are like others!!!!!!!" Some even try to provoke others to hate crimes (see Yep 2003: 22–23). The users of this discourse separate themselves strictly from gays. Before the registration of same-sex partnerships was legalized in Finland in 2002, the *discourse of nature* and the *discourse of religion* were central in public debates about same-sex marriage (Charpentier 2000). In *Demi* these discourses are used not only against homosexuality but also for defending it. Within these discursive frames homosexuality is defined as unnatural because same-sex couples cannot reproduce, or as natural because there is homosexuality among animals too. It is found objectionable on the basis that it is a sin, the same basis on which it has long been objected to in the Lutheran state church (Stålström and Nieminen 2000: 128), or it is defended as a part of God's creation.

Sexual orientation is defined through love and sex, and as identity. In the *discourse of love* sexuality is connected to romantic feelings and love is seen as an important human right, while in the *discourse of sex* sexuality is connected to sexual behavior or strong sexual desires. In the *discourse of identity* humans are born to be heterosexual, homosexual, or bisexual. Sexual identity is understood to be singular and permanent. One can hide it but one cannot choose or change it. This discourse is similar to many identity development theories and models (see, for example, Lehtonen 1998: 186–187, 191). Identity can be found through self-analysis, by falling in love or performing a sexual act. In the *individualistic discourse,* the categorization of one's sexual orientation is resisted as unnecessary. This individualistic discourse often conflicts with the discourses of humanity and love.

In the *discourse of majority* heterosexuality is self-evidently normal and the expected sexuality. A common assumption is that everyone—or at least everyone here—is heterosexual (Lehtonen 2000: 284). For example, in the opening messages of the analyzed conversations no one writes, "I am heterosexual." It is not necessary because one is automatically considered heterosexual if she or he does not say otherwise, it is the unmarked category. Girls who reflect on their sexuality on *Demi* are defined by others more often as heterosexuals than bisexuals or lesbians. Their sexual feelings toward other girls are seen as a normal part of growing up as heterosexual, or as fashionable or experimental behavior (see Kangasvuo 2002: 228). This kind of heterosexism is contradicted by the *parodic discourse.* In a conversation on the topic "What do you think about straight people?" participants question conventional discourses by replacing the word "gay" with the word "straight" but otherwise repeating discourses from word to word. This offers a reformulation of heteronormative discourses as ridiculous, through parody, and it questions the whole "originality" of heterosexuality itself (see Butler 1990: 136–138).

In the *closet* participants talk, for example, about crushes, music, school, free-time, and how they are feeling at the moment. When an outsider sends a message to the *closet* and asks what it is about, she is told, "Well this just is . . . uh . . . well . . . very likely a conversation with an emphasis on girls." The answer is suggestive like the title itself. This helps to avoid both homophobic harassment and a flood of acceptance inside the *closet.* In our culture heterosexuals are never in the closet. It is a metaphorical and concrete space for non-heterosexuals. In the *closet* nicks praise, encourage, and advise each other. Nobody is rude or insulting, which strongly contrasts with conversations in the public *Demi.* The most common type of discourse in the *closet* in which sexual orientation is constructed is the *discourse of adoration and liking.* Some participants also talk about their romantic relationships with their girlfriends through the *discourse of relationships,* and a few talk about their sexual desires and fantasies through the *discourse of sexual desire.* Sexual orientation is constructed in these three discourses implicitly. A user represents herself as a girl or is assumed to be a girl, and she talks romantically or sexually about other girls. These discourses are much more personal and commonplace than the discourses of love and sex outside the *closet.*

Bisexuality has a contested status in heterosexual Western cultures, but it has also been ignored or even despised in lesbian and gay cultures (see

Albrecht-Samarasinha 1997; Dollimore 1997). It is often negated in the public *Demi* too. In the *closet* bisexuality is constructed together with lesbianism. One nick can talk about cute boys and girls, and another can say that she only likes girls. Nobody questions the authenticity of these feelings. Acceptance in the *closet* is expressed without questioning, while outside the *closet* it is expressed with a flood of accepting discourses. Thus in the *closet* lesbian and bisexual identity is normalized. In the *closet* hostility against non-heterosexuality is processed through the *ironic discourse,* for example, by calling oneself "perverted." Self-irony has traditionally been a popular way to protect and defend oneself in gay cultures (Dyer 2002: 49–62).

In the *closet,* being out or closeted is a negotiated and fluid identity status (Phillips 2002: 410). Users talk about how open or secretive they are regarding their non-heterosexuality in different situations and with different people through the *discourse of openness.* Because of the heterosexual presumption, being open about a non-heterosexual orientation is an ongoing process in Finnish society (Lehtonen 2000: 286). In the *discourse of finding and identifying* participants speculate where they could meet others like themselves, and how they could identify them among straight people. In the *discourse of minority community* girls are happy to be in a peer group and they are delighted that there are "so many others.=) I'm not alone after all." The three discourses identified above are similar to two discourses outside the *closet,* namely the discourse of identity and the discourse of majority. In all these discourses identity is understood as a permanent and singular concept, and heterosexuality is seen as the identity of the majority.

The analysis of the online conversations shows that in the public space of *Demi* non-heterosexuals are constructed mainly either as invisible, when sexual orientation is not an explicit topic, or as "the others," when it is an explicit topic. Their self-representations, especially bisexual self-representations, can be openly questioned, even negated. The *closet* began from this hegemonic and heteronormative space with the question "Am I the only one?" and the answer turned out to be something like "No, we are not alone." According to Teresa de Lauretis, who refers to Louis Althusser, the process where an individual starts to represent herself as female is the process where social representation is accepted and absorbed by the individual as her self-representation. This is how social representations become real for individuals (de Lauretis 1989: 11–12). Sexuality is "one form of (self-)representation" (de Lauretis 1994: 303). The public *Demi* and the *closet* enable the production of different social representations and thus different self-representations of sexuality. In the *closet* non-heterosexuality is taken for granted and non-heterosexual self-representations are produced mainly implicitly, like heterosexual self-representations in the public *Demi*. In both spaces transgendered social representations and thus self-representations are invisible, or as Namaste (2000) suggests, erased.

Queering the Self in the #Closet

In spring 2003 users of the *closet* created their own IRC room. At first the *#closet* was a quiet place, according to its founding members, but soon more members joined in. When chatting became lively in the *#closet* it started to fade in the *closet*. Many closeted persons still used *Demi* but the space of their community had moved to IRC. After analyzing discussions as an outsider on *Demi* I wrote an article based on the analysis (Laukkanen 2004). In the summer of 2004 the article was soon to be published, but I started to feel uncomfortable about it. Those who participated in the analyzed discussions were not aware of the research, which is ethically questionable (see Hine 2000: 24, Sarf 1999: 253–255). Even though I did not mention any nicks and left the most personal messages out, I felt that I had an obligation to inform the *closet* group about the coming publication and to give them a possibility to protest against it. I wrote an e-mail to some addresses that I found on the group's home page. In the e-mail I introduced my research, requested the receivers to comment on the attached manuscript, and asked if they would be interested to take part in my study as interviewees. I got answers from two nicks, clown and drop_out, who both accepted to be interviewed. Drop_out said that s/he[6] spoke on behalf of the group and invited me to the *#closet*. S/he turned out to be the key-informant of my research and the one who not only invited me to the *#closet* but also helped me to enter IRC, and the only one I ever met face-to-face.

Altogether fourteen members of the *#closet* participated in my study as informants, and interviewed subjects. I also observed conversations in the *#closet*, but my focus here is on the analysis of the first group interview. It was followed by one-on-one interviews and a second group interview. The interviews were made in the *#closet* in the autumn and winter of 2004. IRC enabled real-time conversations, which made the interviews interactive (Mann and Stewart 2002: 612). The *#closet* was the interviewees' own space where I as a researcher was a visitor. The first time I entered the *#closet* was also the first time I ever used IRC, so those who were interviewed were more accustomed to the interactive situation than I was as the interviewer.

The founding members say that they created the *#closet* because they wanted to chat together in real time. There is also a significant difference in terms of levels of privacy between *Demi*'s discussion forums and IRC rooms. *Demi* has tens of thousands of different users monthly. Users can lurk in *Demi*'s discussions without registration, and all discussions are available to everybody, including the *closet*. The discussions are available for at least couple of months if they are not censored before this. The rules and supervising is organized by the site, not by the users. The *#closet* has only few dozen regular users. Everybody's nicks are visible whether they chat or not, and there is a possibility for private one-on-one chat. In the *#closet* the regular members make the rules and supervise them. The users of both *Demi* and the *#closet* organize face-to-face meetings, but on *Demi* only a fraction of the users participate in these events while in the *#closet* almost all regular members have seen each other offline. Altogether, these online spaces are constructed in a completely different manner (Gustafson 2002), and, consequently, the *#closet* is clearly more private space than the *closet*.

All but two of the informants have participated in the discussions on *Demi*. In order to do this, they have been obliged to fill in the registration form and represent themselves as either male or female. During the time of outside observation on *Demi* I visited some of the users' home pages. I noticed then that at least two closeted users have named themselves on their homepage as androgynous while on *Demi*'s registration form they represented themselves as female. I assumed that many users of *Demi* or any other site answer the question of sex/gender more or less "automatically." However, I thought that non-heterosexual users might start to question the marking of binary sex/gender, which some of them had already done on their homepages.

Before starting the interviews, I told the informants that I study sexuality in "girls" online conversations.[7] Therefore, the informants attend the first group interview as "girls." In the beginning of the interview I tell the participants that first I am going to ask for some background information about them, and I start with "your age?" The answers vary between sixteen and twenty-one years. Then I ask, "Your sex?" Out of eleven informants two answer quickly "woman" and eight answer "girl." One informant, Erzbischof, answers "I don't know." His answer creates the first crack. The answer is noticed by Vendetta who at the time is dating Erzbischof and who defines herself as a girl. She says, "A difficult question," and Erzbischof continues, "(papers say a girl. as a grown-up, hopefully, a boy)." He is defined as a girl on the outside but he hopes to be a boy as a grown-up. However, in the answer he does not define himself as either at the moment. Another informant, pilli, says to Erzbischof, "I still consider you as a girl." The comment reveals that Erzbischof is not regarded as a girl only on paper. The word "still," however, implies that the change is possible. Erzbischof's reaction to this is a smiley where he sticks out his tongue and the words, "I'm hurt." I continue the interview by asking the following:

[21:10] <marjotutk> your sexual orientation?[8]

[...]

[21:10] <Vendetta> Lesbian.

[21:10] <pulla> more like gay

[21:10] <Kabaree> something towrds girls

[21:10] <Kabaree> towards even

[21:10] <Mininabla> Lesbian

[21:10] <Erzbischof> heterosexual male. transsexual then. temporarily lesbian.

[21:10] <drop_out> same

[21:10] <lupu> At the moment I think bi. I'd rather not categorize.

[21:10] <pilli> Hard to define. I'm interested in girls, don't know about boys.

[21:10] <Merlot> Do you have to know what to answer?

[21.10] <drop_out> as former

[21:10] <marjotutk> Merlot: no, you don't have to

[...]

[21:11] <Merlot> Good.

[21:11] <Kabaree> pilli, said it quite well

[21:11] <Merlot> After all: undefined

[21:11] <Diane> Umh. I like both. It varies in phases. Bi?

More cracks begin to form after the question of sexual orientation. Where naming one's sex/gender seemed to be quite easy for all but one, defining one's sexual orientation seemed to be much more difficult. Only Vendetta and Mininabla, who define themselves as lesbians, answer with just one word. Lupu says later during the interview that she could "slide back to straight" because of her current heterosexual phase and relationship. Erzbischof, who could or would not define his sex earlier, says now that he is "heterosexual male. transsexual then. temporarily lesbian," and drop_out defines hirself to be alike even though s/he previously defined hirself as a girl. Now they both define their sexualities in three different categories of social representation and their sex as males and indirectly as females. The first category is something Erzbischof and drop_out feel they belong to (see Griggs 1998: 90–93; Wickman 2001: 195). They are men who have sexual desires toward women, thus heterosexuals (Butler 1990: 22–23). However, they are aware that they are not unambiguously heterosexual males. The second category describes them as members of a sexual minority, as "males" in "female" bodies, thus transsexuals (see Wickman 2001: 141). The third category, lesbian, falls on them in the dichotomized sex/gender system (see Kangasvuo 2002). They are temporarily women who have romantic and sexual desires toward other women, thus lesbians.

After this, some of the other informants also start to redefine their sex. Pulla, who is at the time dating pilli, says, "I like girls but I don't like to call myself one. but not a boy, either." Erzbischof agrees with pulla's definition. This surprises Vendetta who asks for an explanation. Erzbischof answers that if he would say that he is a boy "well, it would be lying. like saying I'm big and tall and scary. it would be nice if it would be the truth but." He leaves the end of the sentence open. Lupu says that she finds "the definition of sex/gender to be a good thing, but somehow the girl/boy division is incomplete (my pseudonym: medically a girl, but otherwise not a boy or a girl)." Later she accepts the word "androgyny" from my account to describe her gender. When I tell the informants that in *Demi*'s registration form one has to mark oneself as male or female, pilli says that she is physically definitely a girl but she is not "what a girl is expected to be." She continues by saying that if there were no presumptions about how sexes differ from each other, maybe the whole defining would be unnecessary. A few informants start to propose alternative models for marking the sex in forms. Vendetta says that there could be a possibility to mark a cross between the boxes or, as Kabaree proposes, to mark both boxes.

When apparently simple-looking questions about sex/gender and sexual orientation are asked on the #*closet,* the informants start to define themselves in the *discourse of (fluid) identity,* in the *discourse of love,* and in the *individual discourse.* The informants weigh up different social representations and negotiate which ones to accept as their personal self-definitions. A single individual can define her-/himself differently in different messages, and some of these definitions seem to include contradictions. Some participants accept other's definitions of themselves, and many define their self outside the existing social categories. Social scientist Jukka Lehtonen has also noticed in his study that some young non-heterosexual Finns define themselves in many different ways and through many words. According to him, they have "tried to accept and promote a philosophy of individualism and empowerment that encourages people to develop and define their own categories to describe themselves" (Lehtonen 2000: 281–282; see also Lehtonen 1998). Almost all my interviewees share an outlook that deems the categorization of sex/gender, or at least that of sexual orientation, unnecessary. Even Vendetta, who defines and represents herself without hesitation as a girl and a lesbian, says, "Defining of both (for me) is quite easy, but I don't know how wise it is."

There are two crucial differences between the sexuality constructed in *Demi* and the sexuality constructed in the *#closet*. First, in *Demi* sexual identity is usually understood as something permanent, singular, and stable, while in the *#closet* sexual identity is understood as something unstable, multiple, and fluid. Diane summarizes the group's thoughts about sexuality by saying that "sexual orientations can yield/change/stretch." Secondly, in *Demi* sexuality is based on a binary understanding of sex/gender which is located in the body, but in the *#closet* sex and gender are seen separate. Sex is based on the body, while gender is not. All informants are still aware that in the eyes of the others they are "girls," or as far as Erzbischof and drop_out are concerned, they are not accepted as boys. One could add to Diane's summary that while "sexual orientation can yield/change/stretch" in analyzed online self-definitions and self-representations binary sex seems to stick like "a wet silk dress."

Doing and Being the Sex in Photographs

Online pseudonymity enables sustaining a digital closet, as Phillips's (2002) analysis shows. One can create different nicks for different purposes and keep online personality apart from offline identity. When I first contacted the members of the *#closet* community I only knew them by their nicks. After a while some of them started to sign their e-mails with their first names and some gave me their official e-mail addresses instead of the free commercial addresses. However, before I learned the first and family names of some of them, I had already seen their faces. During the years of my research in *Demi*, a group of users had their own unofficial website in the *Demix-Gallery*,[9] where they published their self-portrait photographs. The writing in the research diary in September 2003 shows how surprised I was when I found the gallery site: "How dare they?! I couldn't do that. To undress yourself and let others criticize. To remove your own anonymity and surrender yourself to the gazes of those who stay invisible." Later, lupu told in the interview that she was partly and rudely outed because of her anonymous involvement in the *closet*, which was seen and gossiped by one of her offline acquaintances. Other informants did not relate negative experiences about "being out" online.

When David F. Shaw explored how gay men use IRC, he noticed that, ironically, while the physical absence of others is appealing, all the interviewed men transgressed the bounds of disembodiment. They exchanged photographs, phoned each other, and ultimately they met face to face while searching for friends and "significant others" online. In other words, they actively filled bodily gaps (Shaw 1997: 141–143). This seems to be the situation with my interviewees as well. Many of them have seen each other's photos and met face to face. They are friends, and many also dated or had dated each other. However to unmask oneself in a small group of people is different from unmasking oneself publicly in a popular online gallery.

In the time of the research, almost all of my informants had their pictures in an *IRC Gallery*,[10] which is aimed for Finnish users of IRC. In spring 2005, the *IRC Gallery* had more than 200,000 registered users and a significant amount of invisible lurkers. When joining the gallery users are forced to represent themselves either males or females. It is separately emphasized that a user should enter his or her sex "correctly at once because it cannot be changed afterwards." The rules of the *IRC Gallery* control what kinds of pictures are permissible. The body plays a critical role in the identification process (see Poster 2002: 232–233), so the gallery demands a recognizable and relatively new picture that shows the user's face. It censors pictures that represent "overflowing violence or sexuality" because the meaning of the gallery is "to show what people look like and not to present naked skin." Sexuality seems to be a troublesome topic in the gallery particularly because teenage girls are its biggest user group.

Some members of the #*closet* say that they control sexiness in their pictures. For example, Vendetta says in the group interview that she wants to look good in her pictures but not "too obscene :D." Two other girls say in private interviews that they intentionally avoid putting pictures that are too revealing in galleries because of male users. Altogether three of the interviewed girls say that they have received some sexually disturbing comments because of their pictures, for example, "I could fuck you in the ass, you're quite hot." In their pictures all of the sexually harassed girls represent a clearly feminine look. The interviewees see girl-kissing-girl pictures, which some of them have on their gallery sites, not as sexual but as romantic. This is taken into account when selecting pictures: "You don't need to put any soft porn there but appropriate pictures which show that I love that woman, those are fine."

Pictures in galleries are often considered as documents (see Rugg 1997: 5–6, 12–13) even though users are aware that they can be and often are digitally edited. For example, in May 2004 in the *Demix-Gallery* one user of *Demi* had a picture where the face was only seen from nose up, and a blue cowl covered almost all the hair. Another nick commented on the picture: "In *Demi* I always feel like you"re a boy. It's that nick of yours . . . :D Maybe I now learn that you're not." I have witnessed many similar comments during the time of my research. Sex/gender is recognized when looking at photographs because it is placed in the material body, and photographs are seen as documents of this body, and less as representations. It is possible to try to produce androgynous self-representations, but it is likely the person is still recognized as either male or female. Some of my informants say that they also try to recognize or guess other' sexual orientation by looking at their pictures. They lean on certain signs, like boyish looks (see Crowder 1998), while identifying non-heterosexuals.

The first time I looked at Erzbischof's and drop_out's pictures, I looked at two boys. They were boys not only by their looks but also in the way they have placed themselves in pictures. The poses were cocky and expressions almost defiant. Their self-representations as boys were visually clear and easily recognizable. In the first group interview Erzbischof tells that "based on my picture a girl has said that a cute boy." After this Vendetta says that she was shocked when she heard that drop_out was a girl. She had thought him to be a boy based on his chatting and his pictures. Drop_out comments that Vendetta is not the first one who has thought so. Vendetta answers to drop_out as follows:

> [22:23] <Vendetta> drop_out, yes, but I thought that I'd be somewhat experienced in this stuff :)
>
> [...]
>
> [22:24] <Erzbischof> I saw drop_out's picture and I was like "fuck. how come everyone does it so much better than me?"
>
> [...]
>
> [22:24] <drop_out> Erzbischof, I don't do anything special. I just am.
>
> [...]
>
> [22:25] <Erzbischof> drop_out, why d' you then look more like a man than I do? I don't do anything either
>
> [22:25] <Erzbischof> :P
>
> [22:25] * Erzbischof whines
>
> [...]
>
> [22:25] <drop_out> Erzbischof, I'm just so cool.
>
> [22:25] <drop_out> Erzbischof, well I don't know. :P

While talking about photographs and sex/gender, Erzbischof and drop_out talk about "doing," "looking," and "being." Erzbischof refers to sex/gender as something that can be done, but drop_out denies doing anything special and says that s/he just is. After this Erzbischof says that he "doesn't do anything either." However, when Erzbischof describes the pictures he has chosen for gallery, he says that he selects those "where I look big and scary and have my skateboard with me if possible." Culturally these characteristics are considered as masculine. In some captions he also directly calls himself a boy. Thus, in pictures he represents himself clearly as a boy. It is something he cannot unambiguously define verbally to be because "being big, scary and boy" is something he earlier said that "would be nice if it would be truth but."

Erzbischof and drop_out express that they have found girls' heterosexual attention both amusing and flattering. O'Brien suggests that binary gender is transferred to online interaction as perhaps the most significant category of self. Thus presenting oneself as belonging to a "wrong" gender is seen as a great deception (O'Brien 1999: 86–89). It is a deception that drop_out does not want to be guilty of. Even though s/he defines hirself as a "heterosexual male," s/he feels that it is also something s/he cannot be. S/he is afraid that a person who thinks that s/he is a boy will feel betrayed if hir "true" sex is revealed. S/he understands sex/gender as a form of *being* and consequently a "faith." This is the reason why drop_out usually represents hirself verbally as a girl online, if the sex is asked directly. For example, s/he marks "male" only if the site is not important to hir. If there is a possibility of becoming friends with other users, s/he does not want to risk it with self-representation that can be seen as a betrayal by others. Erzbischof, on the other hand, understands sex/gender as something that is changeable, thus *doing*. He represents himself online almost always as a straight boy. For example, he says that he always marks "male" when filling registration forms on the internet. In photographs they can both represent themselves as boys. Photographs allow such self-representation for drop_out that is not always possible in verbal interaction. She can "be" hirself—a heterosexual male—without claiming that s/he is one.

Relative Freedom

When considering self-representation on the internet, the possibilities might at first seem unlimited. The analysis of online conversations and online interviews suggest, however, that this freedom is relative at least in three ways. First, the different discursive spaces enable different social categories and thus different self-representations. If a user's self-representation does not fit into socially constructed and negotiated (self-)representations, it is unimaginable and thus it does not exist for others. Even those who would not want to or will not categorize their sex, gender, or sexuality are often categorized by others inside the existing representations. In *Demi* the group of young non-heterosexuals created their own space inside the public space and named it the *closet*. While in *Demi*'s public space users were automatically considered as heterosexuals, in the *closet* they were automatically considered as non-heterosexuals. The non-heterosexual self-representations were supported by taking them for granted. After a while the same group of users moved to IRC and created the space that was completely their own and thus safe (see Campbell 2004: 53–55, 90). It enabled fluid understanding of not only sexual orientation but also of gender. In the *#closet* one does not have to categorize one's gender or one can define it separately from one's sex. Thus the *#closet* enables transgendered self-representations that were not possible in *Demi*.

Second, each participant's current understanding of sex, gender, and sexuality defines the self-representations that are available for them in different interaction situations. Understanding of sex as changeable, for example, enables different self-representations than understanding of sex as fate. Third, the most remarkable limitation of self-representation seems to be the binary understanding of sex, which is based on a user's material body even online. Even though the queer space like the *#closet* enables a fluid understanding of gender and sexual orientation, binary sex is reproduced intensively. The male/female binary is cracked only in the account of one informant, who represents his sex as unknown. Even he is categorized as a girl from outside. Social representations, self-representations, and self-definitions intertwine with each other in the analyzed online conversations and in the interview accounts of the informants. I contend that the process of this intertwining is the same process that Teresa de Lauretis calls "experience." De Lauretis is inspired by theorizing the concept of experience using an episode from Virginia Woolf's famous book *A Room of One's Own*. In the episode Woolf's fictional "I" becomes by instinct aware of herself as a woman when a man's horrified look awakens her to notice that she is in a place that belongs to men. De Lauretis asks if instinct is the right term to describe this "understanding," and continues, "And yet, to call it "instinct" is not quite so inaccurate, for what is instinct but a kind of knowledge internalized from daily, secular repetition of actions, impressions, and meanings, whose cause-and-effect or otherwise binding relation has been accepted as certain and even necessary?" (de Lauretis 1984: 158).

De Lauretis proposes that the term experience could designate this process of self-representation, which defines "I" as a woman. According to her, experience is the process by which subjectivity is constructed for all social beings, and through what one places, or how one is placed in social reality. It is not an individualistic process, but a social process. For each person, subjectivity is an ongoing construction, and the effect of this experience. As de Lauretis points out, experience is produced by one's personal engagement in the practices, discourses, and institutions that lend significance to the events of the world (de Lauretis 1984: 158–159; see also de Lauretis 1989: 18–19). I propose that different discursive spaces—like the heteronormative public space of *Demi* and the queer spaces of the *closet* and the *#closet*—produce a different experience of the "self." The analyzed queer spaces have been productive and safe spaces for a group of young Finns who represent themselves as non-heterosexuals, and as such these spaces have enabled experience that can support the participants' ongoing subjective construction of non-heterosexuality. However, because even in the analyzed queer spaces the experience of the material sexed body seems almost impossible to crack, the construction of subjectivity becomes difficult when sex, gender, body, and desire are not definable through existing dichotomies.

Notes

1. http://www.demi.fi
2. All empirical material is originally in Finnish. Quotes in this text are translated from Finnish to English.
3. The nicks of the interviewees are changed for the study, so that the interviewees cannot be recognized from the text. Interviewees have chosen themselves fake nicks for this purpose, except lupu, who I was not able to reach for this purpose. Nicks are not translated.
4. http://www.gallupweb.com/redmeasure/MonthReport/default.asp, November 20, 2003.
5. I selected three *closets* (including 428 messages) and eleven conversations about sexual orientation (including 379 messages) for closer analysis. Altogether 217 nicks have sent messages to the conversations about sexual orientation, and three-quarters of them have sent only one message. In the *closet* only 28 nicks have participated conversations, and a quarter of them has sent only one message.
6. In Finnish "he" and "she" are the same word, "hän." I have used pronouns she/he and his/him/her like Jan Wickman who has studied Finnish transgender communities. He uses them in accordance with the assumed preference and gendered presentation of the person in question. When gender is ambiguous pronouns s/he and hir are used (Wickman 2001: 9).
7. Sexuality in girls' online conversations is the original subject of my doctoral thesis in preparation.
8. The extract of the interview is similar to what chatting looks like in IRC. Every line begins with a time and a nick which appear automatically.
9. www.demix-galleria.net; in August 2005 the site was replaced by www.hype.fi.
10. www.irc-galleria.net

References

Albrecht-Samarasinha, L. L. 1997. "On Being a Bisexual Femme," in L. Harris and E. Crocker (Eds.), *Femme. Feminists, Lesbians & Bad Girls* (pp. 138–144). New York, London: Routledge.

Brown, G., Maycock, B., and Burns, S. 2005. "title-bold-large>Your Picture Is Your Bait: Use and Meaning of Cyberspace Among Gay Men." *Journal of Sex Research 42*(1), 63–73.

Brown, M. P. 2000. *Closet Space. Geographies of Metaphor from the Body to the Globe.* London: Routledge.

Butler, J. 1990. *Gender Trouble. Feminism and the Subversion of Identity.* London: Routledge.

Butler, J. 1993. *Bodies That Matter. On the Discursive Limits of "Sex."* London: Routledge.

Campbell, J. E. 2004. *Getting It On Online. Cyberspace, Gay Male Sexuality and Embodied Identity.* New York: Harrington Park Press.

Charpentier, S. 2000. "Gender, Body and the Sacred: Heterosexual Hegemony as a Sacred Order." *Queen. A Journal of Rhetoric and Power 1*(1). Retrieved September 26, 2005, from http://www.ars-rhetorica.net/Queen/Volume11/Articles/ Charpentier.html

Crowder, D. G. 1998. "Lesbians and the (Re/De)Construction of the Female Body," in D. Atkins (Ed.), *Looking Queer. Body Image and Identity in Lesbian, Bisexual, Gay and Transgender Communities* (pp. 47–68). New York, London: Harrington Park Press.

Dollimore, J. 1997. "Bisexuality," in A. Medhurst and S. R. Munt (Eds.), *Lesbian and Gay Studies. A Critical Introduction* (pp. 250–260). London and Washington, DC: Cassell.

Dyer, R. 2002. *The Culture of Queers.* London: Routledge.

Fairclough, N. 1995. *Critical Discourse Analysis. The Critical Study of Language.* London: Longman.

Griggs, C. 1998. *S/he. Changing Sex and Changing Clothes.* Oxford, New York: Berg.

Gustafson, K. E. 2002. "Join Now, Membership Is Free: Women's Web Sites and the Coding of Community," in M. Consalvo and S. Paasonen (Eds.), *Women and Everyday Uses of the Internet: Agency & Identity* (pp. 168–188). New York: Peter Lang Publishing.

Hine, C. 2000. *Virtual Ethnography.* London: Sage Publications.

Kangasvuo, J. 2002. "Sexually Dichotomised Culture in the Lives of Bisexual Youth in School Context," in V. Sunnari, J. Kangasvuo, and M. Heikkinen (Eds.), *Gendered and Sexualised Violence in Educational Enviroments* (pp. 216–230). Oulu, Finland: Oulu University Press.

de Lauretis, T. 1984. *Alice Doesn't—Feminism, Semiotics, Cinema.* London: Macmillan Press.

de Lauretis, T. 1989. *Technologies of Gender. Essays on Theory, Film and Fiction.* London: Macmillan Press.

de Lauretis, T. 1994. *The Practice of Love. Lesbian Sexuality and Perverse Desire.* Bloomington: Indiana University Press.

Laukkanen, M. 2004. "Kaapitetut. Seksuaalinen suuntautuminen nuorten nettikeskusteluissa [Closeted. Sexual Orientation in Young People's Online Conversations]." *Tiedotustutkimus* [*National Journal of Media Studies*] 27(3), 49–62.

Lehtonen, J. 1998. "Young People's Definitions of their Non-Heterosexuality," in H. Helve (Ed.), *Unification and Marginalization of Young People* (pp. 185–192). Helsinki: The Youth Research Programme 2000/ The Finnish Youth Research Society.

Lehtonen, J. 2000. "Non-Heterosexual and Transgendered People in Finland," in I. Lottes and O. Kontula (Eds.), *New Views on Sexual Health. The Case of Finland* (pp. 280–289). Helsinki: Publications of the Population Research Institute, Series D37/2000.

Mann, C., and Stewart, F. 2002. "Internet Interviewing," in J. F. Gubrium and J. A. Holstein (Eds.), *Handbook of Interview Research. Context & Method* (pp. 603–627). Thousand Oaks, CA: Sage Publications.

Namaste, V. K. 2000. *Invisible Lives. The Erasure of Transsexual and Transgendered People.* Chicago and London: University of Chicago Press.

O'Brien, J. 1999. "Writing in the Body. Gender (Re)production in Online Interaction," in M. A. Smith and P. Kollock (Eds.), *Communities in Cyberspace* (pp. 76–104). London: Routledge.

Paasonen, S. 2002. *Figures of Fantasy: Women, Cyberdiscourse and the Popular Internet.* Ph.D. thesis. Annales Universitatis Turkuensis, Humaniora 251.

Phillips, D. J. 2002. "Negotiating the Digital Closet. Online Pseudonymity and the Politics of Sexual Identity." *Information, Communication & Society* 5(3), 406–424.

Poster, J. M. 2002. "Trouble, Pleasure and Tactics: Anonymity and Identity in a Lesbian Chat Room," in M. Consalvo and S. Paasonen (Eds.), *Women and Everyday Uses of the Internet: Agency and Identity* (pp. 230–252). New York: Peter Lang Publishing.

Pulkkinen, T. 1996. "Keinotekoista seksiä? Luonto, luonnottomuus ja radikaali sukupuolipolitiikka [Artificial Sex? Nature, Unnaturalness and Radical Gender Politics]," in P. L. Hekanaho, K. Mustola, A. Lassila, and M. Suhonen (Eds.), *Uusin silmin. Lesbinen katse kulttuuriin* [With New Eyes. Lesbian Look at Culture] (pp. 165–182). Helsinki: Helsinki University Press.

Rich, A. 1996. "Compulsory Heterosexuality and Lesbian Existence," in S. Jackson and S. Scott (Eds.), *Feminism and Sexuality. A Reader* (pp. 130–143). Edinburgh, UK: Edinburgh University Press.

Roberts, L. D., and Parks, M. R. 2001. "The Social Geography of Gender-Switching in Virtual Environments on the Internet," in E. Green and A. Adam (Eds.), *Virtual Gender. Technology, Consumption and Identity* (pp. 265–285). London and New York: Routledge.

Rugg, L. H. 1997. *Picturing Ourselves. Photography & Autobiography.* Chicago: University of Chicago Press.

Sarf, B. F. 1999. "Beyond Netiquette. The Ethics of Doing Naturalistic Discourse Research on the Internet," in S. Jones (Ed.), *Doing Internet Research. Critical Issues and Methods for Examining the Net* (pp. 243–256). Thousand Oaks, CA: Sage Publications.

Sedgwick, E. K. 1990. *Epistemology of the Closet.* Berkeley: University of California Press.

Seidler, V. J. 1998. "Embodied Knowledge and Virtual Space. Gender, Nature and History," in J. Wood (Ed.), *The Virtual Embodied. Presence | Practice | Technology* (pp. 15–29). London: Routledge.

Shaw, D. F. 1997. "Gay Men and Computer Communication: A Discourse of Sex and Identity in Cyberspace," in S. G. Jones (Ed.), *Virtual Culture. Identity and Communication in Cybersociety* (pp. 133–145). London: Sage.

Stålström, O., and Nieminen, J. 2000. "Seta: Finnish Gay and Lesbian Movement's Fight for Sexual and Human Rights," in I. Lottes and O. Kontula (Eds.), *New Views on Sexual Health. The Case of Finland* (pp. 119–139). Helsinki: Publications of the Population Research Institute, Series D37/2000.

Taylor, A. 1997. "A Queer Geography," in A. Medhurst and S. R. Munt (Eds.), *Lesbian and Gay Studies. A Critical Introduction* (pp. 1–19). London and Washington, DC: Cassell.

Wakeford, N. 1997. "Cyberqueer," in A. Medhurst and S. R. Munt (Eds.), *Lesbian and Gay Studies. A Critical Introduction* (pp. 20–38). London and Washington, DC: Cassell.

Wickman, J. 2001. *Transgender Politics. The Construction and Deconstruction of Binary Gander in the Finnish Transgender Community.* Åbo, Finland: Åbo University Press.

Wittig, M. 1992. *The Straight Mind and Other Essays.* Hemel Hempstead, UK: Harvester Wheatsheaf.

Yep, G. A. 2003. "The Violence of Heteronormativity in Communication Studies: Notes on Injury, Healing and Queer World-Making," in G. A. Yep, K. E. Lovas, and J. P. Elia (Eds.), *Queer Theory and Communication. From Disciplining Queers to Queering the Discipline(s)* (pp. 11–59). New York, London and Oxford: Harrington Park Press.

6. Belonging through Violence: Flaming, Erasure, and Performativity in Queer Migrant Community

Adi Kuntsman

This chapter explores flaming as a queer migrant practice of belonging. Departing from scholarly debates on flaming in online communities, and in particular, in online queer spaces, the chapter aims to problematize a simplistic understanding of flaming as an act of violence on one hand, or as a playful ritual, on the other. Following different ways in which flaming can be understood as a culturally embedded performance of queerness or as a linguistically and ethnically specific rhetorical stance, this chapter also challenges the reading of flaming based on English in Anglo-dominated cyberstudies.

Most discussions of flaming (online fights) and trolling (deliberately provocative messages that intend to incite) tend to see them as negative and disturbing. Susan Herring et al., for example, describe them as "mechanisms of online deception and disruptive behaviour" (Herring et al. 2003) that are particularly threatening for what they call a "vulnerable online community"—a feminist discussion forum. Gay, lesbian, bisexual, transgender, and queer online spaces are often seen as vulnerable, too, subjected to homophobic intrusions, "online gay bashing" and hate speech (Campbell 2004; Corell 1995). They can also be disrupted by violence caused by newcomers and those who don't obey the collective rules, as David Phillips demonstrates in the case of GLBT Usenet group (Phillips 1996). At the same time, however, flaming and trolling were described as having a mobilizing effect in those communities: Herring et al., for example, show that the feminist discussion forum they studied organized to deal with trolling. Paul Baker (2001) demonstrates how one person's provocative postings to a usenet group caused "moral panic," and brought up several strategies of response, flaming being the most common. Phillips similarly describes how flaming was used to defend community boundaries in part by reinforcing the coherence of the community itself, by establishing "bona fides"—the ability to flame well (Phillips 1996).

Flaming and trolling, in short, can both disrupt the community and serve to maintain and even strengthen its boundaries, by exercising violence toward intruders and outsiders. But what if the violence is directed toward the insiders? How can flaming within the community be understood? Is it always necessarily a disruption?

Some scholars have argued that flaming has mistakenly been analyzed as violence. Instead, they see it as sporting relations, a game, or a ritual stance that often produces a sense of belonging (Baym 1995; Campbell 2004; Vrooman 2002). Such conceptualization of flaming suggests that once understood as a game or ritual, flaming ceases being violent. I wish to complicate what seems to be an all-too-easy dismissal of the hurtful effects of flaming while remaining attentive to the culturally and linguistically specific rituals and rhetorical stances involved in it. I will do so by showing the complex structure of online fights and their multiple, and often contradictory, meanings and effects. The main argument of this chapter is that cyberviolence, and in particular, flaming and its erasure, problematizes the understanding of violence and queer belonging as incompatible with each other. Online spaces are a fruitful ground for exploring the relations between violence and belonging: as my analysis of flame wars in a queer migrant community will show, there is a need to examine violence as a *constituent of spaces of belonging*, rather than merely as the background against which belonging takes place. At the same time, such examination has to work against essentialized ideas of sexuality and culture and against simplistic notions of flaming as either aggressive, violent, destructive or sporting, constructive and playful.

Violence and Belonging or "Why Do We Always Fight?"

"Why is it that every time "At Roby's" is mentioned, there are always fight, floods of insults and curses?"—writes Alex,[1] a gay man and a frequent visitor to the website of Russian-speaking GLBTs in Israel.[2]

"At Roby's" is the GLBT Russian-speaking immigrants' club established in Tel Aviv around 2000. Since 1989 more than a million people have immigrated to Israel from the former Soviet Union.[3] This wave of immigration created a significant Russian-speaking presence in Israel, and around 1999–2000 the gay, lesbian, bisexuals, and transgendered among them began organizing. The website, called "The Forum,"[4] was created at about the same time as Roby's club, to host information about queer places, culture, and politics and to provide Russian-speaking immigrants an opportunity to meet online. Today the Forum is the main online Russian language resource for queers living in Israel. It contains information, photo galleries, news, and essays. It also hosts a vibrant discussion forum, structured as bulletin board. While for some participants the Forum is the main (and in some cases, the only) queer place they visit and socialize in, for others it is yet another part of the Russian-Israeli queer scene, concurrent with offline events and places. "At Roby's" club, in particular, is closely linked to the Forum: its events are advertised there, and many participants in the discussion forum end up meeting at the club. The Forum often becomes a place to plan events at the club (for example, when someone proposes a karaoke night), or to arrange a lift for those coming from another town. It is also a space to discuss the club itself, and such discussions often turned into vigorous fights, known in cyber-cultures as flame wars. Personal attacks and insults that the participants directed at one another often turned the forum into a battlefield. The fights also caused calls for censorship that resulted in acts (or threats) of the erasure of words, whole threads, and even users. The insults were condemned by many participants as acts of violence, while embraced by others as legitimate and even entertaining. The latter saw the censorship of flaming, rather than the flaming itself, as an act of violence.

The social studies of queer spaces (bars, community centers, gay neighborhoods, and recently also newsgroups, chat rooms, and websites) frequently examine gays and lesbians as objects of violence. These studies describe GLBT spaces as constituted around the feeling of safety vs. the potential threats of homophobia-related hostility and attacks (Moran et al. 2001, 2003; Moran and Skeggs 2004). They also examine the symbolic violence of heteronormativity, by looking at social landscapes as "liberatory or oppressive sites for the performance of <. .> sexed selves" (Bell and Valentine 1995: 98; see also Kitchin 2002; Knopp 1995). Similarly, researchers of cybercommunities note the potential for establishing online queer spaces of belonging (Alexander 2002; Campbell 2004; Munt et al. 2002; Wakeford 1997). Other scholars also highlight the role of class, race, ethnicity, and migrant status (Binnie 1995; Knopp 1995; Manalansan 2004; Moran 2000; Rushbrook 2002; Skeggs 2000) in creating spaces of safety and security. In particular, scholars of "queers of colour" and "queer diaspora" note that queer migrants navigate not only homophobia but also nationalism and racism, and that the spatiality of queer belonging cannot be separated from questions of race and ethnicity (Manalansan 2004).

There is very little research, however, on gays, lesbians, bisexuals, and transgendered as subjects of violence. With the exception of some research on domestic abuse in same-sex partnerships (Cruz 2000; Mason 2002), there are not many accounts of how relations between GLBT themselves can be based on violence—physical, verbal, or symbolic. What's more, there is little conceptualization of how violence from within, as a culturally complex phenomenon, can work to produce queer belonging. It is precisely the violence from within, generated in flame wars, that interests me here. Although there were few cases of straight-identified people who posted on the bulletin boards to express hostility or mockery toward same-sex relations, most of cyberviolence that took place within the Forum came from and was directed toward queers themselves. The community's club, "At Roby's," was one of its frequent epicenters[5]: among dozens of discussion threads about the club that I observed and collected from the archives of the bulletin boards, about one third were passionate and long-lasting flame wars.

My understanding of flaming—as well as some attempts to control it—as violence is informed by the concept of "words that wound" (Delgado 1993). Lawrence et al. in their analysis of assaultive language point out that racist speech not only represents racism and its effects, but also is in itself injurious (Lawrence et al. 1993). I follow their conceptualization when I examine how words or their erasure can have a wounding effect. The idea of wounding words has been taken up by Judith Butler who suggested that violent language—and its censorship—composes of performative speech acts that constitute the very subjects they aim to wound or protect (Butler 1997). Adopting Butler's theory of performativity (Butler 1990, 1993), I also address "Russian," "migrant," and "queer" not as preexisting categories of identity but as products of performative repetitions and collective negotiations. Moving away from essentialized notions of sexuality and culture, I approach online space as a site where individual and collective identities can be constituted through speech acts, but also where notions of what it means to be an immigrant, a "Russian," a "queer" can be disrupted or redefined. Flame wars about the club "At Roby's," as I will show, simultaneously challenge and constitute an online queer migrant space, through choreography of interpretations, performative acts, and wounds. Importantly, however, I do not see online communication as an idealized site where all power relations or hegemonic discourses can be easily dismantled.[6] Rather, my emphasis on violence suggests that the online performance of migrant and queer collectivity is intertwined with injuries and vulnerability. I will follow this intertwinedness by describing how the choreography of a fight moves between many topics and genres, *inseparably binding* the playful and the hurtful. I will then show that flaming employs ritual stances of queerness and Russianness, assuming their already existing audience, and demonstrates that these stances are at the same time (mis)read as and responded to with violence. I conclude the chapter by looking at how the very boundaries of flaming are imagined through acts of erasure.

Flaming Choreography

Most of the fights about "At Roby's" last for days and sometimes weeks, and share the same trajectory. The thread usually starts with an opening post that describes the club in an extremely negative way. Sometimes it also includes personal insults to Roby—the club's owner, or to her employees: the barwoman, the DJs, and the security guard. The opening post contains a critique of—or a list of complaints about—the club and the quality of service (food, drinks, and music) provided there. These complaints are often written in an aggressive or sarcastic style. They are met with protest by the satisfied club-goers. The service was ok, they say, we enjoyed it there and everyone had a great time. Then one of the satisfied visitors attacks the person who complained, and dismisses the critique of the club. Someone else supports the attack. It is not the high-quality service we are looking for at the club, they say. We go there to see friends, to have fun, to feel at home, and you dickhead, if you don't like the place, go to hell. Personal attacks start a flow of mutual insults. Someone posts a flirtatious message, a few others respond. The flirt, accompanied by smiling (:)) or winking (;)) "emoticons," turns the thread into a playful exchange that breaks the tension of the fight. Someone else rejects the flirtation, and insults its author. In the meantime, someone calls on the administrator[7] to erase the "provocateur"—the author of the original complaint. Another one threatens to expose the provocateur's offline identity. A few participants oppose this call for erasure and attack the intimidation of exposures and the tyranny of censorship. This brings up another exchange of personal insults. Then comes another critique of the club, or a passionate defence of the latter.

Due to the structure of the bulletin boards, readers can reply to the opening message of the thread before seeing the rest of the discussion. The thread is divided into short pages of about 10–15 postings, and one can post a response from any of them, before reaching the end of the thread. New arrivals to the thread, therefore, often respond out of synch, and the discussion returns again and again to the original message: the critique of the club "At Roby's." Other times the thread is artificially kept "on topic" by some participants, reminding others the subject of the debate, or by the moderator, who warns against or deletes postings that he decides are "off-tops." Then someone says "good, finally there is a good fight, we have been missing one." Someone else complains about the fight, and attacks participants whose tone is rude and aggressive. Styles of writing, the use of language, opinions, and spelling mistakes are all picked up as targets for mockery.

Then someone criticizes "us, Russians," who prefer complaining to actually doing something about a problem. Others angrily disagree. Another person exclaims "why do we always fight?" Someone suggests that the intention of the first complainer was to simply have some fun, or to open up a debating space, or to actually improve the club. More people respond to the original message with laughter, usually marked by multiple smiling (:) :) :)) or laughing (: D) emoticons. This laughter often dismisses the critique of the club by ridiculing its author. The debate changes direction several times, moves away from the club "At Roby's" to the experience of migration, the meaning of Russianness, racism, and discrimination.[8] Disagreements of these and other issues bring not only another explosion of insults, but also more laughter and flirtations. Someone raises the subject of "At Roby's" again. Another complaint about the club follows. "These are cloned nicknames, generated by the same person," states the administrator, referring to the complainers. "I am issuing the last warning to the clown, before I ban them from the forum. This discussion is now closed."

Although the original message often seems deliberately provocative, it is also described by some as positive: many of the participants seem excited about the fight, some explicitly expressing their enjoyment. At the same time, many appear to be distressed about name-calling, personal attacks, and brutal sarcasm. Some of the club's regulars feel offended by what they see as disdain for the place they appreciate and cherish. Others are annoyed by the administrator's censorship, suggesting that his personal connection to the club and his friendship with the owner make it impossible to criticize Roby. There are "lurkers," too: those who enjoy "watching" (reading) the fights, yet seldom participate in them; and those who are repelled or hurt, but choose to remain silent. Among the latter, notably, is Roby herself, who very seldom responds to critique and insults, yet is very aware of them.[9]

"Flaming as a negotiation of the individual and the social, the oral and the literary, can no longer be looked at as monolithic," suggests Steven Vrooman (2002: 54). Indeed, harsh critique of the club and vicious personal insults, threats to disclose one's offline identity and calls to erase someone's postings, coexisting with smileys, flirt, laughter, and ongoing debates on the meaning of Russian-GLBT community, suggest that "flame wars" cannot be examined as homogeneous. Instead, I propose to look at the complicated work these "wars" do, precisely because of their heterogeneous structure and multiple meanings. I choose to use the term "flaming choreography," inspired by Charis Cussins' work in science studies and her concept of "ontological choreography" as "the coordinated action of many ontologically heterogeneous actors in the service of a long-range self" (Cussins 1996: 600). "Flaming choreography" signals the dynamic and shifting presence of cyberviolence, which is constantly challenged or neutralized (by smiles, laughter, and moments of playfulness) yet never disappears. The choreographic work of violence is clearly seen in the two examples of rhetorical stances—complaining and queerspeak—that I describe below. The first positions online space as a Russian place where one can engage in the cultural ritual of litanies. The second turns it into a stage for a post-Soviet drag show. The two can be seen as tools of imagining a Russian-speaking queer online community (Anderson 1991) and excluding those who cannot recognize its codes. But in both, the flaming doesn't simply draw boundaries of in- and outsiders. Rather, it crafts a complex texture of online belonging through embrace, rejection, and reconfiguration of the two rhetorical stances.

The Performativity of Complaining

<Nice Tree> Friday night, the eternal search for entertainment . . . Where should we go? For the Russian gay scene there isn't much choice—all roads lead to "Roby's."

I remember the old place[10] where everything was nice, and the music was good, although the place was tiny. <. .> My last visit to the place brought only negative impressions. The music at the club is such a mishmash that you don't want to dance at all. "First we need to have vodka," I heard two women saying when entering the club. Indeed, if you want to stay at this place for even 5 minutes you must be drunk.

And the window display [that looks like] of a Russian shop with all kinds of products. Barbeque made in the morning, reddish, and hell knows what else . . . it doesn't look particularly tempting. So what is it? Remind me of a soviet [public] dining center of the late 1980s. And the prices at the bar are so expensive they scare me away. . . . And the crowd is no longer the same. . . .

I felt so sad, and afraid. Its 2004 now, but feels like 1989. Roby's lack of taste and business initiative makes turns place from bad to worse. Of course, the administrator will erase my terrible thoughts, but I am posting them not to hurt anyone, I just want Roby to take this into account.[11]

This is an opening of one of the threads. Like many other postings that criticize the club, Nice Tree's message generated a wave of responses that very fast developed into a fight. While some of the participants argued with Nice Tree's critique of the club, others specifically ridiculed or condemned him[12] for the very fact of complaining (instead of being positive, giving advice, or doing something to improve the club).

The rhetorical act of complaining is an interesting one. Nice Tree's message is written in a genre that Nancy Ries characterizes as "litany" (Ries 1991, 1997). In her work on distinctive Russian speech genres, Ries describes litany as

passages in conversation in which a speaker would enunciate a series of complaints, grievances, or worries about problems, troubles, afflictions, tribulations, or losses, and then often comment on these enumerations with a poignant rhetorical question ("Why is everything so bad with us?"), a weeping, fatalistic lament about the hopelessness of the situation, or an expressive Russian sigh of disappointment and resignation. (Ries 1997: 84)

Indeed, Nice Tree's posting has fatalistic elements of lament about the fate of gays in general ("eternal search for entertainment"), and of Russian gays in Israel, in particular. He mourns the good old days of Roby's club, and is sad and pessimistic about the future. Many other complaints about "At Roby's" are structured in a similar way, some poetically abusing the tool of "poignant rhetoric questions." For example, in the thread started by Nice Tree's critique, another person posted:

<Spring Breeze> I probably have really strange demands of the owners of "At Roby's" . . . if I order something non alcoholic, why do I have to wait until the woman serves everyone who came after me? Why can't I drink from a clean glass (I don't even dream about special glasses for wine or juice),why do I get my orange drink in a disposable plastic vessel? And by the way, drink and juice are not the same, so why if I asked for juice, do I get a drink? Why is the change always either sticky or wet? < . . . > Why is the toilet paper more like a glass paper (?), and runs out after midnight? Why does the security guard protect the entrance and not me? Why is the music (I won't say a word about the selection!) so loud, that I can't talk? < . . . > This is all so sad, and there is no hope for change. That's why I don't come to "At Roby's," and go to meet women in Hebrew-speaking places, where the unexpected native speech comes like life's unintentional gift.

The range of demands presented by Spring Breeze is a subject for a separate paper.[13] What interests me here is the rhetorical structure of this (and other similar) posts and the way they can produce a sense of belonging. Ries points out that litany, widely used by people in Russia in their everyday conversations as well as in public performances in media and politics, constitutes a recognizable[14] Russian stance, a "posture that expresses particular perspectives, values, desires or expectations" (Ries 1997: 88). This is often the stance of the victim, the perpetual sufferer, whose suffering gives him/her a position of moral sanctity. At the same time, litanies are an important cultural tool to "create multiple fields of identification and belonging" (113). Complaints about the club, expressed by Spring Breeze, are an act of distinction between the "Russian"/immigrant and the "Israeli"/Hebrew-speaking spaces. But the role of these complaints is far more complicated. Ries emphasizes that litanies that she observed in Russia at the same time expressed and created the collective Russian self at the time of the political and economic changes of *perestroika*. Taking Ries' argument further, I would suggest that litanies can be seen as performative speech acts (Butler 1990, 1993, 1997), that constitute the collective "we" by weeping about its misfortunes, troubles, and losses. The critique of the club "At Roby's" expressed by Nice Tree and others constitutes the suffering Russian-queer community as an already existing collectivity through lamenting what they need but can't get at "Roby's. This is not just a community of suffering but of suffering that is imposed by the community itself.[15]

At the same time, constant objection to these complaints from the part of some participants problematizes the unquestioned emphasis on (Russian, or Russian-speaking) collectivity. Common as the litanies are on the forum, they are far from taken for granted. Both the content and the very fact of these complaints are challenged and often aggressively attacked by some participants. Spring Breeze, for example, was criticized for her "claims to aristocratism." She and others who complained about the service provided at the club were labeled as poisonous, snobbish, and ungrateful. Such violent responses suggests, while for some they are that poetic weeping by others litanies are experienced as acts of symbolic violence. They are read literally—as humiliation and insult to those who run the club and to those who hang out there.

> \<Nikolavrus\> [summarising the thread and responding to the range of complaints about the club- AK] The most refined and at the same time bitchy complaints belong to "Spring Breeze" (toilet paper, sticky change), whom I would rather call "Stale Air." Everything is so nice that it makes me sick.
>
> Her advice makes one thing clear: it's purely an act of promotion of other places. "Go to the places I go, I am so aristocratic, so mysterious"
>
> About the critique. Ladies and gentlemen, don't critique, don't give advice. You can express your wishes in a calm and respectful tone.

Nikolavrus reads Spring Breeze's as a direct attack on the community club and its visitors. Once refigured as violence, her posting and her construction of cyber-self become the object of sarcasm and disdain: Spring Breeze's desire for cleanliness is described as sickening; her nickname, bearing the connotation of lightness and freshness, is distorted into "Stale Air," and her stance of "moral sanctity" is presented as arrogance.

The ritual mourning of Russian-queer collectivity *becomes* violence once it is read as such. It is this precise moment that shifts a rhetoric stance into a chain of words that wound. The rejection of the complaints, however, does not diminish their performative role. On the contrary, refiguring the litanies as acts of violence also has constitutive power: it performs the collective "we" that is injured or offended by the complaint.

Queerspeaking

This is how another thread began:

> <Crazy Ala> "At Roby's." (Administrator, you can delete this post)

> I would like to comment on my first and last visit to the cult club "At Roby's."
> I was expecting a friend from Moscow, and decided to kill two birds with one
> stone: to go and see the club "At Roby's" and to surprise my pretentious
> Moscow guest with the Israeli gay scene. I took the address of the club from the
> internet, sent the driver from the airport with the luggage to the hotel, and took
> my Moscow friend straight to the fashionable Russian club. The advertisement
> said it was going to be a "boys" night, an evening of poetry, dance and song. . . .
> My friend, inspired by all this, also desired to see this fashionable and glamorous
> place.

The rest of the posting described the club in the most unpleasant way, scorning the place, the music, the service, and the people. It ended with the following words:

> <Crazy Ala> If anyone wants to talk to us, you can call the "Intercontinental"
> hotel, room number 106. We would be happy to talk to you.

The whole posting was written in a female gender by "Crazy Ala," a person
who had appeared on the forum shortly beforehand, criticizing the club's
advertisement. She then opened a new discussion thread, describing her supposedly first visit to the club.

Crazy Ala's mockery of the club caused an immediate and outraged
response. "We love our club, and your floods of dirt won't change that,"
stated one woman. Another participant wrote:

> <Margaret> Crazy Ala, get fucking lost! That's a hello from Margaret. If you
> want to respond—come to Roby's tonight.

Another two cursed her. And yet another one posted:

> <Butterfly> Why did you bother to describe this in so much detail? . . . Starting
> with the airport and the taxi?. . . . I called the hotel and found an Israeli guy
> there, who was totally freaking out. He didn't know any pretentious homosexu-
> als from Moscow :)

> I am asking everyone here (who goes to the club) to support Roby. And Felix,[16]
> I am asking you to erase these kind of messages. It's fucking enough!

Butterfly opposes Crazy Ala's critique by questioning the credibility of her
story. She follows the details provided by Crazy Ala and rings the hotel where
her friend supposedly stays. Butterfly also takes the position of a community

leader, calling others to speak out for the club and the moderator—to police the critique. Crazy Ala's response follows immediately:

> <Crazy Ala> I am reading it and laughing to myself. I can't believe someone took it seriously, so seriously that they called the hotel, probably to curse me there, no less. "I am asking to support . . . I am asking to erase . . ."—well, I myself asked to read this piece and then throw it away, since it was *habalstvo*.

Crazy Ala presents her earlier posting as a joke. She ridicules Butterfly's calls for support and discipline, and describes the story of visiting "At Roby's" as *habalstvo*. *Habalstvo* is a name of Russian gay slang. Like other gay jargons, such as Polari, *habalstvo* is both a language—a use of certain words—and a form of speech (Cox and Fay 1994: 103). *Habalstvo* is characterized by the use of feminine gender by male speakers, a mannered tone, and theatricalized aggression and rudeness; defining a conversation as *habalstvo* is often used by speakers to describe themselves as gay ("we sat at a café and *haballed*," Zapadaev 2001: 4). Crazy Ala's response to Butterfly signals that the author is not a woman but a queerspeaking gay man.

The thread, generated by Crazy Ala's posting, develops like other flame wars about the club. Some defend the club, others attacked Crazy Ala, some laugh, and some fight among themselves, criticizing each other's way of arguing and moving away from the topic of the club to issues of politeness, manners, ethnicity, culture, gender. Crazy Ala's position as *haballing*—that is, squabbling for the sake of fun—isn't supported by other participants, until much later in the thread, when another gay man refers to those fighting in an exaggeratedly rude manner:

> <Kikis> YOU NEED SOME DISCIPLINE!!! Here I come, my dear, my sweet pussies. You need some beating up, and here I come, my lovely faggots, my little cunts!

Crazy Ala immediately responds to Kikis, and the two exchange several messages, that look more and more like a dialogue of two drag queens. Crazy Ala's image as a scandalous *habalka*[17] becomes much clearer. Her name is explained, too, when after a long exchange with Kikis and others she writes:

> <Crazy Ala> Ala Borisovna leaves the scene, covered with confetti and flowers.

Ala Borisovna is a full name of a Russian pop-singer, mainly known as Ala Pugacheva. Pugacheva became famous in the late 1970s and is still performing today. She also serves as a favorite icon for drag queen shows. In particular, the Russian-Israeli drag queens have impersonated her several times, including in their performances at Roby's. Crazy Ala's position as a campy performer transforms the flaming from a fight into a drag show; when supported by others it resembles the dialogue a drag queen often initiates with the audience. Many participants are now smiling or sending Crazy Ala virtual kisses.

Like litanies, *habalstvo* can be seen as a form of ritualized speech. John Campbell in his book on gay chat rooms discussed flaming as a particularly queer ritual (Campbell 2004). Gay chat rooms, and cyberspace in general, are seen here as a site of queer performance whose origins predate the Internet but are then transferred into online communication. "[It] is not inconceivable to compare witty insults and snappy posturing of online flaming to the queer practice of camp," he suggests (Campbell 2004: 89–90). Indeed, the impersonation of a Russian pop-star frames the thread as campy performance, making flaming an explicitly queer act. If camp as (gay) aesthetics is based on "artifice and exaggeration" (Sontag 1964), then Kikis' posting that may at first appear as heterosexist can be read as parody on heterosexual gender norms. Similarly, Crazy Ala's defiant and theatricalized attack on "At Roby's" can be understood as a satire on the constant complaints about the club that galvanizes the forum. What's more, this satire constitutes the online forum as a site of queerspeak.

Describing a fight as *habalstvo* can alter the meaning and the effect of flaming and trolling. Crazy Ala's scorning of the club and Kikis" heterosexist threats, taken literally, appear as assault and aggression. Yet once classified as *habalstvo* they become a drag, a performance of queerness. It is also a performance of diasporic Russianness: the image of Crazy Ala, as well as the framing of her postings as *habalstvo,* links the participants of the Forum to other Russian-speaking queers, as well as to the (post)Soviet legacy of popular culture.[18] Such a performance assumes an already existing collectivity that shares not just sexual identification, but also language, cultural codes, and willingness to play the game. In Crazy Ala's earlier response to Butterfly ("I can't believe someone took it seriously") violence and queerness are juxtaposed: presenting one's speech as *habalstvo* assumes that it will not cause an injury. But is that always so? Can the performance of queerness and the violence coexist?

The distinction between a game and an injury becomes complicated once queerspeak is (mis)read. The assumed queer collectivity explodes when Crazy Ala's *havalstvo,* performed in a GLBT forum, meets with refusal by some participants, men and women alike. In fact, most of the participants of that thread took Crazy Ala's critique seriously. Some accepted his/her gender appearance as a game, yet replied firmly to protect the club. Others "got it" only toward the end, when Crazy Ala conversed with Kiky. And yet others continuously *refused* Crazy Ala her status of a (harmless) drag queen. When Crazy Ala first defined her posting as *habalstvo,* Butterfly, for instance, wrote that it was just an excuse Crazy Ala was making up once caught lying about the hotel.

Anger, curses, and threats directed toward Crazy Ala suggest that *habal-stvo* was perceived/misread by some as an act of aggression and harm. These clashes of intention and interpretation challenge that all-too-easy embrace of flaming as a game of ritual insults, differentiated from "real" violence. Just as in the case of litanies, the content and the effect of *habalstvo* were multiple. It incited some, and entertained others. But the understanding of Crazy Ala's message and of her cyberpersona didn't divide the community between those who "played the game" and those who refused or misunderstood it: the perception of Crazy Ala kept changing during the thread, working choreographically through various forms of individual and collective subjectivity, queer flirtation and diasporic imaginary.

Community of Erasures

Flaming choreography of fights about Roby's club didn't simply challenge and refigure ritual stances and their meanings. It also questioned the boundaries of cyberspeech itself, repeatedly evoking erasure and censorship. Censorship is a common practice in many online communities encountering flaming and trolling. For example, in a usenet group studied by Paul Baker participants contacted the net-administrator demanding to take e-mail rights from a person who had been provoking them (Baker 2001). Herring et al. in their description of flaming in a feminist forum note the call for administrative banning issued by some participants and the technical and ideological obstacles it encountered (Herring et al. 2003). So what can be the meaning and the effects of censorship when it takes place? When is it experienced as violence and by whom?

Technically, any participant can start a new discussion thread on the forum. They can also suggest that the thread should be closed, although only the administrator can do so formally. He is also the only one who can delete entire threads, while individual participants can edit or delete their own postings. Crazy Ala, for example, claimed that she was going to delete her critique of "At Roby's" some time after she posted it:

> <Crazy Ala> I will erase my posting in the evening. I would like people to read it with humour, to have a laugh and to draw their conclusions, when they read it after the good sleep that follows an exciting night of clubbing. I am sure there are people like that here

> <TT> Don't expect that. The admin will come from his holiday, and will restore everything :) Or will himself erase EVERYTHING to fucking hell

While Crazy Ala promises to erase her own post, TT suggests that the power to do so is no longer in Crazy Ala's hands. TT hints at the unrestricted power of the administrator and scoffs at the irrationality of his censorship. The style of TT's post ("will erasure everything to fucking hell") suggest that he sees the arbitrary erasures—or their reversals—by the administrator as acts of violence.

In another message TT notes the violence again, half-jokingly and half-seriously. He responds to one person who was speaking against "At Roby's" with the following:

> <TT> There is one thing I don't understand. Did you really need to create a new nickname to write all this? Are you afraid of revenge, my dear? :)

TT's apparently refers to several earlier incidents on the forum, when those who had been criticizing the club or the administration, were threatened with the revelation of their offline identities or with banning. Some were indeed banned, and later returned under new nicknames, only to be "detected" by the administrator and some other participants (who claimed to have seen their IP numbers) and threatened again.[19] This collapse of all the critique into the single figure of a "troublemaker" is mocked by BOBOO. When TT writes that he finally went to see the club only to discover a "smelly foul place," BOBOO responds:

> <BOBOO> Oh, TT, dear. Now you are at risk of being banned from the forum, thrown out of "At Roby's," and called all the nicknames that have ever criticized that "foul place."

The ghostly presence of those who had been banned and the threat of "detection" haunt many of the flame wars. If a person who criticizes the club or speaks negatively of the administrator bears a new, unfamiliar nickname, he or she is immediately suspected of being such a returnee. The relations between the administrator and the Forum's visitors are complicated by the fact that he is himself part of the Russian-Israeli GLBT community.[20] Rather than being a neutral third-party, he is actively involved in the community's life, as well as in Roby's club, where he occasionally performs.

Censorship of speech and appearance on the site is presented by the administrator and indeed perceived by some participants as a necessary measure of protection. While TT, BOBOO and some others mock and criticize the administrator, other participants support the banning of those they define as "provocateurs." Some specifically request for the administrator's intervention. For example, in response to Crazy Ala's critique Butterfly called him to erase this and other similar posts that offend the club. Butler in her discussion of censorship notes that it "is a productive form of power: it is not merely privative, but formative as well" (Butler 1997: 133). Censorship, according to Butler, produces the subject through regulating speech in the public domain and law. Reading online censorship as performative (rather than simply punitive or protective) suggests that the repeated calls to delete some messages and cyberpersonae work to constitute migrant queer subjects and their collective spaces, on- and offline. Both Roby's club and the Forum come into being as spaces of Russian-Israeli queer belonging, through constant negotiation of what they should be like and who they should welcome. The sense of collectivity, in other words, is performed through repeated critique of community spaces and the censorship of such a critique.

But there is an affective aspect, too: these subjects are constituted through the *desire* to erase and/or be erased. The erasure on the site is not only an act of violence, but also is imposed on those defined as hostile troublemakers. Some of the posts that criticize "At Roby's" and cause flame wars already embed the possibility of their deletion. "Administrator, you can delete this post," called Crazy Ala her *haballing* message, somewhat tongue-in-cheek. "Of course, the administrator will erase my terrible thoughts," Nice Tree completes his weeping complaint. These two references to erasure can be each read within the framework of their genres. Provoking the administrator from the first line of the thread fits well into the queer ritual of *haballing* tease: here I am to annoy you, see who loses it first. Completing one's long lament with "of course this will be deleted" contributes to the Russian stand of eternal hopelessness used in litanies. Yet the repetitive mentioning of censorship and deletion also suggests that erasure has an important role in constituting a *feeling* of belonging (and not only a discursive possibility of such). Both sides of the debate about "At Roby's" imagine the Russian-queer cybercommunity and their place in it though fantasies and fears of banning and deletion.[21] The community here is constituted not through erasure of hostile outsiders and their violent speech, but by marking the insiders as those whose speech was/is/might be erased. In other words, belonging is constituted by being (potentially) subjected to violence from within.

Belonging through Violence

So what can flame wars in and about *community spaces* teach us about the relations between violence and belonging?

My discussion of the flame wars about the Russian-Israeli club "At Roby's" brings up several issues that contribute to the understanding of queer spaces, and in particular, online spaces, and their relation to cyberviolence. First of all, it challenges the approach to flaming as an act of intrusion of—or protection against—outside violence. The flame wars described here were undoubtedly violent. Yet despite the many forms of violence they generated, fights about the club also appeared as something the participants of the community had (and wanted) to take part in, something that would mark them as insiders. Rather than seeing flaming as acts of disruption, I propose looking at flame wars as a form of *being together*. Similarly, erasure acted in these fights as a form of violence from within that was employed in multiple ways to protect, imagine, and perform the cybercommunity of Russian-speaking queers. Far from being a (necessary or unfortunate) result of online communication-going-wrong, it emerged here as a basis of collectivity. Flaming and erasure were at the same time condemned and desired, embraced and rejected.[22]

Second, this chapter addresses flaming as embedded in culturally and linguistically specific forms of communication. Flaming, as I showed here, was seen by some as an essentially queer practice. Yet it is also a practice of diasporic identity where, as Martin Manalansan points out, language plays a central role in "moving through imagined spaces and across borders," marking one's queerness as well as one's migranthood, diasporic location and resistance to the dominant language of the "host" society (Manalansan 2003: 51). At the same time, my discussion complicates the rhetoric or ritual analysis of flaming. Such analysis is undoubtly useful in recognizing distinct cultural forms of speech (such as litanies and *habalstvo*) and their meaning that might escape English-centered theorizing of online communication. And yet, rhetorical analysis tends to ignore the multiple (mis)readings of rhetorical stances. In the case of queer migrants and diasporic subjects, misreading or demanding translation are usually acts of power directed toward those on the margins (Manalansan 2003). A refusal to translate or adapt to the dominant language, as Manalansan shows, can create a space of resistance, however frail. But what about the misreading or refusal within the migrant queer space?

Following Gajjala (2002, 2004) I see these refusals as an invitation to explore the complexity of migrant queer identities instead of assuming a single "Russian" or "queer" voice. Focusing on flaming only as a playful ritual can miss this complexity because it overlooks the moments of slippage when an acceptable form of speech that is supposed to evoke migrant collectivity or signal queer performance is refused its status. At such moments the flaming "ritual" is (mis)read literally, or confronted with its (often unaware) wounding effects. Ritual forms of speech, such as litanies or *habalstvo*, are in themselves neither inherently violent nor simply and unproblematically playful: they turn into "words that wound" at the moments of misunderstanding or refusal from within the queer migrant audience. Importantly, each of them contains its own legacy of violence and oppression (for example, the harsh conditions of Soviet life; or the tyranny of heteronormativity) as well as the ways of resisting them, sometimes through humor or sarcasm. But each is also open to negotiation from within those legacies. Rhetorical analysis often assumes collective agreement on interpretations, as long as people belong to the same social group. Following the multiple meanings and effects of ritual stances, this chapter suggests instead that flaming choreography both constitutes and disrupts litanies and *habalstvo* as forms of Russian-speaking, migrant, queer collective subjectivity. Such a reading proposes a much more complex approach to online interactions and queer cyberspaces.

Online migrant queer spaces, then, emerge here as complex sites where identities are imagined, performed, negotiated, and refused. Violence is constantly present in these spaces also because for queer migrant subjects their identity is far from taken for granted: it comes into being through contestation and daily struggle. Far from seeing online spaces as a way to resolve this struggle, this chapter showed that queer and migrant belonging can work against, alongside, or through violence.

Acknowledgments

I would like to express my gratitude to Dr. Anne-Marie Fortier, Dr. Jennie German-Molz, Dr. Adrian Mackenzie, Dr. Gail Lewis, and Prof. Lucy Suchman for their careful reading and helpful comments on earlier versions of this chapter. I am also grateful to David Phillips for his comments on the earlier draft and for his guidance through the revision process. And last but not least, I am indebted to my partner, Yehudit Keshet for her editorial assistance with this chapter and for her overall invaluable help and support.

Notes

1. All nicknames have been changed. I tried, however, to keep some resemblance to the originals.
2. This chapter is part of my PhD project based on a ten-month-long ethnography, conducted on the website and complemented by several visits to Israel. The ethnography included participant observations on the website, online and face-to-face interviews, and archival analysis of hundreds of discussion threads for the period of two-and-a-half years. I received permission from the website's two co-administrator to use the archives. Other participants have been informed about my research.
3. The political implications of this wave of immigrants is complex and lies beyond the scope of this chapter. The relations between Russian-Israeli queers and Israeli ethnic and national politics are discussed extensively in my dissertation.
4. Both the name of the club and the website have been changed.
5. It was of course not the only one. Another frequent subject of fights, which I discuss in my dissertation, was politics and the Israeli-Palestinian conflict.
6. Ananda Mitra in his classic discussion of on-line community, suggests that "[t]he internet space is indeed a cacophony of voices, all of whom feel empowered, and the traditional definition of dominance becomes nearly inapplicable" (Mitra 1997: 73). But as Radhika Gajjala accurately points out, the multiplicity of voices does not ensure the disruption of hegemony; what's more, some voices are always appropriated, outnumbered or silenced (Gajjala 2004).

7. The website has two co-administrators, one is responsible for news and articles, the other is responsible for the technical running of the site and is in charge of the bulletin board. From here on I refer to the latter as the administrator.

8. A detailed discussion of the relations between Russian immigrants and Israelis, and the analysis of the ways Russian-speaking queers are radicalized within the Israeli GLBT community lie beyond the scope of this chapter and are specifically discussed in Kuntsman (2005).

9. Based on my observations and personal communication with Roby on- and offline.

10. One year after opening, the club moved to another venue.

11. All the translations are mine.

12. Although the gender of nicknames is not always clear, the performed gender of the participants is marked by their speech: Russian language distinguishes between male and female forms of verbs, adjectives, and nouns

13. One particularly interesting issue is the question of hospitality embedded in the complaints about and the defence of the club (Kuntsman 2005).

14. Importantly, Ries also reminds us that it is easily stereotyped and parodied.

15. I thank Gail Lewis for pointing this out to me.

16. The name of the administrator.

17. The person who speaks *habalstvo*.

18. For an excellent account of the use of gay languages by diasporic queers, see Manalansan (2005).

19. Baker makes a similar observation when he describes that one of the protection measures against a troll was to check his online profile (Baker 2001).

20. For the discussion of the complexity of moderating from within see Phillips (1996: 53–54).

21. For an interesting discussion of online communities as created through erasure and self-erasure, see Ferreday (2003).

22. I thank Anne-Marie Fortier for drawing my attention to the fact of simultaneity here.

References

Alexander, J. 2002. "Queer Webs: Representation of LGBT People and Communities on the World Wide Web." *International Journal of Sexuality and Gender Studies* 7(2/3), 77–84.

Anderson, B. 1991. *Imagined Communities*. London: Verso.

Baker, P. 2001. "Moral Panic and Alternative Identity Construction in Usenet." *Journal of Computer Mediated Communication* 7(1). http://jcmc.indiana.edu/vol7/issue1/baker.html

Baym, N. 1995. "The Emergence of Community in Computer Mediated Communication," in S. G. Jones (Ed.), *Cybersociety: Computer Mediated Communication and Community* (pp. 138–164). Thousand Oaks, CA: Sage.

Bell, D., and Valentine, G. 1995. "Sexualized Spaces: Global/Local," in D. Bell and G. Valentine (Eds.), *Mapping Desire: Geographies of Sexuality* (pp. 97–98). London and New York: Routledge.

Binnie, J. 1995. "Trading Places: Consumption, Sexuality and the Production of the Queer Space," in D. Bell and G. Valentine (Eds.), *Mapping Desire: Geographies of Sexualities* (pp. 182–199). London and New York: Routledge.

Butler, J. 1990. *Gender Trouble: Feminism and the Subversion of Identity.* London: Routledge.

Butler, J. 1993. *Bodies That Matter.* London: Routledge.

Butler, J. 1997. *Excitable Speech.* London: Routledge.

Campbell, J. E. 2004. *Getting It On Online: Cyberspace, Gay Male Sexuality, and Embodied Identity.* Binghamton, NY: Haworth Press.

Correll, S. 1995. "The Ethnography of an Electronic Bar: The Lesbian Cafe." *Journal of Contemporary Ethnography* 24(3), 270–298.

Cox, L. J., and Fay, R. J. 1994. "Gayspeak, the Linguistic Fringe: Bona Polari, Camp, Queerspeak and Beyond," in S. Whittle (Ed.), *The Margins of the City: Gay Men's Urban Lives* (pp. 103–127). Aldershot, England: Ashgate Publishing.

Cruz, J. M. 2000. "Gay Male Domestic Violence and the Pursuit of Masculinity," in P. M. Nardi (Ed.), *Gay Masculinities* (pp. 66–82). Thousand Oaks, CA: Sage.

Cussins, C. 1996 "Ontological Choreography: Agency for Women Patients in an Infertility Clinic" *Social Studies of Science 26*, 575–610.

Delgado, R. 1993. "Words That Wound: A Tort Action for Racial Insults, Epithets, and Name Calling," in M. J. Matsuda, C. R. Lawrence III, R. Delgado, and K. W. Crenshaw (Eds.), *Words That Wound* (pp. 89–110). Boulder, CO, San Francisco, and Oxford: Westview Press.

Ferreday, D. 2003. "Unspeakable Bodies: Erasure, Embodiment and the Pro-Ana Community." *International Journal of Cultural Studies 6*(3), 277–295.

Gajjala, R. 2002. "An Interrupted Postcolonial/Feminist Cyberethnography: Complicity and Resistance in the "Cyberfield." *Feminist Media Studies, 2*(2), 177–193.

Gajjala, R. 2004. *Cyberselves: Feminist Ethnographies of South-Asian Women.* Oxford: AltaMira Press.

Herring, S., Job-Sluder, K., Scheckler, R., and Barab, S. 2003. "Searching for Safety Online: Managing 'Trolling' in a Feminist Forum." CSI Working paper, No. WP-02–03. Retrieved November 2005, from http://rkcsi.indiana.edu/archive/CSI/WP/WP02–03B.html

Kitchin, R. 2002. "Sexing the City: The Sexual Production of Non-Heterosexual Space in Belfast, Manchester and San Francisco." *City 6*(2), 205–218.

Knopp, L. 1995. "Sexuality and Urban Space: A Framework for Analysis," in D. Bell and G. Valentine (Eds.), *Mapping Desire: Geographies of Sexualities* (pp. 149–162). London and New York: Routledge.

Kuntsman, A. 2005. "Violent Hospitality: Queer Immigrants and Community (Cyber)spaces." Paper presented at Mobilizing Hospitality Conference, Lancaster, UK, September.

Lawrence, C. R., III, Matsuda, M. J., Delgado, R., and Crenshaw, K. W. 1993. "Introduction," in M. J. Matsuda, C. R. Lawrence III, R. Delgado, and K. W. Crenshaw (Eds.), *Words That Wound* (pp. 1–16). Boulder, CO, San Francisco, and Oxford: Westview Press.

Manalansan, M. F. IV. 2004. "Where Are the Piers? Race, Space, and Violence in the Global City." Paper presented at *Queer Matters* Conference. King's College, London, May.

Manalansan, M. F. IV. 2005. *Global Divas: Filipino Gay Men in the Diaspora.* Durham, NC, and London: Duke University Press.

Mason, G. 2002. *The Spectacle of Violence: Homophobia, Gender and Knowledge.* London and New York: Routledge.

Mitra, A. 1997. "Virtual Commonality: Looking for India on the Internet," in S. Jones (Ed.), *Virtual Culture* (pp. 55–79). London, Thousand Oaks, CA, and New Delhi: Sage.

Moran, L. J. 2000. "Homophobic Violence: The Hidden Injuries of Class," in S. Munt (Ed.), *Cultural Studies and the Working Class: Subject to Change* (pp. 206–218). London: Cassell.

Moran, L. J., Skeggs, B., Tyrer, P., and Corteen, K. 2001. "Property, Boundary, Exclusion: Making Sense of Hetero-Violence in Safer Spaces." *Social and Cultural Geography* 2(4), 407–420.

Moran L. J., Skeggs B., Tyrer P., and Corteen, K. 2003. "The Constitution of Fear in Gay Space," in E. Stanko (Ed.), *The Meaning of Violence* (pp. 130–146). London: Routledge.

Moran, L. J., and Skeggs, B., with Tyrer, P., and Corteen, K. 2004. *Sexuality and the Politics of Violence and Safety.* London and New York: Routledge.

Munt, S. R., Bassett, E. H., and O'Riordan, K. 2002. "Virtually Belonging: Risk, Connectivity and Coming Out On-line." *International Journal of Sexuality and Gender Studies* 7(2/3), 125–138.

Phillips, D. J. 1996. "Defending the Boundaries: Identifying and Countering Threats in a USENET Newsgroup." *The Information Society* 12(1), 39–62.

Ries, N. 1991. "The Power of Negative Thinking: Russian Talk and the Reproduction of Mindset, Worldview, and Society." *The Anthropology of East Europe Review* 10(2), 38–53.

Ries, N. 1997. *Russian Talk: Culture and Conversation during Perestroika.* Ithaca, NY, and London: Cornell University Press.

Rushbrook, D. 2002. "Cities, Queer Space, and the Cosmopolitan Tourist." *GLQ- A Journal of Lesbian and Gay Studies* 81(2), 183–206.

Skeggs, B. 2000. "The Appearance of Class: Challenges in Gay Space," in S. Munt (Ed.), *Cultural Studies and the Working Class: Subject to Change* (pp. 129–151). London: Cassells.

Sontag, S. 1964. "Notes on "Camp." Retrieved February 2006, from http://pages.zoom.co.uk/leveridge/sontag.html

Vrooman, S. 2002. "The Art of Invective: Performing Identity in Cyberspace." *New Media & Society* 4(1), 51–70.

Wakeford, N. 1997. "Cyberqueer," in A. Medhurst and S. R. Munt (Eds.), *Lesbian and Gay Studies. A Critical Introduction* (pp. 20–38). London and Washington, DC: Cassell.

Zapadaev, A. M. 2001. *Dictionary of Habballic Words and Expressions.* St Petersburg: Self-published (in Russian).

Part III
Reformulating Identities and Practices

In this part of the collection the focus is on the reformulation of identity and practices in relation to the image and the screen. All of the chapters deal with desire, affect, subjectivity, and performance. In each chapter the practices of image, screen. and identity are reconfigured in relation to desire and intimacy; race and visuality; and image and virtuality, respectively.

In chapter 7, "Virtual Intimacies: Love, Addiction, and Identity @ The Matrix," Shaka McGlotten draws the reader through an intense poetic examination of screen affects. The emotional pull and push of desires in relation to screens and images is articulated and illuminated in this focused meditation on the visual and affective. Drawing on traditions of dealing with digital media in a visual frame and focusing on visual and aesthetic affect this chapter provides a set of challenges to, and reformulations of, human computer interactions.

Chapter 8 on identity and practice examines the visual construction and intersection of race and desire. In "Brown to Blonde at Gay.Com: Passing White in Queer Cyberspace," Andil Gosine shows that the discursive work of race is both reiterated and resisted in its travels through chat room interaction. Both these chapters point to the significance of the visual in contemporary communication technologies and in this chapter it is not the capacity of the visual to open up proliferating meanings that is foregrounded, but the closures produced through visual racializations. The construction of race and desire through the assumptions of sight as knowledge reformulates discourses of racialization and visualization in the sense of "re-forming"; setting back into form. Reformulation in this instance looks back to reiterate rather than looking forward to transformation. The potentially unruly slippage of bodies and images is secured through interactions which relocate race as an essence that can only be visually recognized. Race then becomes further commodified as aesthetic property that must be known through sight. In this reformulation race is constructed through sight, image, and textual anchorage as a reducible field where political imperatives are displaced through/as aesthetics and desire.

In chapter 9 Debra Ferreday and Simon Lock examine the identity work of cross-dressers. Linking the practices of cross-dressers with discourses about the cybersubject, they argue that cross-dressing has been used as a metaphor for cybersubjectivity and that this operation fails to account for cross-dressing as an identity practice. They examine the websites of cross-dressers who use the Web as an integral aspect of identity work to argue that these practices are not commensurable with cybersubjectivity and that the metaphor elides important ways in which cross-dressing needs to be considered in its own right. This account of the intersection of metaphors and practices allows an examination of strategies of gendering in practice and illuminates some of the ways in which these are material and virtual; body and image invested. Through examining some of the complex threads of gendered embodiment in relation to communication technologies, the chapter illustrates some of the operations of the material-semiotic nodes of bodies and technologies as they interact.

7. *Virtual Intimacies: Love, Addiction, and Identity @ The Matrix*

SHAKA MCGLOTTEN

Virtual Intimacies[1]

> It is the edge of the virtual, where it leaks into the actual, that counts. For the seeping edge is where potential, actually, is found. (Massumi 2002: 43)

Virtual intimacies are intimacies mediated by technologies, by screens in particular, but as the discussion that follows shows, these intimacies are no less real for the fact that they take place in virtual contexts. Indeed, the intimacies that emerge from virtual spaces proliferate opportunities for new and concrete events to emerge. Virtual intimacies transform the intimacies we already have and they condition the possibilities for as yet unknown forms of intimacy to be cultivated.[2]

The feelings of connection that come from our relationships to ourselves, to one another, and to screens open up inquiries into the nature of intimacy itself. How do the stories, events, contacts, encounters, and impacts effected through the space of the screen help us to think about the bleed between categories like the virtual and real, inside and outside, public and private?

Virtual intimacies always start somewhere: at homes, coffeeshops, or libraries; somewhere, there's flesh and blood: eyes scanning personal profiles on the surface of Web pages, people hooking up, bodies desiring. However, my efforts here focus not on arguing for the "realness" of the virtual but on tracking the ways that searching for love or identity in the matrix produces profoundly felt responses that register on the level of the intimate, as that which is perceived as inmost to oneself or to one's relationships. I further suggest that intimacy is itself essentially marked by virtuality, by being in a tense relationship to the concrete. In this chapter, I use ethnographic examples to explore the virtual, concrete, and affective sites in which the virtual and the intimate rub up against one another. I argue that virtual intimacies are ephemeral, ambivalent, and constituted by a messy and violent bleed between categories.

I focus on trying to understand, and reproduce in my own account, a range of emergent structures of feeling (Williams 1977). I try in my ethnography to *enact* desire, the pleasure and danger of sexual practices, and the deep attachments to narratives of intimacy gone right or wrong. In this chapter, experience is something that resonates in particular moments and places, and on various levels of abstractness and concreteness, with things like the virtual or the intimate, as well as with bodily agitations, habits, and surges of affect.

I use a range of methods for tracking this notion of experience. I began, simply, by collecting stories. Friends and lovers would talk to me about the kinds of things they did in real and virtual spaces and they would recommend others with whom I could speak. Although I may have intended to conduct my research with disciplined effort, as it progressed, I became subject to a different set of disciplines, logging on to feel connected, or to escape, or in states of anger, distraction, or lust. Like my informants, I had intimate relations, that is, I had talk and sex, through virtual queerspaces. And these encounters affected my intimate relations; indeed, they often troubled them. My own experiences are not presented here as representative absolute truths, but as creative non-fictions. I have created composites of people and of events. I have mixed stories in an effort to create productive confusions that disarticulate stories from their individual narratives so that they become something else, something collective, something which might be taken as a mix of my own experiences, those with whom I worked, and even those of you the reader, who I take to be an active producer of this text. Thus the research draws on and creates an ephemeral "archive of feelings" (Cvetkovich 2003)—attachments, memories, and dreams lodged in my own situated knowledges as a queer person of color and those of the men I worked with. The narrative of this chapter, then, as well as the stories that make it up, are best thought of as an assemblage, a mix of disparate things sutured together by a formulation that is itself awkward, ambivalent, unstable, and also profoundly alive.

Theoretical Orientations

My efforts here draw on two bodies of theory. My discussion uses Deleuzean understandings of the virtual as that which is real but not actual to think about the structural and everyday instances in which the virtual has *impact* on individual and collective lives. In this regard then, the stories I tell here function as case studies that mark the passage from the virtual to the actual, show-ing how "it is the essence of the virtual to be actualized" (Deleuze 2004: 28). I draw as well on feminist and queer investigations of intimacy as an affectively charged field that circulates in and across a range of private and public domains, as well as a kind of heternormative meta-cultural narrative, a forceful imperative that equates having an intimate life with having "a life" at all (Berlant 1997, 2000; Berlant and Warner 2000; Cvetkovich 2003).

I hope that by foregrounding articulations of the virtual as immanence, as the force of potential, to provide a productive interrogation of intimacy that resists neat summary and categorization. Even when virtual intimacies index failure, I hold on to the belief that these failures can be productively and creatively read. Even when my informants narrate experiences of partic-ular kinds of truth, of, say, addiction and recovery, this does not close off dis-cussion; rather, it forms the ground for new lines of inquiry. One of my key objectives in this chapter, then, is to keep in tension the many different pos-sibilities that inhere in the phrase "virtual intimacies."

Insofar as all of the stories presented here trace the realness of the virtual viz. its effects, this work contributes to efforts to underscore the promiscuous trafficking between categories and experiences of the virtual and the real. My interest in the notion of virtual intimacies, however, has increasingly swerved toward a related but altogether more ephemeral and experimental line of questioning, namely an investigation into the ways intimacy can itself be understood to be virtual. I am trying to get at intimacy as it is constituted by affects, gestures, memories, and dreams. In this way, I am engaging with a wide range of cultural theorists who are trying to trace things in their emer-gence, as structures of feeling, inchoate significances (Barthes 1982; Fernan-dez 1986), and the fleeting, half-glimpsed sensations and movements of vitality or aliveness (Stewart 2006a, 2006b).

My use of the "virtual" is inspired by an intellectual genealogy that includes Gilles Deleuze and Felix Guattari (1994) and, most recently, Brian Massumi (2002). In this line of thinking, the virtual is opposed not to the real, but to the concrete present or actually real. In *The Virtual*, Rob Shields provides a concise gloss of the ways these thinkers use the virtual:

> The virtual is ideal but not abstract, real but not actual. It is ideally real, like a memory. Of more significance is the weaving together of these ontological cate-gories in our representations of reality, of the past and of the future. Virtual ele-ments are embedded in everyday activities and the language we use. Ritual, miracles, understandings of risk and fate all involve slippage between categories as the virtual is actualized, the probably takes place—as our fears and dreams "come true." (Shields 2003: 43)

On a broad level, thinking about the virtual helps us to ask what's real—what's real when it comes to intimacy? Is it the intense feelings, the longing that comes even when people are together, or worse, after the end of things, after abandonment or estrangement? The narratives we attach to intimacy try to snap into place, make sense of, the often confused pulsations of affect that are the heart of what we call intimacy. The narratives attached to intimacy gone wrong are particularly illustrative in the ways they try to ground the floating ambivalences that the endings of intimacies can generate: "He's afraid of commitment," "I drank too much," "There was just this emotional disconnect," "It was addictive and codependent." These narratives try to get us out of our ambivalence, the ambivalent fears that things were never as they seemed; that what seemed so real was in fact unreal, projected, transferred, dreamed, fantasized, virtual. Of course, what we experience when we dwell in the virtuality of intimacy isn't just fantasy gone right or wrong, but the discomfort of actually not knowing what our attachments are about or where they come from. This ambivalence, the virtuality of affect and of intimacy, may be what is actually at stake when we seek succor from lovers, former lovers, therapists, recovery programs, spiritual retreats, etc., from stories that make sense, that try to get us to come back to our senses. The confused anxiety with which we grapple with intimacy means that we can say, then, with more than a little assurance, that *virtual intimacies are ambivalent.*

In her introduction to the anthology *Intimacy,* Lauren Berlant says, "to intimate is to communicate with the sparest of signs and gestures" (Berlant 2000: 1). Intimacy is something you can only just barely put your finger on. It can in fact be the wagging of a finger, or the arch of an eyebrow. Like sex, it's something that is supposed to belong to private people; yet, also like sex, it's something that we can't stop talking about. Indeed, intimacy occupies a central place in our therapeutic culture, from the analyst's office to Jerry Springer, from coffee klatches to every pop song on the radio; intimacy is a key, if ghostly, presence that saturates the cultural landscape. But is it a thing, is it actually concrete? Surely, these spare signs and gestures exist in relation to the probable (there's still a relationship because there are signs of intimacy) and the actual (an intimate gesture is an event that might lead to other events, to lovemaking or argument). "At its root," Berlant says, "intimacy has the quality of eloquence and brevity" (1). With whispers, glances, soft or hard touches, something is getting passed on in these intimate communications. Do we know what this thing is? Isn't it the case that the sparest sign paradoxically communicates not a single thing, like "you know what I mean" or "I love you," but instead indexes a whole range of past intimations—"you know what I mean because we've intimated this before"? Intimacy is a sign of past and future connection, of things just barely communicated. Communicating with the barest of signs is like having a secret language, a language whose secrecy runs so deep that neither oneself nor the other with whom one communicates briefly, sparingly, can claim literacy in it. You can't grab intimacy easily. It's like love and other dangerous dreams, about which people say, "you know it when you got it." To the ambivalence of virtual intimacies, we can add that *virtual intimacies are ephemeral.*

Ambivalent and ephemeral, constituted by memories and dreams, intimacy is itself virtual, indexing as it does past intimations and the desire for their continuance, intimacy's future actualization: a wink, rolled eyes, a stuck out tongue, the brush of fingers across a nipple, hands clasped under sheets even when bodies face opposite directions. Using the virtual to think through intimacy reveals the degree to which our intimacies are terribly fragile and delicate things. The fragility and delicacy is best revealed when intimacy gets taken for granted or when it's lost; it appears when things come apart, when one can see the frayed edges, the broken threads of the intimations that used to tie people together. At the end of things, the virtual, the always-still-becoming of the relationship's intimacy, becomes something else, it becomes actually over, undone.

Everybody's Doing It

As Donna Haraway notes, "the promise of technoscience is, arguably, is its principal social weight" (1997: 41). The promise drew us in. The hype was too big to ignore. There were worlds to explore, worlds animated, above all, if also a bit obviously, by desire—the desire for new worlds.

Certainly this is part of what attracted me to these virtual spaces; my desires were reflected back to me on porn sites or in the interactive exchanges I could have in chat rooms. I'd made contact and felt like I'd found a community before community started to sound like a dirty word, stained by liberal delusion or a desperation for togetherness. My longing for intimacy was being realized. Finally, technology was allowing us to *really feel connected* to strangers in new and novel ways. We could learn about ourselves and explore our fantasies from the safety of our home or office. We could even become other people, people of other genders, sexes, or races. Maybe we could even learn to love ourselves. In these moments of pure potential, virtual spaces promised us freedom from all constraint (of identifications, obligations, roles) and failure (not getting "it" right, or not getting "it" at all, of breaking down before we got to "it"). They promised us an interactive freedom from *all that shit.* Freedom from everything. Except, of course, from the constraints and failures that come with the meaty territory, the matrix, of desire and sex. Or capitalism. Or consumption, production, labor. . . .

So the promise may be the principal social weight of every new technology, but this promise always cuts both ways. It promises that things will go bad, that we'll get alienated (from our labor or our friends and lovers) and addicted, that we'll lose touch, or, worse, just lose it. Virtual intimacies might mean "getting dick to your house faster than a pizza," as one lover/informant/friend told me, but there is no guarantee that it'll still be hot when it gets there.

Virtual intimacies thus also came to be about the half an hour you spent talking to a spambot, the stranger's rejection because you weren't "what they were looking for right now," the ways people lied and told you that they were what you were looking for when they were really fat and old, how you started to get bored, how you started to want more than a session of hot chat or sloppy blow job from "vgl, 29, frat cock."

Eventually, the promise and the threat of virtual intimacies collapsed into the ordinary. Sure, there were these occasional irruptions around privacy, or kiddie porn, or Friendster, but the idea of using the net to connect, of putting up personal ads at Myspace or looking for hot chat on Aim, or using Facebook to set up some casual sex wasn't abnormal anymore. Virtual intimacies were no longer this throbbing point of conversation and contention on the cultural landscape. They'd faded, like the radio we put on in the morning, to the status of background hum. Everyone just took it for granted that they'd spend too much time at ebay sometimes, that they'd scan the job ads at craigslist, or that, in a pinch, wikipedia might answer some basic questions about Deleuze. Everyone just took it for granted that their real life was their virtual life, and vice versa.

Still, you held onto the promise, the dream that connection was possible, and that, if you set up the right conditions (time of day, clear profile picture, knowing what you wanted), you could get the possible to slip into the probable, the virtual to pass into the actual, the intimate to metamorphose into something concrete, something you could sink your teeth into. You could find love and sex and equality.

Interactivity

Unlike technologies of film and television, chat rooms are situated within the history of interactive communications media such as the telegraph and phone, technologies that make it possible to "reach out and touch someone," but also to be touched back.[2] Chat rooms are important for many reasons, not least of which because they helped make porn interactive.[4] Rather than drive to the gay video store or the XXX Megaplexxx, you could log on and find someone to help you get off. Chat rooms made real the possibility for constructing interactive intimate scenarios, ones less beholden to some of the rules that govern relating intimately (let's talk about this, tell me what you're feeling, I don't think we're on the same wavelength). Chat rooms let you sidestep the rules about talking in the right way, about being honest, they let you, in short, sidestep "good" communication as the defining index of the worth or success of a relationship's intimacy. Instead, in chat rooms, what mattered was your ability to draw someone out, to get beyond they initial "hey, how's it going," to get someone interested or engaged, to get them turned on by your ability to quickly construct hot chat scenarios.

In video chat, the possibility for constructing alternate intimate scenarios was intensified, no longer requiring theories of active masochistic spectatorship. You could literally turn yourself and the friend or stranger on the other end of the screen into objects. You might do something a stranger asked you to do without question, an act that carried none of the delay or frustration that might come with having to explain to your partner why spanking doesn't necessarily mean you want to be abused. A stranger asked you do stand up, undress, bend over, turn around, show face, show dick, show ass, and you might do it. With pleasure. These were, arguably, those rare moments of freedom, in which desire was unfettered, when its actualization followed uncertain lines of expression. And if it didn't work out, if you weren't into it, then so what, you could tune out, log off, and live.

In contrast to this ideal, what seemed more the case among the men I spoke with was an ambivalent, changing relationship to interactivity, the space of the screen, and desire. For instance, Joseph, a white graduate student in his late twenties described his use of video chat rooms as part of an evolving relationship to screen cultures. While he initially used the Web primarily for pornography and then for text-based hot chat, he eventually found that the interactivity of video chat rooms appealed to him the most.

I use video chat, it's interactive porn.

It's like after a while, it just wasn't satisfying to have these cyber [role-playing] chats. Maybe I just graduated or evolved to using other kinds of porn things. . . . I think maybe you feel more connected to the person on the other end, because you're not just chatting with them, you can see them at the same time that they can see you. But most of the time, these days anyway, I don't really know how connected I feel, even when I'm doing video chat. Sometimes I can't tell whether it's just narcissistic, whether I'm looking at myself getting off for these other people, whether these other people even interest me. I wonder, why not just masturbate, you know, in front of a mirror?

But I like the idea that I might be able to excite someone else. I like the feeling of being wanted. . . . I like to be able to hear someone getting off. . . . I can imagine how this looks from the outside—here's this guy jerking off on his bed, staring at a screen, while juggling a cell phone [laughs]. But is it really any different from someone getting of to "just porn" in their living room? I think these new technologies have definitely made porn more interesting in some ways. I mean, in video chat you know there's someone there actually interacting with

you—you type or you see them or you chat on the phone. People might even do
things you ask them to do, you know, show off different parts of your body or
play with toys, stuff like that. But I get irritated when people do that too much
to me.

In popular culture as in intimate life, porn is both productive of particular
kinds of intimacy and an index of its failure. For Joseph, virtual intimacies
were undoubtedly real; they aided in the exploration and expression of particular kinds of desire, perhaps most important among them, the desire to be
desired. But it is a virtual intimacy too, and here I let the meaning of virtual
bleed into a negation, because he's doing it alone, uncoupled, in his room.
Because porn is a substitute for the real thing. (These aren't usually the kinds
of intimacies that you parade in public or advertise to the neighbors. They
aren't, then, the kinds of intimacies that require other people for their
authentication.)

Interestingly, even as certain kinds of intimacy are valorized, so too are
particular sorts of virtual intimacies. Video chat was better for John because
it was more interactive. More interactive meant, somehow, less virtual. For
John, the better virtual intimacies were the ones in which *he knew he was connected:* "people might even do things you ask them to do, you know. . . ."

A couple of years after I interviewed John, I ran into him at a local
leather bar. He told me he'd been off interactive screen-mediated virtual intimacies for a while. "I'm back in the real world," he told me. But he complained, too, about how hard it was to meet guys, date, and negotiate sexual
relationships. He wondered if he hadn't substituted one kind of virtual intimacy for another.

The Bleed

Over time, I discovered that there were no clear lines between virtual and
real life. Virtual and real life bleed into one another, as do public, private and
intimate lives.[5] I was often struck by how events in bars, relationships, or even
previous chats were recounted in both face-to-face encounters and, in a feedback loop of infinite regression, in chat rooms as well: "Did you see X with Y
at the bar last night? Can you believe it? X and Z only just broke up." The
bleed implies a kind of mixing, things get jumbled up together; it's hard to
sort out where things end and where they begin. It also, importantly, implies
a kind of violence.

Pedro, a self-identified cyber-Chicano, who was almost always online
when I was, told me the following story about the bleed between real and
virtual life:

One time I went to a bar with a guy I knew from online. I'd been worried about going because my ex went there sometimes, and I didn't want to see him. I told this guy that, but he said not to worry. Well, sure enough, we go there and not ten minutes after we arrive, there's my ex along with his new fuckbuddy. I drank a few drinks fast, then bolted out of there. On the car ride to my friend's place, I asked him if he'd known my ex was gonna be there. He said no. But later on, I found out from my ex that he and this guy I went to the bar with had both been online, and that my ex had been seeing if anyone wanted to go to this bar. So I stopped hanging out with this guy, figured he was a total pathological liar, which was a pattern for me anyway.

When Pedro elaborated on his story, he told me that one of the reasons he'd started using the internet was in an effort to make better judgments about potential romantic and sexual partners. He said he'd had a (pre-internet) pattern of getting into relationships with people he felt were liars. Yet, rather than offering an escape from this pattern, his use of chat rooms, at least in this story, seem to indicate the pattern's repetition, albeit in a virtual context.

Pedro might have tried to use the net to become a different kind of person, but the virtual doesn't necessarily provide any kind of escape from repetition compulsion. Indeed, as I discuss below, the virtual can simply provide a new space for acting out. Peter, a bisexual man in his early 20s, told me all about the bleed. The bleed might be a dream world but that doesn't mean it isn't *intense*. Screen-mediated intimacies carried the force of a blow as recollections surged to the surface of consciousness and the body, as the past was made present, as the virtual put life on hold. For Peter virtual intimacies were about getting put on hold; the looking-glass of the screen only intensified his longings for connection with lost loves.

I'd been looking for [my ex] for a while, and then one day he was there [on Instant Messenger], and it just totally freaked me out. We had this totally fucked up conversation, and I asked him to remove me from his buddy list. Wasn't that I didn't want to be his friend anymore, at least I don't think so. It was more like I just didn't even want to be reminded of him. I'd tried to talk to him once through [Instant Messenger], but it wasn't even him, it was his new boyfriend. And I asked something stupid, like "are you okay," cuz he'd gotten with this guy just a few days after he left me, and then he moved like 1500 miles away. Turns out it wasn't even him that time, but his boyfriend who'd been logged into his account. When he talked with me, he started by telling me that. I mean the whole thing was just so fucked up. So I stopped trying to find him online.

But I'd still go to these websites where he had profiles up. One of them . . . was set up so that you could see who'd looked at your profile. I kept a profile there basically just to see if he'd looked me up. It was the same as with my last boyfriend—every time I'd look him up I freaked out, even after I waited five months or so, the results were the same. I'd think, "oh, I feel a lot better about this now, so I'll just take a peek and see where he's at," you know, wondering and hoping he and this guy would have broken up by now. And I'd look up his profile and see things like "monogamously coupled" and I'd freak out all over again. I'm probably just a jealous person, but in a way, I think it was like I was thinking, "he'll be single now and come back to me." I'd look up his profile, he'd still be with this guy, and I'd have to go through all the feelings of the breakup over and over again. Every time, it just totally freaked me out for days—more like weeks—to read his profile—like where it said "monogamously coupled." I don't know why it affected me so much. The reactions were totally physical. My hands would shake, my heart would race, I'd start crying and just generally freaking out.

What's weird about it was that it was like a way to hold on to the relationship after it had ended. I mean, for a while it had been phone calls, or trying to meet in person. Hopefully now I've learned my lesson, though I just got a letter from my last ex, and it was the same. I was so angry to hear he was still with this guy, and I was terrified that he'd be coming back to town. He wanted to know if I wanted to see him. I don't know. I wonder if I should have written him back. I did, and I told him he could contact me by e-mail, but I bet even that was a mistake. Probably best for me to just not do anything, and let it work itself out. I'm still angry and jealous, and my experience has taught me that I can't really have a decent relationship or friendship or whatever with my exes until they're not with anyone or a lot of time has passed.

Q: How did you get over that longing to connect with your former lovers?

A: I didn't. I still long for them, for renewal, for closure, whatever. I'm usually focused on the most recent one, though. I guess I've just learned to live with it better. For now anyway. I do wonder though if I hadn't kept reopening the pain of the relationship by looking up my lovers online and stuff, if it wouldn't have been easier for me.

Like the rest of us, Peter held onto a dream, a dream of intimacy, a dream of union, a dream that the matrix could deliver. The dream or the memory of the thing we had or don't have or want to have is virtual.

In Peter's story, virtual technologies helped him to hold on to past relationships. While virtual technologies helped him to reach out and touch someone, he wasn't always prepared for what happened to him when they reached out and touched back. Telecommunicative touches don't always help us feel connected; they don't always ease the pain of separation or of distance. Sometimes they're toxic and produce dis-ease. Or, maybe the contact and communication has gone bad. Or, maybe it was bad to begin with. Or, maybe contact opens up grief or longing. Now, is the grief about the end of things or did the mourning come prior to the end? Maybe mourning's object here was intimacy itself.

Distraction and Addiction

In this reaching out, a lot of folks went hunting for fantasy, for the promise or actual realization of pleasure. But not everyone had a plan. In fact most folks thought of what they were doing in terms of distraction or, worse, addiction. Whether they were running toward or away from intimacy is probably irrelevant. There were almost definitely doing a bit of both—they got intimate with themselves as they found themselves at this or that porn site again, less intimate with their friends and lovers, and more intimate (if not comfortable) with the notion that their intimacies in their real and digital lives were equally virtual.

As a kind of active escape, distraction has a tendency to bleed into a death drive that manifests most typically as repetition compulsion. Given the American preoccupation with sex, and our obsessive-compulsive preoccupation with obsessive-compulsive disorders, it's not surprising that cybersex has not only raised the ire of conservatives, but also continues to preoccupy pop psychology. Are you addicted? You can take the quiz yourself at www. cybersexualaddiction.com.

I didn't do so well, but I'm also skeptical of most efforts to produce "normal" sexualities; nonetheless, I want to believe that "good" and "healthy" sexual behavior are free from guilt and shame, or fear that you may be hurting yourself or others. I recognize of course that my text walks a fine line here. I want, on one hand, to critique normative discourses which figure sexual behavior in relation to some "statistically imagined norm" (Berlant and Warner 2000: 321). On the other hand, I want to mark the importance in my own narrative and the narratives of the men with whom I spoke of the feeling (cognitive and affective) of being overly attached, of being addicted, of dwelling in, at, or beyond the periphery not just of a statistically imagined norm, but of one's own limits.

Many chat users frequently used the term addiction to describe their own relationship to virtual technologies. John, a self-employed graphic designer who works from home was explicit in describing his online wanderings as addictive.

> I found a lot of this stuff really addictive. I'd work on a project for a couple of hours and then I'd get bored and so I'd look for a distraction. Since I do my [design] work on a computer, it was easy to log into gay.com or look for porn. Before I knew it, I'd be downloading a dozen porn movies from some site or I'd be chatting in gay.com, even arranging for a hookup.

> I always thought it'd be nice to just have the program up and running and if someone interesting wanted to chat with me, great, then I'd chat for a bit and get back to work, but I always ended up giving this distraction my full attention. . . . And I did start thinking, you know, maybe this is a problem, because I can't

seem to work at the computer and stay focused on what I need to do. I had a friend who was a sex addict, but he was into public sex stuff; he didn't even have a computer. He got in trouble for it even, with citations and what not, but I don't think he was ever arrested. Anyway, he started going to these sex addicts meetings that are structured like AA [Alcoholics Anonymous] and that seemed to work for him. I borrowed this book from him about sex and love addiction and that gave me some perspective. You know, I really saw myself in it. But I was resistant to going to any kind of meetings. I mean that would be admitting I had a real problem, and I didn't think it was that bad yet. But it was interesting to think of this thing that had started out being a kind of distraction as being connected to other stuff. . . .

Like . . . maybe I was online or looking for distraction because I was really look- ing for something else, something deeper, like sex, I guess, but also stuff like attention, affection . . . or love. . . .

At one point, I installed all this software to block stuff, and that usually works, but then sometimes, you know, I'll disable it all. Makes me more conscious of what's going on anyway. I still use the computer for porn. And sometimes, I'm like, "oh, this isn't a problem at all" and I'll go without going to these sites or even thinking about them for a few weeks. And then other times, I'll find myself spending a few consecutive days downloading porn and chatting or whatever. Then the cycle happens all over again. I mean, I'm totally aware there's a com- pulsive aspect to what's going on . . . to how I relate to this stuff and that it can affect, that it does affect, my work habits. I dunno, maybe I just need to get a boyfriend. That's probably what I'm looking for. For me it's hard, because I'm not super gay—I don't go to bars or do gay pride or anything like that. I don't have a lot of gay friends. Maybe this is just my way of participating in gay culture.

For John, porn and chat rooms helped him to feel a part of gay culture. But his feeling that he was addicted to these things also mark a degree of dis- tance between himself and other gay men; the internet allowed him to con- nect virtually but not actually ("maybe I should just get a boyfriend").

John wasn't the only one addicted to notions of addiction. After word of my research gets out through an article I wrote for Texas' statewide gay weekly, I was contacted by the host of a syndicated gay and lesbian radio pro- gram who wanted to talk with me about cybersex and addiction. I agreed to talk to him and a few weeks later he called to do the interview. Even though I'd written about addiction and found myself and the men I worked with using the term more and more, I refused to give this guy what he wanted. I was probably in denial, but instead of talking about how fucked up chat rooms were, or how disease clusters had been traced to them, I talked about the ways chat rooms helped create feelings of community, something which I no longer really believed (but still dreamed of). During the course of the interview he became increasingly angry. He didn't call back, and the program never aired.

Indeed, I strongly identified with John's sentiments. After a breakup, I sometimes joked with my ex, perhaps inappropriately, "the computer made us break up." Chats in gay.com, video chat rooms, and compulsive visits to porn sites had provided the evidence for my meandering gazes, my untrustworthy love, and my desire for extra-relationship sex. Hurt and sullen one day, my lover said, "I read that thing from the boy from Belgium, who said, 'what about your ex?' I don't appreciate being called your ex."

Somehow having an actual relationship, a face-to-face, skin-to-skin feeling of intimately relating wasn't enough. I looked to the matrix to give me more. Though more of what is difficult to say—more attention, more sex, more stimulation? Whether trying to supplement or intensify my relationship with virtual intimacies had to do with lack or excess hardly matters anymore: my desires produced effects, they changed things.

Now, part of me wants to return to simpler times, when all I had to do to get off was spit and fantasize, when all I did to meet people was take a walk down the street or go to a coffeeshop. In a strange way, being online, at least my being-online, means giving something up. Getting online to get off, I sacrificed a sense of proximity and touch: his hand across the back of my neck, his love.

Conclusions

In the contemporary moment the virtual saturates cultural life in technophilic and technophobic nations like the United States. In our everyday lives, the virtual bleeds into the actual as what was once private goes public. There are other bleeds as well in which promises pass into failures, desires into dreams deferred. And everything bleeds into commodification as the authenticity we seek in our relationships to ourselves and to others becomes another set of lifestyle options.

The bleed is messy and violent. Categories don't just break down, they move into one another, they pass from one state to another in a movement of becoming that can be wrenching. The bleed indexes that fact of what is sometimes a fatal breech in the wall. Flows can't be stopped, and things leak or gush out.

Messy and violent, the bleed is also, of course, productive. Worlds get built when the virtual gets actualized. And worlds get built when things get virtualized too: dream worlds. In terms of intimacy, those intimacies that are virtual and real and actual and concrete, the bleed helps us to resist normative models of intimacies, those social imperatives to have an intimate life *or else;* it encourages us to attend to the emergence of new forms of intimacy, digital or otherwise; and it challenges us to think of intimacy not as a static, fixed, or firm thing but as a living assemblage of spare communications, ephemeral gestures, and ambivalent affects.

Notes

1. Portions of this chapter originally appeared, in very different form, in the August 2, 2002 issue of the *Texas Triangle*. My title borrows in part the subtitle of Paige Baty's 1999 book, *Email Trouble: Love and Addiction @ the Matrix.*
2. I am thinking here, in particular, of various posthuman intimacies, intimacies with machines, animals, and other nonhuman becomings. On the surface it seems as if the posthuman properly belongs to the past. See Halberstam and Livingston 1995; Hayles 1999; Weinstone 2004. Still, it is both possible and probable that forms of intimacy outside the human and the posthuman are currently being experienced on the ground, and that new forms of posthuman embodiment will continue to be cultivated.
3. See Kittler 1990 and Postman 1985.
4. While it is difficult to find precise figures, many Web industry experts estimate that nearly half of the bandwidth of the internet is used for pornography.
5. In different context and with different aims, both Brian Massumi 2002 and Rayna Rapp 2000 offer examples of "the bleed." Massumi's discussion centers on Ronald Reagan's image and body, of the way Reagan's speech and performance of various events bled into his everyday reality. For Rapp, her own firsthand experiences with amniocentesis and the loss of a child inspired her to delve more deeply into research into on reproductive technologies, their effects on women, and to develop a feminist methodology that looked at amniocentesis "against a larger social background" (Rapp 2005: 5).

References

Barthes, R. 1982. "The Third Meaning: Research Notes on Some Eisentstein Stills," in S. Sontag (Ed.), *A Barthes Reader* (pp. 317–333). New York: Hill and Wang.
Baty, S. P. 1999. *Email Trouble: Love & Addiction @ the Matrix.* Austin: University of Texas Press.
Berlant, L. 1997. *The Queen of America Goes to Washington City.* Durham, NC: Duke University Press.
Berlant, L. 2000. "Intimacy: A Special Issue," in L. Berlant (Ed.), *Intimacy* (pp. 1–8). Chicago: University of Chicago Press.
Berlant, L., and Warner, M. 2000. "Sex in Public," in L. Berlant (Ed.), *Intimacy* (pp. 311–330). Chicago: University of Chicago Press.
Cvetkovich, A. 2003. *An Archive of Feelings: Trauma, Sexuality, and Lesbian Public Cultures.* Durham, NC: Duke University Press.
Deleuze, G. 2004. "Bergon, 1859–1941," in D. Lapoujade (Ed.), Trans. M. Taormina, *Desert Islands and Other Texts: 1953–1974* (pp. 22–31). Los Angeles: Semiotext(e).
Deleuze, G., and Guattari, F. 1994. *What Is Philosophy?* New York: Colombia University Press.

Fernandez, J. W. 1986. *Persuasions and Performances: The Play of Tropes in Culture.* Bloomington: Indiana University Press.

Halberstam, J., and Livingston, I. (Eds.). 1995. *Posthuman Bodies (Unnatural Acts).* Bloomington: University of Indiana Press.

Haraway, D. 1997. *Modest-Witness@Second-Millennium.FemaleMan-Meets-OncoMouse : Feminism and Technoscience.* New York: Routledge.

Hayles, K. 1999. *How We Became Posthuman.* Chicago: University of Chicago Press.

Kittler, F. A. 1990. *Discourse Networks 1800/1900.* Stanford, CA: Stanford University Press.

Massumi, B. 2002. *Parables for the Virtual: Movement, Affect, Sensation.* Durham, NC: Duke University Press.

Postman, N. 1985. *Amusing Ourselves to Death.* New York: Viking.

Rapp, R. 2000. *Testing Women, Testing the Fetus: The Social Impact of Amniocentesis in America.* New York: Routledge.

Shields, R. 2003. *The Virtual.* New York: Routledge.

Stewart, K. 2006a. *Surface Tensions.* Durham, NC: Duke University Press.

Stewart, K. 2006b. "Cultural Poesis: The Generativity of Emergent Things," in K. Denzin and Yvonna S Lincoln (Eds.), *Handbook of Qualitiative Research* (pp. 1015–1030). London: Sage.

Williams, R. 1977. *Marxism and Literature.* New York: Oxford University Press.

8. Brown to Blonde at Gay.com: Passing White in Queer Cyberspace

ANDIL GOSINE

> I am in love with the image and idea of white manhood, which is everything I am not and want to be, and if I cannot be that at least I can have that, if only for the night, if only for one week or the month. (Shepherd, 1991)

> I would love to be white. Not forever, but perhaps a weekend. Don't you ever get sick of being a minority? . . . I have posed this question to other minority artists, and get stumped by answers like "No, not ever have I ever wanted to be white." And I just don't buy it. Why would you not want things to be easier? (Cho 2005)

So much social, economic, and cultural capital is invested in the idealization of white bodies (and in the devaluation and denigration of non-white ones) that neither Shepherd's confessional yearnings nor Cho's caustic daydream is surprising—nor are the disapproving reactions from those whom find their declarations uncomfortable, even upsetting. Fantasies and anxieties about the realization and loss of whiteness inform the configuration of social relations and production of knowledge in much of the contemporary world. Since at least the fifteenth century, white has connoted purity, virginity, beauty, and even Godliness in European nations, and the accident of white skin has authorized its bearers to claim, conquer, and colonize the lands and cultures of non-white peoples of Africa, Asia, and the Americas. Whiteness, writes Kalpana Seshadri-Crooks, is a "master signifier that establishes a structure of relations, a signifying chain that through a process of inclusions and exclusions constitutes a pattern for organizing human difference" (2000: 3–4). Through the production of Orientalism, non-white subjects are characterized as a function of the white subject and are allowed no autonomy, and purpose except as a means of knowing the white self (Said 1978). Consequently, white people are systematically privileged and enjoy "unearned advantage and conferred dominance" in Western societies (McIntosh 1992: 74). They "create the dominant images of the world and don't quite see that they construct the world in their own image," and "they set standards of humanity by which they are bound to succeed and others bound to fail" (Dyer 1997: 9). Frantz Fanon concludes: "Sin is Negro as Virtue is white" (1967: 138).

There are longstanding rituals through which white people are able to perform non-white racialized ethnicities (e.g., casting white actors in Asian roles in films, donning kimonos or turbans to play Japanese or Indian at costume parties) and for non-white people to perform exaggerated expressions of racialized identities (e.g., American Minstrel shows, representations in television and film), but not many choices exist for a Korean-American comic like Cho or an African-American like Shepherd to assume white racial identities. The advent of cyberspace provided a new venue for non-white people to experience racial crossing into whiteness—an experience that was part of a parcel of opportunities being trumpeted by queer, feminist and cyberculture critics anticipating the liberating potential of virtual worlds (Turkle 1995; Plant 1996; Sunden 2001; Gross 2004).

In November 1998, I engaged "race" play in cyberspace as a way of examining claims about its revolutionary promise, and of racial crossing. For five consecutive days, I participated in conversations in the "Toronto" chat rooms at gay.com, and kept a journal of my online interactions. Selecting a gay website feature to consider the operation of "race" in cyberspace made sense for several reasons, including my own ties to and investments in queer culture, and the fact that queer scholars were among those leading the celebration of this technological advance. Many of them, including Larry Gross, for example, imagined that for queer men and women, the net would present more opportunities to inhabit sexual desires and identities, connect and create community, and refuse gender and class restrictions that structured their offline, "real world" lives (2004). A focus on chat rooms also seemed appropriate. As Lisa Nakamura observes, "cyberspace is a place of wish fulfillments and myriad gratifications, material and otherwise and nowhere is this more true than in chat spaces" (2002: 32). Textual chat spaces, she says, "encourage users to build different identities, to take on new identities . . . to describe themselves in any way they wish to appear (Nakamura 2002: 32).

My chat room experiences did not prove to be as liberating an event as proclaimed in the cyberutopian rhetoric. Although opportunities to unfix and reconstitute meanings of identities and social markers were certainly available, processes of racialization were evident in and seemed to have an important structuring influence on the organization, flow of dialogues and relationships between users in the chat rooms. Returning to review the site seven years later, in 2005, I also found that whatever potential may have existed for dominant, colonial narratives of "race" to be displaced or undermined in cyberspace are fading (or have faded). Changes to gay.com's chat services since 1998 appear to have further reinforced racial categories and ensure the reproduction of "real life" racism. In this respect, the development of virtual worlds has been shown to be not unlike other technologies, merely mimicking dominant socioeconomic relations rather than challenging them.

What also emerged from this study of the chat rooms were compelling insights about desires for passing white. Very often, racial crossing from non-white to white is read as evidence of investments in racial imagery and symbolism. This presumption underlies the outrage expressed by Cho's friends about her wanting to be white for a weekend and the persistence of epithets to describe non-white people accused of "acting white" (e.g., "coconut" for South Asians, "banana" for East Asians). But analysis of the operation of "race"-racism in the gay.com chat rooms suggests that passing white is not simply the exercise of desires by non-white people to become white or fetishize whiteness, but, rather, to experience the privileges afforded to whiteness. Passing white expresses longing for the experience of racial disembodiment that cyberspace promises, but does not ultimately appear to fulfill.

Toronto@gay.com, 1998: Identity Play (and Its Limits)

"Race" traps the body in real life. It attaches meanings to skin, hair, and bones that have been organized around the ambitions of colonialism/imperialism, capitalist exploitation and psychoanalytical differentiation, and which have proven difficult to destabilize. Ideologies of "race" are so purposefully and intensively repeated and circulated in Western cultures, whether through institutional practices (policing, education, etc.) or the production of popular culture, that despite overwhelming evidence that "race" is a lie, its mythological links between skin and thought continue to shape most (if not all) aspects of living in most (if not all) parts of the contemporary world. But early on in the development of virtual worlds, optimists hoped that cyberspace might offer opportunities to usurp "race." In 1995, Sherry Turkle observed, "in simulation, identity can be fluid and multiple, a signifier no longer clearly points to a thing that is signified, and understanding is less likely to proceed through analysis than by navigation through virtual space" (1995: 49). This fact, cyberutopians argued, would create conditions that diminished or refused the structuring power of narratives of gender, "race," class, and sexuality.

In November, 1998, chat rooms at gay.com allowed, even encouraged, users to actively shape their identities, to create and recreate themselves, whatever the motivation: to express anxiety, to deceive, to fulfill deep-seeded fantasy or indulge more fleeting pleasures, or to engage idle curiosity. Entering a gay.com chat room involved only a few steps: setting the Web browser to gay.com and clicking the "chat" icon. Users were then directed to a tree menu of room locations, which in 1998 consisted of a limited number of geographic regions, countries and cities, including Toronto. Due to the high volume of traffic, Toronto was assigned three rooms: Toronto 1, Toronto 2, and Toronto 3. As the first room filled (fifty chatters were allowed entry to each room), users would enter the second, and so on. During the five consecutive days that I entered the rooms Toronto 1 was always full, but the population sizes of Toronto 2 and 3 varied with the time of day (late evenings and nights were more active). Once the list of cities appeared, users only had to submit a "handle" (a name identifier) of their choosing to enter a room. Users could also—but were not required to—compose a tag line describing themselves.

Bragh, McKenna, and Fitzsimons suggest that internet interactions are analogous to those one sometimes has with "strangers on a train,"

> in which one opens up and self-discloses intimate details to the stranger sitting in the next seat, details that one might never have told one's colleagues at the office or even one's family and friends back home. (2002: 35)

My single sentence tag-line description presented only the aspects of myself that I wanted to share at the moment of participating in the chat, details which could change with each entry into a chat room. "Online queerness pushes you to push," suggests Jacqueline Rhodes, "to follow your desires to (il)logical conclusions" (Alexander et al. 2004: 28). The possibility of imagination, the sense of boundlessness, the absence of the more rigidly policed social regulations of the world, and the play of language and identity permit new excursions, the release of inhibitions, travel into unexplored bodies; virgin, slut, whore, prude, pervert: some, all or none—online, performance of any, some or all of these and other personalities seemed possible.

In real-life encounters between queer men (between any sighted individuals, for that matter), the moment of meeting is usually the same moment in which racial identification is rationalized. With no visual or aural clues as clearly and readily available in chat rooms (in 1998), control of the terms of representation would appear to rest with the users themselves. But the absence of visual and aural signifiers, or descriptors identifying "race"/ethnicity, does not actually make users "race"-less. As Nakamura points out, "the decision to leave race out of self-description does in fact constitute a choice: in the absence of racial description, all players are assumed to be white" (2002: 33). Campbell also believes this presumption "indicates these channels are implicitly understood to be white spaces rather than raceless spaces; that is, white is viewed as the norm in these particular online communities"

(2004: 81–82). Their analysis is strongly supported by several empirical studies of cyberspace conducted in the United States, all of which conclude "white" is viewed as the "normal" racial condition of cyberspace users[1]—but not entirely by my experience in the Toronto chat rooms.

In the absence of information stating my "race" or ethnicity, some men with whom I engaged in conversations at gay.com appeared to assume I was white. But whether due to the particular demography of Toronto (a city where half of its resident population of five million consists of non-white peoples), the influence of prevailing Canadian discourses on multiculturalism that encourage strong ethnic identification, more equitable access to internet technologies in Canada, or some other reason, most of the users with whom I interacted did not seem to immediately assume I was white. This response did not mean, however, that Canadian chatters engaged a more critical understanding of "race" than their American counterparts. Rather, they tended to insist that users be "transparent" in naming one's racial identity.

Four main strategies were employed to encourage, if not ensure, racial identification in the Toronto chat rooms at gay.com. First, many users adopted handles that indicated ethnic or racial identities, e.g., "Chinese23," "Blackboi20," "FlyWhiteGuy," or "PakiStud," or suggested them, e.g., "Chc18dream" (chocolate dream) or "Brown_dt" (Brown, downtown). Second, some used the short descriptor profile to state their own identities or racial preferences. Information listed in this space typically included three items—age, height, body weight/type and race/ethnicity—and sometimes others: penis size, chest width, sexual position preference (top or bottom), and hair and eye color. Sometimes, the latter two items substituted for mention of race/ethnicity (e.g., "bl/bl" would read as blue-eyed blonde, i.e., white). Often, messages such as "white guys only please," "looking for Asians," or "any race ok" would appear. Third, users avoided asking for "race" information by offering to send or requesting pictures sent through e-mail; by far, the most common request was for "face pics." Fourth, chat room users who did not identify "race" or ethnic markers were prodded to do so. When I did not indicate a racial identifier, usually my chat room encounters at the Toronto gay.com chat rooms began with or eventually arrived at this inquiry: <What's ur background?>. When I still didn't include information about race or ethnicity in response, a more pointed question would follow, such as "So you're white?" or "What is your race?" Inquiries for "Stats?" also demanded a particular form—height, weight, build, hair and eye color, and sometimes, penis size, ethnicity, and chest size—to which chatters are expected to comply. If information about any of these items were left out, chatters would again pose a more specific question, requesting clarification.

Such demands for racial identification may be read as merely attempts by chat room users to more clearly imagine interacting parties and advance fantasies. But the flow of dialogues in the chat rooms often revealed the persistence of racism in organizing online interactions. For example, reactions to answers stating a non-white ethnicity were almost entirely limited to three types, whether my correspondents were white or non-white. A few users continued our conversation, some expressed enthusiastic appreciation, and a third group dismissed me immediately. On several occasions, long and engaged, flirtatious, even salacious chats would reach an abrupt end once I confessed non-white ethnicity. Several conversations took this form:

<badPup> What's ur background?

<Garf23> Indian

<badPup> Oh

<Garf23> "Oh?"

<badPup> Not into that Sorry

badPup's response was among the more polite dismissals; on very many occasions, no disappointments were expressed, no reason given. Chatters would simply end the conversation, and a notice that "*badpup has left the chat room or is ignoring you" would appear as the last entry on my private chat window.[2]

Toronto@gay.com, 2005: Pictures, Power, and Capitalist Expansion

Changes implemented to the gay.com chat services since 1998 have only encouraged processes of reification, and the reproduction of "real life" racism through their interface. In 1995, Tom Reilly, the founder of PlanetOut, the parent company of gay.com declared, "traditional mass media is cost-intensive. . . . The Internet is the first medium where we can have equal footing with the big players" (cited in Gross 2004: x–xi). Reilly's dream has been realized. According to Nielsen Net Ratings, in June 2004, gay.com ranked second in terms of average time online per person and sixteenth in terms of visit per person among all websites measured. On November 8, 2005, there were 6, 033, 363 registered members at gay.com.[2] PlanetOut's success with the site has been accompanied by the hyper commercialization of its main features, and the format of the chat rooms has been organized around a primary interest in profit generation. Access to many sections of the site, including most elements of the chat room feature, is now tied to purchase of a "Premium" membership (in November 2005, the fee was set at $19.95 per month, with various promotions available for members willing to commit memberships over longer periods). New general memberships are free, but involve an elaborate registration process and allow only partial access to profiles, pictures and contact information. Both the financial investment and the demanding registration process requirements promote the creation of a stable identity. In 1998, the structure of the chat room interface at least permitted, some would say even encouraged, identity play. Limits to play were not by the technology per se, but by the cultural conditions in which it was used. Eight years later, the form and flow of the gay.com chat rooms more aggressively reinforce stable identities and actively resist identity play.

In 1998, each visitor to a chat room could assume a new identity with each entry into the space, but now chatters must take out a new membership for each identity assumed. Users must also register profiles and select from a range of limited menu items. They are not required to complete all information requested—and many users do not provide fully complete profiles—but the presentation of a form with boxes to check seems to compel most to do so. Users must declare an age, gender, sexuality, height and weight, characterize their build as "athletic," "average," "chubby," "curvy," "large and solid," "muscular," "overweight," "slim," "voluptuous," or "Other," and select their personality from a short list of options: Bitchy, Extroverted/Social, Flamboyant, Flirtatious, Funny, Intellectual, Introverted, Loving, Romantic, Serious. Their mannerisms may be "Masculine/Butch," "Feminine/Femme," or "In the middle." Their politics "lean left" (or right), are "Way left" (or right) or "In the middle," or they might "Avoid politics" or "Prefer not to say." Finally, choices to identify a "race"/ethnicity are limited to the following: African/African American/Black, Asian/Pacific Islander, Latina/Latino, Middle Eastern/North African, Native/Japanese, White/European, Mixed/Multi, or Other. (Having been born in the Caribbean to parents descended from Indian indentures, which category do I now pick in the gay.com chat rooms: am I "Asian," "Black," "Latin," or "Other"? Each category carries a different set of burdens, and each will position me differently in the chat rooms.) This menu-driven interface, which has become the normalized structure throughout the World Wide Web, enforces a sense of personal identity that progressively works by

> narrowing the choices of subject positions available to the user, an outcome that seems to fly in the face of claims that the Internet allows for a fluid, free, unbounded sense of identity than had been available in other media—or, indeed, in the world—before. (Nakamura 2002: 104)

Against the model of "multiple self" imagined by Turkle and others, the menu structure obliges users to declare essentialist identities.

Reification is also accomplished through the adoption of specialized fetish rooms. In the United States, "race" or ethnicity-specific rooms are not the norm, although Spanish-language rooms are included in most major cities.[4] But in Toronto, alongside six rooms marked by geography (East, North, etc.), one for HIV-positive men, one for "Mature" men, a "real-time" room and a bisexuals' room are three focused on fetishes: "Leather," "Bears," and "Asian."[5] Another important shift has been the addition and prioritization of pictures. Throughout, the World Wide Web has become a graphics intense medium that has merely mimicked systems of gendered and racialized representation that are typical of older forms of media. At gay.com, most users now post pictures and many (if not most) limit their online inter-actions to users with pictures attached to their detailed profiles; as declared in the title of a recent study, "your picture is your bait" (Brown, Maycock, and Burns 2005).

All of these changes, especially the addition of pictures, have made racial crossing a much more difficult prospect—one that requires active deception on the part of users (e.g., posting pictures which do not clearly signify "race"/ethnicity or which are not their own)—but they have not rendered it impossible. In fact, the construction of more distinct borders between "races" may also work to simplify the process of crossing: as opportunities for taking on more fluid identities have now disappeared, users wanting to "pass" as a particular "race"/ethnicity now have access to a more structured format in which to constitute themselves. Racial crossing and "passing white" in particular therefore remain interesting events and compelling objects of analysis.

Passing White: Resource Access and the Exercise of Agency

In one of her studies on white people engaging racial passing in cyberspace, Nakamura observed that "many users masquerading as racial minorities in chat spaces tend to depict themselves in ways that simply repeat and reenact old racial stereotypes," including, for example, "users masquerading as samu-rai and geishas, complete with swords, kimonos, and other paraphrnalia lifted from older media such as film and television" (2002: 107). This type of play, she says, "reenacts an anachronistic version of "Asian-ness" that reveals more about users" fantasies and desires than it does about what it "feels like" to be Asian either on- or offline" (2002: 107). Passing white, however, may serve a different purpose, not exclusively an exercise in fantasy or anxiety produc-tion, but an opportunity to experience the material and cultural privileges afforded to white people. Unlike its reverse ritual, racial crossing from non-white to white may not be primarily motivated by fetishistic conscious or unconscious desire, but by struggles for access to resources and for experience of cultural and political agency.

Accessing Resources

One of the reasons queer scholars cheered the development of cyberspace was their expectation that virtual spaces would be better able than bars or clubs to provide affirmation for "many who do not find themselves welcomed or validated by the increasingly commercialized and mainstreamed institutions of the newly respectable GLBT communities, including marginalized sub-culture groups" (Gross 2002: xi). Keith Dorwick argues,

> One thing online communication has changed radically is that men can now speak to men they'd never speak to in the bars. The social barriers between races, between "hot men" and "dogs" or "trolls" and between younger and older men are much lower online. (Alexander et al. 2004)

But characterizations of chat rooms as more egalitarian spaces do not hold up on more attentive examination. Anxieties about race—held by both white and non-white men—may sometimes determine who is solicited for conversation, friendship or sex in bars, but they perform the same function in cyberspace as well, as evidenced by the shutting down of conversations after responses to the "background" question confirm non-white racial identity and, also, by the preferred status afforded to white men.

Of the many identities I adopted in the Toronto chat rooms at gay.com, blue-eyed and blond haired "Robbie" was easily the most fun to inhabit. Robbie fit my own physical description except, importantly, that he was blonde and blue-eyed, I enjoyed the most attention from other online chatters than in any other representation of myself. I was overwhelmed with requests for private window conversations and many times I was chatting separately but simultaneously with five or six of the thirty users in the room. Changing only information about hair and eye color to indicate a white identity, I was invited to participate conversations with many more men and have an altogether different experience than when my descriptor indicated that I was non-white. Others engaged in similar projects have reported similar experiences. For example, one Taiwanese-born college student posting to a Bulletin Board System based in Orange County, California, also found that immediately after changing his ethnic identity from "Chinese" to "Caucasian," he received more queries and invitations to chat (Tsang 2000: 435). Tsang also reports that consequent to their experiences of queer spaces on the Web, many non-white users refused to identify themselves, or identified themselves as "Other" or "Mixed" when given a choice, "in the hopes that their chances [to interact with other men] would be improved" (2000: 435). In the physical world, non-white men have often been refused entry to white-dominant gay bars and clubs; in cyberspace, self-identification as white often serves as a qualifier to access conversations with other users.

Exercising Agency

Interactions in the Toronto gay.com chat rooms make clear that the act of passing white is also an attempt to experience another kind of privilege of whiteness: the opportunity to be viewed as active, dynamic and complex agents. Dominant processes of racialization fix identities for non-white people in ways that generally do not apply to white people. Writing about gay bars and clubs in the real world, Mercer and Julien observe that representations of non-white men are "confined to a narrow repertoire of types—the supersexual stud and the sexual savage on the one hand, the delicate and exotic "Oriental" on the other" (1991: 169). Choices placed to non-white men appear to oscillate between the two:

> Far too many of the white men I see in [. . .] clubs look at me as if to say, "I couldn't sleep with you. You're black. Or they desire me because I am black. (Shepherd 1986: 54)

These representations, rooted in the experience of colonialism and empire, are circulated again in cyberspace. Toronto resident "Marshall," a twenty-six-year-old Asian male who regularly goes online, references a common experience among non-white men:

> I find that a lot of guys won't consider me because of my background . . . a lot of guys are not into Asians, or, if they are, are only into submissive Asians, but I'm a top. [. . .] I've had guys say to me . . . "if I were into Asians I'd totally get with you." I don't exactly consider those compliments, but they're part of my reality and so I deal. (Cited in Sanders 2005: 83)

Similarly, "Big_Wolf" says of his experiences on IRC, "if they suspect or find out you are black MANY immediately go to the penis size thing" (Campbell 2004: 79).

Byron Burkhalter makes the important point that racial identification occurs differently online. "Stereotyping in face-to-face interaction follows from an assumed racial identity," but online interaction, he says, "differs in that the imputation tends to go in the other direction—from stereotype to racial identity" (1999: 73). In real-life situations, the complex, multidimensional realities of racialized peoples also serve to reveal race as a lie. Online, however, fixed stereotypes are the means through which users are received in interactions. "In online interactions," Burkhalter points out, "perspectives resist modification because participants confront an immutable text" (1999: 73). There are of course occasions when the exploration of conversations in cyberspace might engage chatters in critical self-reflection—a user might be surprised about his interactions and be challenged to rethink race-based presumptions. But this happens in the real-world bars as well, and I would even suggest that spontaneous acts leading to confrontations with and challenges to "race"-based expectations may be more likely to happen in bars than cyberspace. For example, suppose that I believe that I am not interested in forming friendships or relationships, or having sexual encounters with Japanese men. I might, however, walk into a bar and encounter an Japanese man whose gestures, body, or manner are attractive to me. Such a real-life meeting might challenge my imagination to be less fixed, resolve sub-/unconscious desires and undermine my investments in "race." If I come to a gay.com chat room with same belief, I simply shut off the possibility of speaking to men identifying themselves as Japanese, allowing no opportunity for challenges to the same investments in "race" to proceed, untroubled.

Insofar as racial identification is concerned, white men are generally not subject to this fixing gaze. As Dyer observes about his study of white representation:

> One cannot come up with a limited range of endlessly repeated images, because the privilege of being white in white culture is not to be subjected to stereotyping in relation to one's whiteness. White people are stereotyped in terms of gender, nation, class, sexuality, ability and so on, but the overt point of such typification is gender, nation, etc. Whiteness generally colonizes the stereotypical definition of all social categories other than those of race. To be normal, even to be normally deviant (queer, crippled), is to be white. White people in their whiteness, however, are imaged as individual and/or endlessly diverse, complex and changing. (1997: 11–12)

When I represented myself as any kind of non-white man in the chat rooms, my "race" almost always figured into users" reactions. Whatever kind of non-white man I claimed to be, even opposed reactions referenced "race"; some respondents shut down conversations because I was non-white, others pursued me because I was Black/Indian/Chinese, etc. But as blonde, blue-eyed Robbie, I was "normal," a complex human whose behavior and personality were not necessarily read through racial tropes. No longer trapped in my skin, I was neither repulsive nor alluring because of it. I was not a member of a group but an individual. I was not a "type" and I spoke for no community but myself. Raced white, I accomplished what Peggy McIntosh identifies as an ultimate achievement of whiteness: the belief that everything a white person does may be accounted for in his/her individuality (1992: 70–81). I was imagined as white people were imagined to be: endlessly diverse, complex, and changing (Dyer 1997: 12).

Conclusion/Epilogue

My experiences as "Robbie" seemed to achieve the kinds of experiences imagined by Shepherd and Cho, and revealed motivations for "passing white" and occupying white identities that were similar to their own. Passing white, whether in a chat room for a few hours, over the course of a trouble-free weekend, or, as Shepherd coyly suggests, for "just one night" if not all eternity, appears to be neither an idle expression of identity play, nor a pro-nouncement of faith in white supremacist mythologies. Those wishing to "pass white" may have no actual desires to inhabit or be with white bodies; I never imagined what "Robbie" might look like, nor was I motivated to undertake this project by conscious desires for white men in particular. Instead, as demonstrated in the analysis of the Toronto chat rooms at gay.com, this act more likely conveys a longing to experience the cultural, social and political privileges afforded to whiteness.

Although Shepherd introduces his "On Not Being White" essay as a reflection on his "obsessive attraction to white men" (1986: 47), he provides no explanation other than a yearning to enjoy the same kinds of liberties enjoyed by them. Shepherd writes, "As a child I would go to sleep wishing that when I awoke I would be white" (1986: 48). Yet, his imaginative ener-gies are less spent on visualizing himself in a white body than in fleeing the restrictions placed on his movements because of the cultural meanings attached to blackness:

> The burden of my identity, one of the many burdens of my identity, has always been the burden of not being white . . . I was the wrong one: wrong lips, wrong nose, wrong self . . .
>
> I've had notions, negative each one, images of what it is to be *seem* black: to look black, to talk black, to walk black. . . . If one didnot say those things, wear those things, if one didn't do things that way, then one would never, could never be branded with that word, that awful word; though of course one was. (1986: 47–49)

Shepherd may want to sleep with white men, but says nothing about what he likes about their bodies. They are described as "beautiful" but no details describing what exactly he likes about white bodies. No yearning is expressed to touch white skin, no allusions to phenotypes associated with white men.

Sexual desires are the consequence of a complicated mess of personal experiences, social relations, and conscious and subconscious anxieties; for Shepherd, a yearning for political liberation is clearly part of that mix:

> If I am seen with a beautiful man, not only am I thus one who can acquire a valuable prize but I am by the same operation (as a man having it both ways) transformed into such a prize myself, sought after and acquired by the man I am

with. . . . By being seen with him, I am made an honorary white man for so long as I am with him. Suddenly I am part of the community. So by being with him I manage almost to be him. (1986: 54)

Writing two decades later than Shepherd, Cho gets right to the point about what motivates her daydreams of becoming white:

What if I didn't have to bend anything? What if there really was a level playing field? I would love to see how far I could actually go. What if all I had to show off was my mad skills? Wouldn't I really be able to fly then? (margaretcho.com/blog, January 23, 2005)

Cho doesn't actually want to be white, just enjoy access to the privileges it affords. Similarly, Shepherd concludes:

My dream? Finally to be 'myself,' relieved of the baggage of my history both as an individual and as a member of an oppressed race and caste, relieved of my self-despisal in the shining warmth of the beloved's blond approbation. (1986: 56)

Passing white in cyberspace makes a similar promise to Shepherd's beloved blond: temporary comfort from—but no absolution from—the inflictions of "race."

Notes

Special thanks to Nell Tenhaaf, Alan Sinfield, Garfield Lemonius, and Frederick Routier.

1. In her study of a social-oriented MUD (multi-user dimension), Kendall observed that when "black participants must state that they are black in order to be recognized as such, [online] anonymity carries with it a presumptive identity of whiteness" (2002: 210). John Edward Campbell reached the same conclusion is his study of gay-themed IRC (Internet Relay Chat) channels. Asked whether he identified his "race" online, the only self-identified African American included in Campbell's study replied, "yes, sometimes . . . sometimes they go on thinking i'm white" (2004: 80). Nakamura's own studies of racial impersonation and identity tourism also conclude that when race identification was left out of descriptors, "all were assumed to be white" (2002: 5).

2. One explanation for this kind of reaction is to be found in the perpetuation of beauty myths that idealize phenotypes associated with whiteness. As suggested in *Shared Lives*, a collection of oral histories about gay Asian men in Toronto, "gay culture focuses on the white male, who is usually blonde, blue-eyed, tall and muscular. We come to believe that this is the look we should all be seeking" (Gay Asians Toronto 1996: iii–iv). "Seeking" in this context suggests both self-representation and desire for sexual partners. Although there is certainly a broader range of ideal types than the blue-eyed blonde model, it is also true that in mainstream gay cul-

ture, dominant representations of "ideal types" mostly correspond to degrees of whiteness or to the desires of white men.

3. This represents the number of searchable accounts, as stated on the gay.com website. It may include accounts that are dormant, or different accounts registered to the same user. Neilsen net ratings data are also taken from gay.com's promotional material.

4. The lack of ethnicity-specific rooms at gay.com is also a consequence of the proliferation and intensified specialization of ethno-specific sites elsewhere, to cater to men interested in black men, Arab men, etc.

5. There is a "Men of Color" room available in Ohio, but its title and form suggest a different political engagement (for meetings, friendships, camaraderie between non-white men) to the Toronto rooms.

References

Alexander, J., Barrios, B., Blackmon, S., Crow, A., Dorwick, K., Rhodes, J., et al. 2004. "Queerness, Sexuality, Technology and Writing: How Do We Queers Write Ourselves When We Write in Cyberspace?" Retrieved January 20, 2005, from http://acadiana.arthmoor.com/cuppa

Back, L. 2002. "Wagner and Power Chords: Skinheadism, White Power Music, and the Internet," in V. Ware and L. Back (Eds.), *Out of Whiteness: Color, Politics and Culture* (pp. 94–132). Chicago: University of Chicago Press,

Bargh, J. A., McKenna, K. Y. A., and Fitzsimons, G. M. 2002. "Can You See the Real Me? Activation and Expression of the 'True Self' on the Internet." *Journal of Social Issues 58*(1), 33–48.

Brown, G., Maycock, B., and Burns, S. 2005. "Your Picture Is Your Bait: Use and Meaning of Cyberspace among Gay Men." *Journal of Sex Research, 41*(1), 63–83.

Burkhalter, B. 1999. "Reading Race Online: Discovering Racial Identity in USENET Discussions," in M. A. Smith and P. Kollock (Eds.), *Communities in cyberspace* (pp. 60–75). London: Routledge.

Campbell, J. E. 2004. *Getting It On Online: Cyberspace, Gay Male Sexuality, and Embodied Identity.* London: Harrington Park Press.

Cho, M. 2005. "I Would Love to Be White." Retrieved January 23, 2005, from http://www.margaretcho.com/blog

Dyer, R. 1997. *White.* London: Routledge.

Fanon, F. 1967. *Black Skin, White Masks.* New York: Grove Press.

Gay Asians Toronto. 1996. *Shared Lives* (pamphlet).

Gross, L. 2004. "Preface," in J. E. Campbell, *Getting It On Online: Cyberspace, Gay Male Sexuality, and Embodied Identity* (pp. ix–xii). London: Harrington Park Press.

Kolko, B. E. 2000. "Erasing @ Race: Going White in the (Inter)face," in B. Kolko, L. Nakamura, and G. B. Rodman (Eds.), *Race in Cyberspace* (pp. 213–232). New York: Routledge.

Kolko, B., Nakamura, L., and Rodman, G. B. 2000. "Introduction," in B. Kolko, L. Nakamura, and G. B. Rodman (Eds.), *Race in Cyberspace* (pp 1–14). New York: Routledge.

McIntosh, P. 1992. "White Privilege and Male Privilege: A Personal Account of Coming to See Correspondences through Work in Women's Studies," in Margaret L. Andersen and Patricia Hill Collins (Eds.), *Race, Class and Gender: An Anthology* (pp. 70–81). Belmont: Wadsworth.

Julien, I., and Mercer, K. 1991. "True Confessions," in E. Hemphill (Ed.). *Brother to Brother* (pp. 167–173). Boston: Alyson Publications.

Kendall, L. 2002. *Hanging Out in the Virtual Pub*. Berkeley: University of California Press.

Nakamura, L. 2002. *Cybertypes: Race, Ethnicity and Identity on the Internet*. Routledge: New York.

Plant, S. "On the Matrix: Cyberfeminist Simulations," in R. Shields (Ed.), *Cultures of the Internet: Virtual Spaces, Real Histories, Living Bodies* (pp. 170–183). London: Sage, 1996.

Said, E. 1978. *Orientalism*. London: Routledge.

Sanders, C. 2005. "M4M Online Chat Rooms: The Use of Gay Websites by Men Seeking Men." MA thesis, York University, York, UK.

Seshadri-Crooks, K. 2000. *Desiring White: A Lacanian Analysis of Race*. New York: Routledge.

Shepherd, R. 1991. "On Not Being White," in J. Beam (Ed.), *In the Life: A Black Gay Anthology* (pp. 46–570). Boston: Alyson Publications.

Sunden, J. 2001. "What Happened to Difference in Cyberspace? The (Re)turn of the She-Cyborg." *Feminist Media Studies* 1(2), 215–232.

Turkle, S. 1995. *Life on the Screen: Identity in the Age of the Internet*. New York: Simon & Schuster.

9. Computer Cross-Dressing: Queering the Virtual Subject

Debra Ferreday and Simon Lock

Histories

Within cyberculture studies, the notion of cross-dressing has been used largely as a metaphor for thinking through multiple forms of identity performance. The term "computer cross-dressing" was coined by Allucquére Roseanne Stone to describe the notorious case of "Julie," a male psychologist who angered an online community by successfully passing as a disabled woman. In her account of Julie's case, Stone gives an exhilarating picture of the practices of virtual passing that prevailed in online culture at a specific historical moment. On the internet, she says, it has become meaningless, to see gender identity as grounded in a physical body, since the anonymous nature of online communication means that anyone is free to experiment with gender by passing, in a safe environment, as a member of a different gender, a "wholesale appropriation of the other" that "has spawned new modes of interaction" in which gender identity is more flexible (1994: 84).

While Stone does not take a wholly utopian view of online identities, she does on the whole present "computer cross-dressing" as emblematic of a largely benign model of shifting and fluid cyber-identities. Nevertheless, she does point out that there is a need for consideration of ethical issues, and of the risks associated with breaching boundaries (which, after all, may be experienced as a source of safety as well as of constraint) (1994: 84). Elsewhere though, computer cross-dressing has been mobilized as a means of thinking through precisely the ways in which cyberspace might be experienced as threatening. Perhaps the most well-known example of this is provided by Lisa Nakamura's influential essay, "Race In/For Cyberspace." For Nakamura, "computer cross-dressing" is a form of "identity tourism," which exemplifies the way in which online gaming provides "scenarios for the fantasies of privileged individuals." "It is commonly known," she says "that the relative dearth of women in cyberspace results in a great deal of "computer cross-dressing," or "men masquerading as women" (Nakamura 1995). Men, she says, do this not because they want to experiment with gender for its own sake, but only in order to seek sexual interaction with other players; and this becomes a "double appropriation or objectification" where players inhabit racialized identities (Nakamura 1995: 187–188). This view of online cross-dressing as a deceptive practice by privileged individuals is supported by the work of Roberts and Parks, who found that while it was common for online gamers to play characters of the "opposite" gender, "the primary barrier to gender-switching was the belief that it is dishonest and manipulative" (1999: 521).

In other words, cross-dressing has historically been used with theories of virtual subjectivity, not in relation to the actual practice of dressing as a member of a different gender, but as a metaphor for any gendered practice that might be regarded as deceptive. This is the case not only within online communities, but in wider theoretical representations of cross-dressing. Although some accounts of gender identity have situated cross-dressing on what might be termed a "transgender continuum" (Ekins 1997; Feinberg 1996; Hegland and Nelson 2002),[1] it has frequently been used as a metaphor for particular forms of identity performance, especially those that involve passing, particularly by members of privileged groups. According to Michael Moon, the use of "cross-dressing" as a metaphor for male privilege has a long tradition both within popular culture, and in gender and performance studies. In an interview with Eve Kosofsky Sedgwick conducted in 1994, Moon said that "[T]ransvestism has often been trivialized and domesticated into mere "cross-dressing," as if its practice had principally to do with something that can be put on and off as easily as a costume" (Sedgwick 1994: 219). As an example of this, he cites an essay by Elaine Showalter (1987) which uses the notion of cross-dressing to critique the notion that male theorists can write on behalf of feminism. For Moon, this exemplifies the extent to which, within feminist theory, the transvestite has become "*the* dominant image . . . for the purely discretionary or arbitrary aspects of gender identity," with the result that

[I]t is sometimes seen as sinister—when men are seen as being empowered by a pretence of femininity that they can doff at will, leaving their underlying gender identity and privilege untouched or indeed enhanced. (Sedgwick 1994: 219)

Here again, we can see that the figure of the cross-dresser is representative of a wider anxiety about the extent to which "cross-dressing" might allow privileged subjects to experiment with identity in a way that does not disrupt or trouble their privilege. This view has also been reproduced in feminist performance studies; as Lesley Ferris has noted, feminist theorists including Amy Dolan and Erika Munk have suggested that cross-dressing performances promulgate "misogynistic images of women" (cited in Ferris 1993: 9).

In contrast to these negative metaphorical uses of "cross-dressing," a potentially more positive approach has been opened up by feminist theorists drawing on the work of Judith Butler, especially her theory of identity as performative. Butler's arguments are founded on a reading of specific forms of cross-dressing practice: drag shows, and lesbian butch-femme identities. It is outside the scope of this chapter to examine the many differences between cross-dressing and drag: however, while Butler does not explicitly deal with cross-dressing in the sense that we are using the term here, her comments are instructive in working toward an understanding of online cross-dressers identity performances.

In *Gender Trouble,* Butler argued that drag "reflects the mundane impersonations by which heterosexually ideal genders are performed and naturalized and undermines their power by virtue of their exposure" (1993: 231). In *Bodies That Matter* she develops this argument, suggesting that "in imitating gender, drag implicitly reveals the imitative structure of gender itself" (1999: 175). She further makes the point that in cross-dressing performances, "the very notion of an original or natural identity is put into question; indeed it is precisely that question as it is embodied in these identities that becomes the source of their erotic significance" (1999: 157).

It is possible, then, to bring online cross-dressing into dialogue with Butler's theory of drag as a means of illuminating the ways in which online texts construct the lived experience of male-to-female cross-dressing. Butler does not deal with cross-dressing directly; instead she is concerned with a specific form of staged drag performance. Nevertheless, we feel that her model of performativity speaks strongly to the experience of online cross-dressers. On one hand, there are significant material differences between the lived experience of her drag queens, who largely identify as gay and often to not "dress" offline, and that of the largely heterosexual and bisexual members of the online cross-dressing subculture, for whom dressing is presented as integrated into their everyday lives. Nevertheless, we would suggest that the staging of online identities, with its awareness of speaking to an audience and its use of visual and textual technologies to construct a gendered identity, also has important similarities with the practices she describes. More problematic is the implicit suggestion within queer theory that cross-dressing performances are always produced in a self-aware manner, with the explicit intention of subverting normative gender identities. Victoria Pitts draws attention to this implication in the work of some poststructural feminists who, following Butler, have produced a celebratory view of "deviant" bodies, seeing technologically mediated bodily practices such as SM, sex radicalism, and various forms of body modification as "performances aimed at subversion" (2005: 232). As Pitts points out, this model risks assuming that the body is freed not only from cultural constraints, but also from social ones: in other words, "the high-tech body appears as *socially* plastic, a space for identity exploration," thus suggesting that technology allows individuals to construct self-created identities that transcend traditional embodied identity categories (2005: 230).

> Feminism has identified how subjectivities—in particular, gendered subjectivities—are linked to the rootedness of bodies in the material, lived realities of gender, race, and other power relations. Unless race, class and gender stratifications actually disappear, individuals can be limited in the ways in which thy can imagine themselves and shape their bodies and identities—even within a culture that celebrates such choice and freedom. (2005: 231)

Such a view, she argues, raises problems of intentionality; as Butler herself has said, body projects are produced within real histories over which "individuals have little control" (Butler 1993, cited in Pitts 2005: 233). In order to address this problem, Pitts argues that there needs to be a feminist perspective that "shifts the focus from intentionality to technology," since, she concludes,

> Body projects can be subversive in their effects . . . but this is in no way guaranteed by subjects" intention. . . . I don't believe that intentionality is unimportant. It's rather that intentionality doesn't determine meaning or effects. What Butler gets from poststructuralism is the point that intentionality is a *product of* rather than the origin for meaning. (2005: 233)

In other words, she says, gender performances, whether intended as subversive or not, are necessarily shaped by gendered norms and identities already circulating in popular culture (2005: 233). Following this point, we must be aware that the imagination does not exist in a separate category, one which is less constrained (and therefore potentially more "authentic") than material reality. Instead, the imagination is itself culturally constructed within the same histories, discourses, and power relations that structure lived experience. This might mean, for example, that "feminine" identities, if they are to be intelligible, can only be produced within the existing discourses of femininity that have emerged from cultures of normative heterosexual identity. In other words, recognizing that identity is discursively produced does not detract from the fact that identities are experienced as authentic; there is no single "authentic" identity that exists outside discourse.

The identity narratives of online cross-dressers support this view. On one hand, online cross-dressers demonstrate a great deal of control over the ways in which their online images are produced, displayed, and consumed. In this sense, intentionality plays an important role in structuring the online performance. On the other hand, a common rationale for producing a blog is that it enables what Mason-Schrock calls the "true self" (1996) to be constructed and made visible. However, we would build on this to suggest that the "true self" in this sense need not refer to a disembodied, "postmodern" self that is seen as authentic in that it escapes bodily constraints (that is, to the view of the self on which Nakamura rightly casts doubts). Instead, online selves make visible both bodily identities, and the fantasies, desires, and narratives through which they are constructed. Online identity, in this sense is no more "true" than the identity positions that are inscribed on the body in offline life. However, we would suggest that the practice of performing gender identities online allows the complex and multiple character of all gendered identities to become visible. For example, as we shall see, online cross-dressers may speak of feeling that they are "in drag" while "in drab," or dressed as men. This, we suggest, is not simply a gesture toward subversiveness, an attempt by a privileged group to lay claim to a marginalized position that is experienced as pleasurable (and which therefore fails to do justice to real dangers and anxieties associated with racial or transgendered passing, for example). Instead, these narratives suggest a desire to construct a uniquely transvestite identity which is nevertheless intimately bound up with anxieties about the transvestite subject's access to privileged, normative masculine identity: this is a recurring theme of cross-dressers' Web pages and discussion groups. Online cross-dressing hence does not deny the reality of masculine or heterosexual privilege. Nevertheless, it does suggest that to read a cross-dresser as unproblematically "male" is to deny the complex web of sometimes contradictory gendered roles and practices that constitute transvestite identity.

The Transvestite as Transvestite

Above, we explored how the figure of "the cross-dresser" has been evoked within histories of both cyberculture and queer studies. A side-effect of this theoretical appropriation of cross-dressing is that "real" cross-dressers have been marginalized and even excluded within the history of cyber-identities. Here, we will expand on our argument that it is necessary to think beyond this view of cross-dressing. However, we do not wish to deny that critiques of some users" appropriation of online spaces as a site of racial and gendered passing is highly problematic. Our point is rather to intervene in the notion of the anonymous identity play that characterized MUDs and chat rooms as the only site of computer cross-dressing. By reading personal homepages and weblogs through queer theory, we aim to distinguish between the disembodied practices of passing that Nakamura identifies, and the embodied experience of what might (somewhat problematically) be termed "real" cross-dressers. Our point is not that it is impossible to experiment with identity online; instead, we would suggest that those experiments are not only produced within the context of offline culture; often, they are also a continuation of offline experiments. In other words, online spaces should not be seen as a privileged space that somehow makes such experimentation possible (although they may allow it to take new forms). Crucially, though, our argument is that online sites make *visible* the processes through which all identities are constructed.

In this chapter, we are interested in the ways in which "computer cross-dressing," as described by Stone, is used by real cross-dressers as a means of performing their offline identities. Our ongoing research is based on close readings of established online constructs within what is often termed "the tranniesphere": a loose collection of sites that includes Web pages, discussion forums, photo sharing sites, and personal weblogs in order to gain insights into the experience of "real" online cross-dressers. However, in this chapter we will focus on weblogs in particular, since we feel they exemplify the ways in which actual practices of identity production have evolved in unexpected ways since the 1990s.

In particular, we would argue that by bringing the embodied practices of transvestite blogging into dialogue with queer theory it is possible to ask new questions about transvestite subjectivity, and also to rethink the notion of online subjectivity more generally. However, we should say a few words here about our use of the term queer. In this context, we use the term not as a means of making generalizations about sexual preference, but to suggest the ways in which cross-dressing "queers" the boundaries between binary categories of gender. This is an important point since our research suggests that while some online transvestites actively seek to align themselves with a queer identity politics, others are more ambivalent about claiming queer as a "label." This tension was clear, for example, in debates around (female) partners' anxieties that cross-dressing meant that their partners were gay. With this in mind, we nevertheless feel that queer theory and online cross-dressers have much to say to one another. Above, we have argued that the contested nature of the term "computer crossdressing" has meant that with very few exceptions (see Nelson and Hegland 2004), "real" transvestites—that is, men for whom engaging in feminine gendered performances is experienced as a central aspect of their identities—have been marginalized. A central concern of our research, then, is to understand how online cross-dressers are resisting marginalization. However, we also see our research as part of the same movement to address the invisibility of "the transvestite as transvestite," and it is for this reason that we have chosen to situate our readings of online communities within the tradition of queer studies.

It should be noted that we do not claim to "speak for" *all* cross-dressers; indeed, one reason for the marginalization of transvestism relates to the heterogeneous and fragmented nature of cross-dressers as a group. The bloggers we focus on in our research can be viewed as a subset of all computer cross-dressers and as a consequence, this small group often becomes lost among all the other different types of people using the Internet to help fabricate multiple identities.[2] In addition to this, within the tranniesphere, there is great range and diversity in the motivation, objectives, destinations, and forms of expression used by individuals. It is impossible to reach a concrete group identity or even a clear definition of what transvestism "is." This is also related to what Marjorie Garber (1997) calls the "category crisis" of transvestism. We found much debate as to whether cross-dressing belongs on a continuum of transgendered or even queer identity, since many cross-dressers identify as heterosexual. This category crisis has, we would argue, resulted in a reticence in claiming cross-dressing as an identity category; instead, it has often been seen simply as a set of practices or a mode of dress. For example, our case studies show that while discourse within the tranniesphere suggests that there is a movement toward claiming cross-dressing as an identity position, this anxiety is implicitly present in the frequently reiterated question of whether a transvestite is (or is seen as) "just a bloke in a dress." What is certain however is that transvestitism implies a disruption of normative gender categories: that is, cross-dressers queer not only traditional gender boundaries, but also potentially the boundaries of what it means to be "queer." It is in this sense of crossing boundaries, and not in any sense of deterministic ideas about sexual preference, that we are using the term "queer."

We would argue, then, that online cross-dressing involves resisting marginalization. In this, they are aided by developments in the production of online identities. In reality, practices of identity production have developed in rather different ways than those predicted in the accounts cited above. Stone's notion of cross-dressing, from which Nakamura's is initially developed, is grounded in studies of chat rooms and gaming; that is, in spaces where users were often anonymous; where identities tended to be fluid and shifting, with some users assuming several different identities; and where characterization was largely textual, for example, relying on users' written descriptions of their character's appearance rather than on pictures (Turkle 1995). As our introduction suggests, this led some theorists including Stone to hail the Internet, and in particular e-mail lists, as spaces that allowed users to experiment and play with identity in a way that seemed to bear out a ludic postmodern model of subjectivity as fragmented, fluid and shifting. At the same time, some feminists expressed a fear that this fragmentation of the subject would lead to a loss of agency for traditionally marginalized groups (see Dean 1999).

What is missing from these historical accounts is the phenomenal growth, since the turn of the century, of the personal homepage, and particularly of personal weblogs or "blogs." It is not clear when or why blogs first appeared, although one study claims that the first online diary to be identified as a log and with the now-familiar characteristics of a reverse chronological structure, frequent updates, and the addition of links appeared as recently as 1997 (Miller and Shepherd 2004). The popularity of blogs has been attributed to a number of wider social developments, including the advent of a wider confessional culture, the visibility of a few famous examples (such as that of Salaam Pax, the "Baghdad Blogger"), and the need for a less playful and more politically engaged stance in the light of developments in Western politics (Miller and Shepherd 2004; Rodzvilla 2002; Gurak et al. 2004).

The metaphor of computer cross-dressing assumes a desire to pass: that is, it involves the construction of gendered and racialized identities that, while they may fail, are intended to convince. Passing thus assumes the existence of an onlooker whose (unmarked) gaze is able to make judgments about the success, or otherwise, of the performance. The notion of passing recalls Marjorie Garber's argument that critics have tended to "look through" rather than at the cross-dresser, to turn away from a close encounter with the transvestite, and to instead subsume that figure within one of the two traditional genders. This, she argues, is "emblematic of a fairly consistent critical desire to look away from the transvestite as transvestite" (1997: 9–11).

As Douglas Mason-Schrock points out in his study of transgendered peoples' autobiographical narratives, the process of storytelling is central to the construction of identity. Mason-Schrock found that there was a need for "stories that feel right, that point to authentic selfhood" (1996: 176). The creation of "new self-narratives" was hence an important strategy in supporting the shift to a "new" identity and in bringing the "authentic" self into being:

> We might find, as Gergen and Gergen (1983: 266) have suggested, that stories are not simply told about a preexisting self, but that stories and their collective creation bring phenomenologically real "true selves" into being. (1996: 176)

There is much evidence to support this suggestion that storytelling is an essential element of online identity expression. Stories often appear as an integral part of many personal website and blogs. One obvious objective of these is to entertain and intrigue, but they also exist to demonstrate the conviction and integrity of the cross-dresser. These personal anecdotes can be seen as integral to gaining acknowledgment and respect of peers. These stories also help in defining an individual much more accurately and in much finer granularly than the existing set of crude (and non-standardized) labels and definitions. Let us also not forget the expressive potential possible through the embellishment and enhancement of factual stories, as well as the descriptive power of fictional narratives.

Online cross-dressing is precisely concerned with the construction of "the transvestite as transvestite," and the existence of websites and blogs presuppose the existence of a reader who specifically desires to look, who does not wish to turn away. While photographs, graphic material and fantasy biographies allow the feminine self to be materialized, the process of identity construction is simultaneously made visible through the deployment of commentary, links, banners and ironic humor. As one transvestite blogger puts it, "many of the photographs are unflattering and unconvincing. If you're looking for a tranny with model looks, then you came to the wrong site. You will just see a guy in a frock" (www.broxie.co.uk), and this is a trope frequently repeated in cross-dressing sites. We find this statement instructive because it not only bluntly sets out the category of "the transvestite as transvestite," but also in that it implicitly engages the viewer, suggesting that gendered performances are not simply created by individuals, but are constantly reproduced through the (privileged) gaze. While identity may be in the eye of the beholder, it suggests, the online space is precisely one in which the beholder's first impression might become problematized. To persist in seeing only a "guy in a frock" is to miss the depth and complexity which characterizes the shifting gender identities and performances though which transvestite identity comes into being.

Welcome to the Tranniesphere: Identity Narratives

Identities in Transit? Rethinking Identity Tourism

> I am a traveller, you are a tourist, he is a tripper. (Keith Waterhouse 1989, cited in frontispiece to Urry 1990)

> By creating this web site, I realized that in some silly way it has helped me find out a little more about myself as well. (Karen's World)

At the beginning of this chapter, we argued that the metaphor of "computer cross-dressing" as a form of "identity tourism" is one discourse through which the experiences of real online cross-dressers have become invisible within the historical position of the virtual subject, as well as in queer studies more generally. While we concur that this use of the term has been used to inform trenchant feminist critiques of a historically dominant model of online subjectivity, the aim of our research is in a sense to reclaim the term as representative of a real, heterogeneous group of online subjects whose highly complex, nuanced and reflective gender performances call into question common assumptions about cross-dressing, as well as about online subjectivity more generally. As part of this work, we would suggest that there needs to be a move from a model of identity tourism, to one of online cross-dressers as identity travelers.

The use of journeying and travel is an ever-popular metaphor for gender exploration; it is, however, interesting to extend this metaphor and follow it though to some of it's logical conclusions. This has been addressed to some degree by Urry's notion of the tourist gaze, which he describes as a mobile privileged point of view which, while taking the exotic Other, does not disturb or trouble the gazer's privilege (white, male, heterosexual) identity (Urry 1990, 2001).

While discourses of gender tourism might make us want to question the representation of the tourist gaze as heterosexual, it is true that the term "tourist" is implicitly overloaded with images of power and exploitation; and it is true that there is widespread criticism within transvestite communities of those who use computer cross-dressing for touristic intent by engaging in practices that are seen as voyeuristic, without engaging with local cultures. However, equally, there is also the notion of the gender "traveler" who is typically motivated more by enrichment, appreciation, and experiencing other cultures and identities. Such travelers use online cross-dressing as a route to personal exploration and understanding. Interestingly, this metaphor can also be extending in order to encompass gender "package tours" offered by dressing services such as the Boudoir (http://www.theboudoironline. com). These holidays away from the day-to-day masculine persona involve literal travel away from the subject's home, as well as the provision of services such as hair and makeup advice, dressing services, and personal shopping.

"Trannies Are Their Own Worst Critics": Identity and Image Production

As we have argued, computer cross-dressing has been imagined in terms of passing: it is imagined as an attempt by a male subject to produce a fantastic, female identity which, while it may or may not succeed, is aimed at convincing the onlooker that they are seeing a "real" woman. Our reading of cross-dressers' weblogs suggests that this definition fails to account for a far more complex relation between the offline masculine self (often referred to as "male mode" or "bob mode"), offline femme identity, and the online identity which shifts between the two to produce a uniquely transgendered self.

It is interesting to note that many of the blogs studied continually drew attention to the creative work that went into producing online images, whether these were deemed to be capable of passing or not. The online image is continually being deconstructed and critiqued such that even where a particular image was considered especially "convincing," the fantasy of passing was disrupted either by reference to flaws in the image, or to practices such as digital airbrushing that were used in its production. Indeed, they are in a sense the same thing since, in blogging culture, skill with an electronic paintbrush is seen as an extension of skill with a makeup brush in the real world.

However, it could also be argued that ways in which images are presented specifically work to queer the traditional model of the transvestite as "just" a man attempting to pass as a woman. One of the ways in which this operates is through the juxtaposition of a feminine image, which is produced both visually and through the adoption of a feminized narrative voice, with text or images that deliberately problematize, disrupt, or subvert this image. For example, Becky provides what she calls a "Face Critique" detailing her transformation http://www.beckysweb.co.uk/beckysblog/2005/07/my-face-critique.html. Her rationale for this practice is that

> Trannies are their own worst critics. This is partly, I think, due to the fact is we've seen the man behind the makeup every day of our lives in the mirror. We know every inch of his face. Whereas a stranger might see a girl's face that looks a bit masculine, we see a man we know very well, who just happens wearing makeup. (Beckysweb)

Similarly, Karen includes large numbers of photographs on her site, but these are presented alongside a highly self-critical text, which draws attention to what she sees as their flaws. Although it is not clear whether she is dissatisfied with the details of her dress and makeup, or with the photographic techniques she uses to present them on her website. This posting is instructive in its use of self-mocking humor to deflect potential criticism and to partially mask the seriousness of her reason for posting the images in the first place:

> I will be honest and tell you that the photos section needs a drastic update and that will happen in time. For now I have posted a small selection of pictures that might give you a giggle or might just scare you away. (Karen's World)

Another example in particular that stands out is Tranniefesto (http://www.tranniefesto.co.uk), the website of Siobhan. This site consists of a personal blog together with links to a Flickr (an online photo sharing and pooling site) profile. The insightful writing and distinctive visual style of Siobhan's site has led to its attracting a great deal of comment in other blogs both within and outside the tranniesphere, including several mentions in the *Guardian* newspaper's News Blog (www.guardian.co.uk/newsblog).

The website portrays a particular "image" of Siobhan, a major component of which is a large collection of photos, the majority of which have been processed and manipulated to some degree by computer. However, this image is not presented as seamless: instead, Siobhan uses the accompanying text to continually question and reflect on the practices and techniques that go into producing her photographs. For example, one entry gives a step-by-step account of how she produces her signature "look" using Photoshop in a post ironically entitled "photographic realism" (http://www.tranniefesto.co.uk/2005/06/28/). Here, she explains that she lacks conventional photographic skill, but goes on to say that she intends to compensate for her lack of conventional skills by working "in the medium that I'm most comfortable: Photoshop." A detailed tutorial follows on how to use this desktop publishing software package to retouch an image in her characteristic style, though this is intercut with discussion of her concerns about possibly "deceiving" the viewer.

A debate follows this posting in which one of Siobhan's regular readers, D, adds a comment in support of her methods, saying "as for the ethics . . . you're offering fantasy here, not reality. The whole Internet comes with a big warning sign saying "Truth may be manipulated for better user experience." Siobhan's response to this is revealing:

> Not just the Internet though D (and your point about offering a fantasy is a very appropriate one), I think this applies to the whole concept of transvestite photography . . . it's not about manipulation of photographs, it's about deception. OK, basically, for some reason (and I have some thoughts as to what those might be) some transvestites blatantly cut-and-paste their faces onto the bodies of models. Now, to some extents, I don't actually have a problem with that. The whole process of dressing up, sticking in falsies, slapping a pile of make-up on your face (something I seem to do a lot more infrequently than some girls—or at least, feel the need to less), to me, is a process to go through to be able to look at myself as if I was a woman. . . . The thing is though, when it comes to doing that then sticking your pictures on a web site, I think there's something else going on. And this is where the deception comes in.

This account suggests a rich and nuanced view of the relationship between online and offline, as well as fantasy and "real" selves. The original comment begins by arguing against simply appropriating culturally prevalent images of female celebrities such as Jordan, positioning this as an act of deception. However, there is then a shift toward imagining a transvestite who is not able to dress and who can, through technology, produce an image of an imagined feminine self *without ever actually putting on a dress*. This suggests that, as in Mason-Schrock's account, transvestite identity is not simply a matter of dress; instead, it is experienced as an authentic form of subjectivity—the "image in my head"—which *becomes visible* through dress, writing, or technologically mediated imagery. The quote from Karen's website above, in all its implicit vulnerability and distancing, self-deprecating humor, also reproduces this anxiety about the gap between mental image and visible signifier. In the second comment, Siobhan goes on to read *all* photography through the lens of transgender identity, suggesting that "transvestite photography" produces an image that is no more or less real than any photographic image. Interestingly, there is another twist here. It might be argued that *feminine* subjects are traditionally regarded as the narcissistic objects of the other's gaze. Far from reproducing this normative image of femininity, however, Siobhan instead presents "obsessing about the way we look" as a specifically *male* trait.

All of the accounts cited above suggest a complex relationship between image and production, one that goes beyond both the notion of passing, and the Butlerian model of subversive identity performances that disrupt normative categories of gender. This is not to say that the question of passing is unimportant; indeed, many of the bloggers devoted extensive space to their often complex and contradictory views on this subject. The blogs and websites that we describe are a safe space for online cross-dressers to experiment with the construction of a gender identity. By revealing the mechanisms of construction and highlighting the flaws in the "end product," cross-dressers may enroll the help of others in improving these aspects and thus the final gender presentation. Gaining feedback is essential in assessing the success of exploration and experiments in gender presentation.

"Breaking the Fourth Wall": Identity as Dialogic Performance

So far, we have focused on the ways in which the subject is presented online; an online expression of gender identity incorporating writing, photography and image manipulation. So far, though, we have only touched on an important aspect of this performance: that is, the relationship between the author and the reader.

Blogging does not take place in a vacuum: blogs may contain private material, but they are designed to be seen. This is evidenced not only in the way that they encourage readers to append comments to posts that interest them, but also in the constant logging of who is accessing the site, where they linked from, what they do once they are there, where one ranks in search engine listings, and so on.

Siobhan's blog (www.tranniefesto.co.uk) demonstrates the importance of dialogue between blogger and (imagined) reader, in an entry posted on October 20, 2005:

Breaking the Fourth Wall

> I'd like to think, that over the course of these past (nearly) four years that I've
> been doing this, you (dear reader) and I have built up a certain level of trust.
> We've gotten to know each other, through incessant accounts of my hangovers
> and Mac-based geekery, and the various comments that have been left that I base
> my opinions of self-worth on, and I'd like to take it for granted really that we
> have an understanding of one another.

From this ironic starting point, Siobhan goes on to problematize this relationship with reference to two literary concepts she has recently discovered
the first is suspension of disbelief:

> See, both you and I know that I'm not really a girl. . . . But the thing is, I think,
> that somewhere along the line, we (I assuming "we," this might just be some-
> thing that applies to me) make that leap of faith and just accept—through the
> tone, the stereotypical language and visual clues (like pink)—that the voice that
> reads this thing is in fact, female. If you read through everything I've ever writ-
> ten with a deep bass, macho voice, then it doesn't make sense. We're willing, in
> a way, to make that illogical assumption because without it, this whole thing falls
> down. It stops being an interesting and slightly self-deprecating piece of writing,
> and starts being, well, kinda creepy. (www.tranniefesto.co.uk/2005/10/20/)

The idea of suspension of disbelief, then is mobilized to produce a sense of
collusion between author and reader. For Siobhan, the reader is drawn into a
relationship with the text, in which he or she chooses to "hear" the correct,
feminine voice. Crucially, this collusion is presented as the effect of both
Siobhan's use of writing style and technology to produce a flawless performance, *but also of constant reminders that this is a performance.* The reader
"knows" Siobhan (the "girl"), but also Siobhan the transvestite *who desires to
be seen as successful at performing femininity.* This is made explicit in her references to the "fourth wall."

The concept of the third wall, she tells us, originated in the theatre. It
refers to the notion that performances involve the audience looking through
an imaginary wall into the world of the play, and which is assumed to be a
defining characteristic of theatrical realism. For Siobhan, the relationship
between blogger and reader generally follows this model of seeing an intentionally realistic performance. However, there is a difference in online performance in that, "this suspension of disbelief is kind of a sacred thing
between us I think. But every now and again, I break the fourth wall, and
things go a little weird."

This occurs when she disrupts the performance of "being a girl" by making statements like "I'm not a girl, I'm a bloke in a dress." It is intensified by
a particular posting in which a programming quirk resulted in a picture of
herself in "male mode" appearing on its own, rather than in its intended con-

text at the bottom of the previous day's diary. She concludes the post by saying, "it's odd isn't it? A moment of unwelcome realism in a fantasy environment. In a way, it's less real, because of the context it's sitting in. True, that's what I look like (sometimes) as a guy, but it's not how I see myself when I write this stuff" (www.tranniefesto.com).

The introduction of these critiques is instructive in that it problematizes the notion of "deception" invoked in the earlier post. The practice of breaking the fourth wall serves to disrupt the verisimilitude of the gendered performance, queering elaborately constructed performance of femininity that Siobhan has gone to such pains to produce through the use of visual technologies. This suggests that transvestism does not involve an unproblematic desire to pass "as a woman"; indeed, it would be easy to remove these traces of the male body from the site. Instead, it is precisely at these moments of disruption, in the tension between the presentation of feminine identity and the experience of inhabiting a biologically male body, that transvestite identity comes into being.

"You Will Just See a Guy in a Frock": Addressing the Bad Reader

In the preceding section, we examined how weblogs work to address a reader who is imagined as sympathetic, so that the performance of gender identity comes into being partly through a dialogue between author and reader. However, while Siobhan's entry above could be seen as being addressed to an ideal reader (such as her fellow bloggers) with whom she has "built up a certain level of trust," this is not to say that the reader is always positioned as a benign figure, as we shall examine here.

In transvestite Web cultures, there is also widespread awareness of a less sympathetic reader: the bad reader. The following example is drawn from Jessica's blog:

> There are people out there who seem to spend a lot of time surfing for websites they don't want to find, are not interested in, or just disagree with, so they can leave some negative comments. The web's a big place! If you don't like my website just try another one!
>
> I just saw a post on my guestbook from yesterday saying 'holy shit srry but wtf.' I thought ok, so he found my site through something none tranny related, but all he had to do was look at the front page and he'd know exactly "wtf" my site's about, and could then click "back."(www.just-jessica.com)

The bad reader may appear in the form of a transphobic "troll" as in this example, or may be a persistent or annoying "admirer": in either case, their comments typify the negative effects of flaming, trolling, and general harassment that can be found throughout internet spaces. More interesting are the ways in which individual bloggers respond to their comments. Jessica's response to this intruder is instructive. Following on from the entry above, she gives an entertaining and detailed account of the flamer's activities on her site, which include playing with dress-up doll (a Flash site which enables readers to dress a cartoon image of Jessica in various outfits), then spending some time looking at her photo gallery. Jessica's gallery uses a rating system, allowing readers to give each image marks out of 10. This particular reader begins by giving each image 1 out of 10, before suddenly giving a rating of 5 and then one of 10, then abruptly leaving the site. She provides links to the last two pictures, so readers can see for themselves.

> All photographs of Broxie can be found in "Girl Power Snaps." There is no nude photography. Be warned though that many of the photographs are unflattering and unconvincing. If you're looking for a tranny with model looks, then you came to the wrong site. You will just see a guy in a frock. (www.broxie.co.uk)

The desirability or otherwise of passing is hotly debated among bloggers (even Siobhan, who is reckoned to be able to pass in her online photographs, decries the impossibility of getting around "My Big Veiny Hands"). However, we need to see the debate around passing in context. Although the ability to pass is seen as desirable, the fact that it is being debated on (highly visible and public) spaces that are coded as being *for and about transvestites* suggests a problematization of the desire to pass. These issues are complex because passing is not a universal objective; some cross-dressers do wish to pass and be taken for women (either online or in the real world), while others however are perfectly happy to be "read" and accepted as the mixed gender identity that this implies. However, the very act of creating a specifically *transvestite* blog suggests that, while some authors may wish to be able to pass, they only desire to do so in particular contexts. Either way, the decision on whether or not to prioritize passing ultimately rests with the author, not with the reader. The bad reader, such as the flamer on Jessica's site, is seen as one who needs the reassurance of "model looks" in order to suspend disbelief, to feel that they are not "just" seeing "a guy in a frock." The repeated use of this phrase can further be seen as a means of managing reader expectations as well as having a practical use in trying to elicit feedback; by stating, "I know I look like a bloke in a frock, so it's OK to say so in your comments," it is possible to encourage critical or reassuring comments, especially from other cross-dressers. However, it can also be seen as a disruption of the assumed privileged gaze of the reader. By pre-emptively critiquing one's own appearance, one denies the reader the dualistic pleasures that are associated with a privileged point of view: that of "seeing" the transvestite as a feminine object of desire on one hand, or at the other extreme of being able to "tell the difference."

In other words, this is not a simple visual economy, where the blogger gives the best performance that he or she can and then offers this up for the approval, or otherwise, of a privileged gaze. Instead, the relationship between performer and reader is imagined as one of trust, in which acceptance (rather than passing) is the result of a dialogue between the two. To see only "a guy in a frock" is constructed as a failure on the part of the reader, whose original (faulty) expectation is to see a reproduction of a normative femininity that, displayed on the bodies of celebrities and supermodels, is already ubiquitous within Western culture. The bad reader is imagined as wanting to return to a traditional visual economy, to scrutinize the image of a "beautiful woman," see that "something is not right," and to speculate: "wtf? [what the fuck]."

Websites and blogs are not simply about gaining pleasure from looking (although this may be a considerable part of the experience, for the authors themselves as much as for the reader). By providing text as well as pictures, by displaying the image but also revealing the technologies, practices and fantasies that feed into its production, the author/performer invites the reader to enter into a relationship. In this relationship what is at stake is not an "imaginary" female self or "female impersonation," but rather a *real, transvestite self:* a self that, following Garber, we might name "the transvestite as transvestite." From the perspective of his privileged (but limited) gaze, the bad reader is imagined as missing out on the complexities of this relationship.

Conclusions

Above, we quoted Marjorie Garber's argument that the ways in which the figure of the transvestite has been mobilized in cultural theory has obscured the lived experience of cross-dressers. That there is an abiding interest in the notion of fluid gender identities, but simultaneously a reluctance to engage with cross-dressers themselves that is "emblematic of a fairly consistent critical desire to look away from the transvestite as transvestite" (Garber 1997: 9–11). This chapter arose in part from a desire to address this; as a result, we have attempted to engage with, but also to think beyond the production of cross-dressing in narratives of online identity, through close reading of the identity narratives and performances of "real" online transvestites.

Not least, we have attempted to show that online cross-dressing is not concerned with the production of disembodied identities; the body, with its possibilities and limitations, is everywhere in these narratives. What is more, this is no postmodern view of identities in constant flux. Indeed, while the blog format may involve the construction of an identity that is distinct from and often an extrapolation of the subject's offline persona, it is relatively stable. It is offline experience, which is forever haunting these narratives, that is presented as disturbingly (and dangerously) fragmented. Far from involving a loss of authority, blogging culture involves the careful construction of a persona through the practices of authorship, including programming techniques, photography, and writing style. Most strikingly, it involves the production of an individualized narrative voice; those bloggers whose writing is seen as especially revealing, perceptive, or funny become almost celebrities, with their own following of admiring readers.

Following from this, we have attempted to complicate Nakamura's view of online cross-dressing as merely involving the playing out of the fantasies of privileged individuals. This is not to say that we are disavowing the importance of fantasy; to be sure, online cross-dressing involves fantasy, and the fantasies of femininity it invokes are the subject of much unease and soul-searching in individual blogs, not least in relation to anxieties about masculine privilege. Nevertheless, it is necessary to recognize that the very desire to engage in cross-dressing may work to destabilize this privilege: cross-dressing, in online as well as offline spaces, involves risk and social stigma as well as pleasure. In their article on a bulletin board for male cross-dressers in Brazil, Primo et al. identified "coping with stigma" as a central concern of transvestite groups (2000: 290). They state that many members had "felt alone in the world" before discovering this online space (291). This hints at an interesting functional use of blogs and personal websites as a safe "thinking space" where identity can be constructed and reconstructed in an attempt to explore personal gender. Various components of personality and identify can be layered in many different configurations and combinations. The act of formally committing thoughts and explanations to (electronic) paper has much to offer an individual in understanding aspects of their identity. When this takes place in an environment where suggestions, assessment, and input from an audience of readers can all be fed back, a powerful creative space is produced. This addresses the fact that, while transvestites might enjoy a privileged position "as men," they are marginalized "as transvestites"; indeed, we would argue that the tension between two identities, one more privileged and one less, is a defining factor of the lived experience as transvestism. What is interesting about online cross-dressing is that it provides a space in which to speak not simply "as a woman" (or as some male fantasy of what it means to be feminine), but also as a transvestite.

It is for this reason that we suggest paying attention to the possibility of thinking through online cross-dressing in terms not of identity tourism, but identity travel. While this model does not foreclose the possibility of acknowledging the ways in which online identity performances are produced within normative categories of gender (albeit in a way that "queers" and disrupts those categories), it also does justice to the time, effort, and care with which transvestites go about constructing, refining, and evolving their online identities. Such activities are typified by long protracted involvements that do not constantly return to the same ground, but seek new territory and additional experiences. As a final example we turn to Karen, who presents her photo album in chronological order, starting with pictures documenting "the Early Years" under the tagline: "See how Karen emerged from the closet: pictures from my deepest and oldest photographic archives" (http://www.karens-world.com/Photo_Gallery.htm). This display is not aimed at suggesting that her transition to a specific gender identity is now complete. Instead, she expresses her belief that her identity will continue to develop, saying that "Karen has her own style, personality and hopes she will make a positive contribution in the communities and world we live in today" (www.karensworld.com).

In other words, Karen's website suggests not only that online productions of the gendered self "travel" by circulating around the globe (potentially giving readers a sense of inclusiveness and belonging that results in their feeling less "alone in the world"), but also that cross-dressing identities, and by extension all identity, are constantly in transit. It is only as a consequence of the explicit and observable nature of online gender identities that the processes involved in their construction are rendered visible. By considering such constructions, it becomes possible for these transient gender identities to become visible in a way that challenges the boundaries, not only of normative gendered identities, but also of what it means to be a virtual subject.

Notes

1. In any case, the tendency to conflate transvestism with transgendered identity is highly problematic, and this is a theme we intend to explore in future research. Whilst we found much debate within online cross-dressing communities about the extent to which transvestites and transgendered people might share political concerns as well as practices of gender transformation, the differences between the two groups need further explication, not least in relation to the very different ways in which they are positioned in relation to the notion of passing explored in this chapter.

2. We use the term "fabricate" here to give an indication of the manufactured nature of the creative process. It is not our intension to imply such identities are false representations, but to pay attention to the work involved in their creation through online technologies of the self.

References

Beckysweb. Retrieved July 3, 2005, from http://www.beckysweb.co.uk/beckys-blog/2005/07/my-face-critique.html

Butler, J. 1999. *Gender Trouble*. London: Routledge

Dean, J. 1999. "Virtual Fears." *Signs* 24(4), 1069–1078.

Ekins, R. 1997. *Male Femaling*. London: Routledge.

Feinberg, L. 1996. *Transgender Warriors: Making History from Joan of Arc to Rupaul*. Boston: Beacon Press.

Ferris, L. 1993. "Introduction," in L. Ferris (Ed.), *Crossing the Stage: Controversies on Crossdressing* (pp. 1–19). London: Routledge.

Garber, M. 1997. *Vested Interests: Crossdressing and Cultural Anxiety*. London, Routledge.

Gurak, L. J., Antonijevic, S., Johnson, L., Ratliff, C., and Reyman, J. (Eds.). 2004. *Into the Blogosphere: Rhetoric, Community and Culture of Weblogs*. Minneapolis: University of Minnesota.

Hegland, J. E., and Nelson, N. J. 2002. "Cross-Dressers in Cyber-Space: Exploring the Internet as a Tool for Expressing Gendered Identity." *International Journal of Sexuality and Gender Studies 7*(2–3), 139–161.

Karen's World, Website, Retrieved July 3, 2005, from http://www.karens-world.com

Mason-Schrock, D. 1996. "Transsexuals' Narrative Construction of the "True Self."" *Social Psychology Quarterly 59*(3), 176–192.

Miller, C. R., and Shepherd, D. 2004. "Blogging as Social Action: A Genre Analysis of the Weblog." Retrieved July 3, 2005, from http://blog.lib.umn.edu/blogosphere/blogging_as_social_action.html

Nakamura, L. 1995. "Race In/for Cyberspace: Identity Tourism and Racial Passing on the Internet." *Works and Days 25/26 13*(1/2), 181–193.

Nelson, N. J., and Hegland, J. E. 2004. "Crossdressing and Cyber-Shopping: The Internet as Consumption Tool and Community." Article published on Association for Consumer Research (ACR). Retrieved July 3, 2005, from http://www.acrweb.org

Pitts, V. 2005. "Feminism, Technology and Body Projects." *Women's Studies 34*(3/4), 229–247.

Primo, A. F. X, Pereira, V. A., and Freitas, A. 2000. "Brazilian Crossdresser Club." *CyberPsychology and Behaviour 3*(2), 287–296.

Roberts, L. D., and Parks, M. R. 1999. "The Social Geography of Gender-Switching in Virtual Environments on the Internet." *Information, Communication and Society 2*(4), 521–540.

Rodzvilla, J. 2002. *We've Got Blog: How Weblogs Are Changing Our Culture*. Cambridge, MA: Perseus.

Sedgwick, E. K. 1994. *Tendencies*. London: Routledge.

Showalter, E. 1987. "Critical Crossdressing: Male Feminists and the Woman of the Year," in A. Jardine and P. Smith (Eds.), *Men in Feminism* (pp. 116–123). New York: Methuen.

Stone, A. R. 1994. "Will the Real Body Please Stand Up? Boundary Stories about Virtual Cultures," in M. Benedikt (Ed.), *Cyberspace: First Steps* (pp. 81–118). Cambridge, MA: MIT Press.

Turkle, S. 1995. *Life on the Screen: Identity in the Age of the Internet*. New York: Simon & Schuster.

Urry, J. 1990. *The Tourist Gaze: Leisure and Travel in Contemporary Societies*. London: Sage.

Urry, J. 2001. "Globalizing the Tourist Gaze." Paper presented at *Cityscapes Conference*, Graz, Austria, November 7–11.

Part IV
Relocating Structures and Agencies

In this final part of the collection the chapters focus on the relocation of structures and agencies in the intersections of contemporary media and communication technologies. In chapter 10, "Is This Because I'm Intertextual? *Law and Order, Special Victims Unit,*" and Queer Internet Fan Production, Christy Carlson argues that we take seriously the intertextual nature of TV and fan texts. In this chapter Carlson relocates the agency of fan producers and television producers, through a close reading of queer intertextual production in relation to the televisual *Law and Order.* This chapter provides an important conceptual synthesis of intertextuality and queer as areas of production that must be understood as relational. Queer intertextuality offers and produces meanings through bringing multiple texts into a relational heteroglossia. This relocation of structure and agency pays attention to the conditions of possibility created in the intersection of agency and structure while examining the productive work that simultaneous reorders this intersection. In chapter 11, "Virtual Citizens or Dream Consumers: Looking for Civic Community on Gay.com," John Edward Campbell also examines the intersection of commercial structures and civic engagement. In this analysis four different case studies based on media and policy events are examined in the context of U.S. politics and LGBTI cultures. This chapter provides a less hopeful contention than that of Carlson's; namely that structural constraint limits agency. The structure and form of the affinity portals that Campbell examines seem to close down the capacity of individuals to act, in his analysis. However, Campbell also provides a nuanced appraisal of the ways in which such structures can be negotiated in such a way that "civically-engaged" community is made possible, even within commercial infrastructures that operate to offer spaces of consumption. Thus, the consumer/civic community opposition is broken down in this chapter and a developed sense of the traffic across this boundary is produced.

In the last chapter of this collection structure and agency are examined through an analysis of HIV and sexual practices among gay men. In chapter 12, "Life Outside the Latex: HIV, Sex, and the Online Barebacking Community," Sharif Mowlabocus illuminates the close, complex, and contradictory relationship between barebacking discourses and practices, and HIV prevention work. By foregrounding the Web as a space where the negotiation of civil rights, in these contexts, is occurring, Mowlabocus also highlights the potential to utilize the Web for health interventions. This chapter usefully points to the ways in which Web interactions can operate as interconnected "outsides" to more mainstream spaces of political negotiation. A key contribution made through this chapter is the contention that structuring discourses and subcultural discourses are produced in relation to each other. A second important point is the intersection of such discourses and bodily health. His arguments stress the importance of taking on board the concerns of such marginalized outsides and bringing them into direct dialogue with the more "normative" debates that are shaped and produced in queer cultures. The political imperative here is life itself.

10. *Is This because I'm Intertextual?* Law and Order, Special Victims Unit, *and Queer Internet Fan Production*

CHRISTY CARLSON

"Our stories are real stories," says *Law and Order: Special Victims Unit* (*SVU*) star Mariska Hargitay, in an advertisement for the television series.[1] A variation on the oft-repeated characterization of *Law and Order* (*L&O*) plots as "ripped from the headlines," this comment describes a relationship between fiction and reality that can't satisfactorily be termed oppositional. The tension between the real and the fictional in *L&O* (and its spin-offs) is, I'd argue, more usefully understood through the concept of intertextuality (which the phrase "ripped from the headlines," of course, signals). I use the term intertextuality here in Roland Barthes' sense, as describing the "text-between" (1977: 160) status of all texts which is necessitated by "the impossibility of living outside the infinite text" (1975: 36).[2] At stake in this way of framing the fiction-reality dynamic is a perception of textual boundaries as fluid and of texts as open to infiltration from the "outside." The focus of this essay is the mutually constitutive and dynamically transformative relationship among *L&O*, *SVU*, and a heterogeneous body of online fan productions (including fan fiction, forum discussions, images, and fan videos).

My analysis is indebted to Henry Jenkins' influential theory of fans as "textual poachers" who remake TV texts and in the process often challenge their ideologies. Jenkins positions his argument as a corrective to critical work that views fans "as constituted by texts" rather than "as constitut[ing] their own varied culture" (1992a: 209). For Jenkins, fans are "active producers and manipulators of meanings" (1992b: 23). But even as he works to challenge the opposition that constructs fans as passive consumers, Jenkins repeats its terms. The assertion that "fans promote their own meanings over those of producers" (1992b: 34) categorizes fans as something other than producers, as does Jenkins' repeated use of the term "producers" to refer exclusively to producers of televisual texts. However productive fans may be, they are not, Jenkins implies, real producers. Jenkins argues that fans' interpretations and the texts which convey them elaborate on "the characters and situations proposed by the primary text" but often push them "into directions quite different from those conceived by the original textual producers" (1992a: 214). In other words, fans respond to producers' meanings rather than originate their own. Fans use "primary" texts—which Jenkins also refers to as "the programs which gave them birth...as a starting point for their own fiction" (1992b: 212). The upshot is that his theory characterizes fan texts as secondary and derivative.

This chapter recasts the TV producer-fan producer relation as articulated by Jenkins. Noting that fans "read intertextually as well as textually," Jenkins remarks that "their pleasure comes through the particular juxtapositions that they create between specific program content and other cultural materials" (1992b: 37). I'd like to propose that we take seriously the intertextual nature of TV and fan texts. To do so would challenge the priority and the originary status of the TV text, both of which are reinforced by Jenkins' observation that the TV text provides "the raw materials" for fans' productions (1992b: 23). These fan productions can't adequately be understood as constructing an alternative narrative that exists in opposition to those of the TV text. Rather, they constitute an intertext that resides within and perpetually transforms the televisual text. As such, these fan productions underline and exacerbate the fragility of the borders that surround *L&O* and *SVU* (as well as borders between actor and character, reality and fiction). Moreover, in disrupting the boundaries between sexual identity categories, these fan productions construct queer texts and subjects in Alexander Doty's sense of queer as occupying a space "beside and within" the heterosexual and the straight while refusing to be contained by these positions, and thereby rendering the borders of these categories unstable (1993: 15).

"Is This because I'm a Lesbian?"

The ou(s)ting of Assistant District Attorney (ADA) Serena Southerlyn during the final scene of the *L&O* episode "Ain't No Love" on January 12, 2005, was a provocative and productive moment in queer televisual history. The two-and-a-half minute scene begins with a discussion between Serena and District Attorney Arthur Branch about the legal case featured in this episode and Serena's assessment of its outcome. After explaining that the ADA would be better suited to advocacy work than prosecution (because she is passionate and favors emotion over facts), Arthur matter-of-factly tells her that she is fired. The question Serena asks in response—"Is this because I'm a lesbian?"—elicits a measured "No, of course not" from the DA, to which Serena replies "Good; good." The screen fades to credits.

Immediately following the airing of "Ain't No Love," fans took to online forums, mailing lists, and blogs in order to discuss the implications of the ADA's simultaneous exit from the show and from the closet. By most accounts, Serena's question was confounding given the absence of signifiers of her homosexuality. In an attempt to determine whether the ADA could have been a lesbian all along, fans re-examined past episodes. While no unambiguous evidence was located, the intertextual nature of television allows Serena's sexuality to be reread and retroactively revised.[3] The seeming stability of Serena's "new" lesbian identity is troubled, however, by the recognition that her sexuality is open to illimitable transformation. Fans posting on both the Usenet group alt.tv.law-and-order and the *L&O* forums at TelevisionWithoutPity.com concluded that the lesson this episode teaches is that sexuality and gender are more fluid than is usually acknowledged on *L&O*.

The extreme lack of context for Serena's question leaves the implications of this scene more than a little uncertain. Does the scene characterize the DA as homophobic? Does it underline the difficulty of proving homophobia? Does it make a (rather ambiguous) statement about people being fired in everyday America because they are gay? Does it suggest that lesbians tend wrongly to see themselves as victims of homophobia? Does it mock anti-discrimination discourse by implying that Serena doesn't mind being fired unless the reason for her firing is discrimination? Arthur's characterization of Serena as passionate and emotional was received by viewers with almost as much surprise as the revelation about her sexuality. While we could read Serena's question as a *non sequitur*, as many viewers did, we could also parse it as "What you just said makes no sense; you're firing me because I'm a lesbian, aren't you?" Does the scene imply that being passionate, biased, and unobjective are euphemisms for what it means to be lesbian?

Serena's "last-minute-lesbianism" (medicminx) can be read as a half-hearted response to criticism of the franchise's representation of queer characters. It allows *L&O* to look (a bit more) inclusive without having to attend to the ramifications of having an ongoing lesbian character. In this way, Serena's outing may function as an ironic self-absolution, a disingenuous attempt to "clear" the franchise of the accusation. The decision to make Serena, one of the least popular *L&O* characters, the franchise's lesbian can also be understood as an assertion of authorial authority—lesbianism is brought to the surface so that it may be more definitively dismissed. Indeed many viewers interpreted Serena's outing as an attempt to "in" *SVU*'s subtextually queer character, Olivia Benson. Does the intertextuality of this televisual moment function to delegitimize Olivia's queerness, or does it suggest that Olivia's subtextual queerness may at some point become textual?

"In the Future, Everyone Will be a Lesbian for Five Seconds." ### *(Tarheel)*

Online fans' critical and creative responses to "The Line," as Serena's question came to be called, took varied forms. Some recontextualized The Line in visual and/or scripted scenarios deemed more appropriate (because better suited to fans' agendas), while others highlighted the absurdity of Serena's question by inserting it into even more surprising contexts. On the *L&O* forums of Television Without Pity, The Line was cited in almost every post for weeks after "Ain't No Love" aired. Further, forum participants reported instances in which they responded to various mundane statements made by friends, colleagues, and market researchers (among others) with the query "Is this because I'm a lesbian?" While some addressees heard the question as a quotation, others didn't. This mass iteration of The Line is significant not only because of its scope but also because it demonstrates the tenuousness of the borders between TV text and fan text, and between online fan production and everyday life. These fan activities aren't contained within the bounds of a website or even the internet in general.

Several forum participants reframed Serena's question in their posts as "Is this because I'm a lesbian even though I just said I wasn't?" In response to such utterances, which both claim and deny a lesbian identity, others asked what is at stake in playing a lesbian on an online forum such as Television Without Pity (or elsewhere in the "real" world) in the wake of "Ain't No Love" and how this performance compares to being an "authentic, pre-Line lesbian" (Frightened Auk). I would argue that one of the more notable aspects of this online coming out scene is that it refuses essentialist notions of sexual identity. A conceptualization of identity as fluid and strategic is particularly evident in a "pixel challenge" (on the Television Without Pity boards) that asked fans to produce a Photo-shopped televisual image based on the topic "Is This Because I'm a Lesbian?" In this challenge, hundreds of queer- and non-queer-identified TV characters, actors, and fans "came out" by citing The Line in ways that magnified the complexities of its televisual utterance.[4] This mass coming out scene can be read as mocking its original iteration and reclaiming it for different purposes. At the same time, this act repeats and reinforces the (ambiguous) agendas of "Ain't No Love," perhaps most obviously by reframing the sexuality of numerous real people and fictional characters in *L&O*'s problematic terms. Indeed a significant number of pixel challenge entries comment on Serena's simultaneous outing and firing by positioning "lesbian" as a category of frightening, monstrous or just expendable otherness.[5]

That so many (lesbian- and non-lesbian-identified) people and characters claimed a lesbian identity at once arguably destabilized televisual and non-televisual heteronormativity, literally overnight. In the wake of this scene, the boundary between homo and hetero came to look increasingly uncertain. Doty argues that we pay "less attention to the proposition that basically het-erocentrist texts can contain queer elements, and basically heterosexual, straight-identifying people can experience queer moments" than we might (1993: 2–3). This mass coming out scene provides an example of queer ele-ments existing within heterocentric texts, and of variously identified viewers experiencing queer moments of reception and production. Viewer response to the "Is this because I'm a lesbian?" moment envisions sexual identity in fluid ways that disrupt borders between entrenched identity categories and between real and fictional worlds, lived and imagined lives.

These fan interventions show that the boundaries between hetero and homo, television and fan productions, TV producers and fans are radically compromised, allowing for movement between these categories that enables their contents to be made over continuously. The repetition of The Line in a seemingly endless chain ensures that its meanings constantly alter and blur, as each new meaning transforms into the next. Put another way, this multiplica-tion of intertexts is also a multiplication of epistemological holes. As the nar-rative chain is extended, it is rendered both more complex and less complete. This logic of the supplement is especially evident in pixel challenge entries that transform "lesbian" into "Les Nessman" (farinacus), "L'Espion" (Gray-donCarter), "Lebanese" (Sleestak Hunter), and "less filling" (quotidian), each iteration further postponing the promise of arriving at a fullness of meaning. We are confronted here not with multiple meanings but with what Barthes calls "the very plural of meaning" (1997: 159).

Several entries feature characters from the *L&O* franchise whose citations of The Line address points of intersection between *L&O* and (its spin-off) *SVU*. Reading a displacement of *SVU*'s queerness onto *L&O* (through the newly outed *L&O* character Serena), one entry juxtaposes a screen capture from the *SVU* episode "Consent" of Olivia Benson and Alexandra (Alex) Cabot in an intense gaze; its caption reads "Serena stole our thunder. Damn her" (swivel135). Another—which shows Olivia straddling Alex's body after Alex has been shot—rewrites The Line as "Okay, this is definitely because I'm a lesbian," thereby explicitly marking the homoeroticism of this near-death scene (sravenk). The meanings produced in these entries derive in large part from the fact that the screen captures used to recontextualize The Line are already heavily laden with insinuation. And yet as I argue more fully below, the endless proliferation of intertexts thwarts any attempt to name a point of origin. In the remainder of this chapter, I examine the interplay between *SVU* and productions of the Alex/Olivia fandom.

"Come for the Line. Stay for the Hoyay." ### (medicminx)

An examination of Alex/Olivia fan productions reveals the limitations of discussing the dynamic between TV producer and fan producer, TV narrative and fan narrative vis-à-vis singular moments. From this perspective, the dynamic tends to look like a competitive, even antagonistic, game in which positions of ironic knowingness are traded. For example, in one LiveJournal post, a screen capture that shows Olivia wearing a pink-striped hoodie is juxtaposed to an animated GIF of Olivia walking in a masculine manner titled "the dyke strut" (aleatory_6).[6] If we interpret these images solely as a competition between dueling versions of Olivia Benson, however, we are likely to overlook the interpenetration and interdependence of these ostensibly opposed terms.

In the context of scenes shared by characters of the same gender, markers of a romantic/sexual relationship are termed "hoyay" (an abbreviated form of "homoeroticism, yay!") by forum participants at Television Without Pity.[7] A group project in process, the production of hoyay-oriented viewer guides and analyses of *SVU* and its intertexts (including media reports and photographs of *SVU* actors), functions not only to critique the show's heterocentrism but also to reveal the extent to which it is built on a thinly veiled homoeroticism. *SVU* icons (thumbnail-sized images that accompany a comment) used on LiveJournal draw out the homoeroticism of particular images from the TV show, often by juxtaposing text (for example, "The top button is unbuttoned for you, Detective" or "Kissing? We weren't kissing! [newbie_2u]) to image and sometimes by using arrows/circles to focus attention on specific elements of the image (for example, "Yes, it's a hickey" or "They're *so* holding hands" [rorschachkit and zuzubailey76]).

It's worth noting that the sharing of and collaboration on icons raises questions about the stability and uniqueness of identity within LiveJournal communities, and that it underlines the extent to which identity is dependent upon (explicitly fictional) texts. Indeed online fans demonstrate a strong belief in the textual nature of identity. One viewer mentions in the *SVU* forum at TelevisionWithoutPity.com that she is new to this forum but not to the phenomenon of hoyay, explaining that she "*come[s] from* the A[ll] M[y] C[hildren] thread" (kariyaki; emphasis mine). Legible in these fan productions is the pleasure their producers take in exposing the extent to which all these texts interpenetrate and thus function to constitute each other. The interconnectedness of TV text and fan text is perhaps nowhere more obvious than in an Alex/Olivia manifesto, "The Case of the Butch and the Blonde" (cabenson), that developed out of a website called the "HoYay Hall of Fame" (bectec), and which links (in both senses of the term) fan fiction to specific scenes from episodes of *SVU*.

That any interpretation is open to intertextual transformation is evident in moments when the TV text attempts to explain its characters' sexuality in relation to singular identity categories. By showing Alex and Olivia on dates with men (but not with each other), the TV text arguably closes off the possibility that the two are romantically involved with each other. Such televisual moments—which introduce a male character as a potential love-interest for Alex or Olivia—are referred to by fans as "manvils," a neologism that combines "man" and "anvils" (anomalys). Despite these manvils, Alex and Olivia's sexuality remains open to debate. Indeed it would seem that these attempts to assert closure serve instead to reveal its impossibility. Ultimately, the interpenetration of TV text and fan text produces sexualities that can't easily be read as heterosexual or homosexual.

We can appreciate more fully the ways in which fan productions exacerbate *SVU*'s fraught presentation of sexuality by examining fan responses to the sixth season episode "Ghost." Although she left the series in November 2003, Stephanie March reprised her role as Alex Cabot in this 2005 episode, which brought the former ADA back from the Witness Protection Program to testify against the man charged with her attempted murder. Much of the fan discussion of this episode revolves around a short exchange that begins with Olivia asking Alex if she is making any new friends. In a pained voice, Alex acknowledges that "there's a claims adjuster at the insurance agency" where she works. She adds that when they are in bed together he calls out her Witness Protection Program name, Emily.

A viewer on the *SVU* board at Television Without Pity explains the way that the exchange as a whole works to equate "friends" with "lovers." Alex responds to Olivia's question—"Are you making any new friends?"—by mentioning a *lover*:

> She didn't say, "Yeah, I go salsa dancing with the girls from the Knitting Club sometimes, and I'm on the insurance company water polo team, but it's just weird when they're like 'Emily! Over here! I'm open!' and 'Emily, it's knit one, purl *two*.'" (Learned Hand)

Especially since she has already used the term "friend" with reference to Olivia in this episode, Alex's response to Olivia's question, Learned Hand argues, reflects the role that Olivia played in her life. She understands Olivia to be asking whether Alex has replaced her. Interestingly, this reading derives from an examination of dialogue that could be understood as an attempt to eclipse the scene's homoeroticism. It is not just Olivia's behavior in this scene that implies that the two were lovers or that Olivia had wanted them to be lovers—her teary-eyed gaze implies that she is experiencing a crushing loss—but also the dialogue itself which can't be contained by a heterocentric reading. Indeed another viewer argues that this is "truly the gayest scene ever" (strangefroote). That Alex has a new male lover doesn't, of course, negate the possibility that she has, had, or will have female lovers; but these viewers are suggesting that, in a certain way, Alex's acknowledgment that she has a male lover makes her seem *less* straight.

Olivia's response to Alex's story about her new "friend"—"It's hard to be something you're not"—was heard by many viewers as a reference to Olivia's and Alex's closeted lives. Filtered through fan fiction, and contextualized by the fact that Alex and Olivia are spending the night together in a hotel room, this line also sounds like a prelude to romance. As one fan mentioned, this conversation between Alex and Olivia was "like a scene out of the best fanfic" (Frightened Auk). The blurring of the line between TV text and fan fiction is also evident in a discussion among viewers regarding Alex's reference to her claims adjuster friend as "a good man." The consensus among posters at Television Without Pity was that this is yet another line that resonates ambiguously. Ostensibly a positive characterization, this descriptor also seems to suggest an absence of deep feelings on Alex's part; it implies a "but" clause. One fan fiction writer supports this reading by pointing to her previous use of the phrase to describe Olivia's "MacGuffin fiancé" in *Spark*, a "Return of Alex" online story: "And you, gentle readers, know how that turned out" (tenblade). Wishing there "had been a bit more *Spark* in 'Ghost,'" another viewer underlines this interpenetration of fan fiction and TV script (jfdb).

One of the more notable elements of this hotel room scene is its textually inexplicable intensity. Many fans account for the emotion the characters display in this scene by inferring that Alex and Olivia developed a much deeper relationship off-screen. Support for such inferences is often located in intertexts. This practice is perhaps most obvious in readings of a three-episode arc (during 2004–2005) in which Mary Stuart Masterson plays a psychiatrist and former-police officer who knows Olivia from their time together at the Police Academy. The interactions between Olivia and Masterson's character, Rebecca Hendricks, were so heated that many fans concluded the two had been involved in a romantic relationship that ended badly. One viewer glosses their interactions by commenting that Olivia displays "completely inappropriate looks of tortured melodrama every. single. time. M[ary]S[tuart] M[asterson]'s character said anything that added to that imagined backstory" (Learned Hand).

In an attempt to make sense of Olivia's extreme (and textually inexplicable) anger in scenes she shares with Rebecca, viewers argued that Masterson's

SVU psychiatrist character carries traces of Idgie Threadgoode—the almost-textually lesbian character Masterson played in *Fried Green Tomatoes*—as her fan-given nickname, "Dr. Idgie," indicates. Due, at least in part, to this intertextuality, viewers found that Masterson's *SVU* character sent mixed messages when she flirted with Olivia's male partner. In the same way, Olivia's heated response can be understood as marking both her jealous possessiveness (with regard to her partner) and her past romantic relationship with Rebecca.[8]

An intertextual blurring of boundaries is also legible in the relation between character and actor. Both John Fiske and John Ellis argue that TV's serial form brings about a merging of character and actor. As Ellis explains, "[t]he two become very much entangled, so that the performer's image is equated with that of the fictional role" (106). Within the *SVU* text, fans and actors exacerbate this blurring of boundaries and demonstrate that the transformation proceeds in both directions. In an imagined account of Mariska Hargitay's Golden Globes acceptance speech (for her portrayal of Olivia on *SVU*), a few days before the actual 2005 ceremony, one fan predicted that "Hargitay" would ask "Is this because I'm a lesbian?" and then explain that in reality she is straight. This parody of The Line calls up remarks Hargitay made in a 2003 appearance on *Late Night with Conan O'Brien*. In the interview, O'Brien asks if people confuse her with the tough character she plays on *SVU*. Nodding in agreement with O'Brien's comment that she is very feminine in real life, Hargitay tells the story of a fan who spotted her walking down a NYC street with her boyfriend, who had his hand on her hip; Hargitay reports that the fan called out to her exclaiming, "Damn, I thought you was a lesbian!" She glosses the fan's comment by explaining that everyone mistakenly believes she is a lesbian because of the character she plays on *SVU*. Hargitay's comments in the interview are noteworthy because she acknowledges that "everyone" believes that Olivia is a lesbian and because in marking the difference between actor and character, she suggests that "everyone" is right. Interestingly, Hargitay herself often blurs the boundary between actor and character. Even as she attempts to emphasize the difference, in an interview with Jay Leno, by telling a story that begins with her walking down the street in heels and a skirt—"very not Olivia Benson"—she ends up emphasizing the similarity. Hargitay mentions that she reverted into Olivia Benson mode, reiterating phrases she uttered as Olivia on *SVU* in her Olivia voice, as she tried to rescue a pregnant woman who fainted in front of her. Hargitay's frequent media references to her real-life self as a "brother in blue" who spends her time "bustin' perps" are clearly tongue-in-cheek, but she nevertheless participates in the blurring of the boundary between actor and character, as we can see clearly in an interview in *Parade Magazine* where she explains that "[she is] an LA girl who became a tough NY cop" (Brady). This blurring of the actor-character boundary is also evident in the season five transformation of Olivia's look and personality. Commenting on the extent to which Hargitay seems to "bleed onto the character of Olivia" (Learned Hand), fans refer to post-season four Olivia as "Oliska."

"Please Continue and Make Them Make Out" ###
(sqully)

In "Starring Lucy Lawless?" Sara Gwenllian-Jones remarks that fans of cult television shows such as *Xena* "favour characters over stars" (2002: 16). She explains that "[d]espite extensive research, [she has] yet to find a single example of a fan fiction story which invokes [Xena's portrayer] Lawless as herself, or indeed even mentions her" (2002: 12). S. Elizabeth Bird finds that some *Doctor Quinn* fans are also primarily "interested in cast members in terms of their . . . roles" (2003: 77); others, however, "are deeply interested in the actors and spend most of their time discussing and speculating about their lives" (2003: 77). Despite this difference in their findings, Bird and Gwenllian-Jones both suggest that fans maintain a rather strict distinction between characters and their portrayers. According to Gwenllian-Jones, the privileging of character over performer "greatly reduces the effectiveness of the performer's star text upon that of the character" (2002: 16). Within the *SVU* fandom, however, significant attention is directed toward the "performers-as-stars" (2002: 16).[9] Moreover, the relation between character and actor is both transformative and bi-directional. Gwenllian-Jones claims that the *Xena* fandom "takes stardom to its logical conclusion, abolishing altogether the need for an obvious referent in the form of a 'real' person" (2002: 12). As I argue below, Alex/Olivia fans tend to challenge the distinction between fictional and real. Indeed they show the real to be as fictional as fiction.

    I take my title for this section from a review of a story (written by an *SVU* fan) that was posted at fanfiction.net. It exemplifies the type of reader feedback that is most often offered to online *SVU* fan fiction writers, namely, pleas for additional chapters and suggestions regarding the direction the narrative could take. Both forms of feedback underline one of the distinctive characteristics of online fan fiction: it consists, to a significant extent, of works in progress. As many stories are left incomplete and a large proportion of completed stories are initially posted chapter by chapter, reviews tend to offer (open-ended) suggestions more often than finalizing critiques. For these reasons, online fan fiction writers/readers tend to conceptualize fan fiction as open and future-oriented.

    We need only turn to Yahoo Groups and LiveJournal fan fiction communities to see that there is considerable pleasure to be found in the postponement of narrative closure. "It's Gotta Be Love," an ongoing Alex/Olivia story that is updated daily by co-writers Katherine Quinn and Adrienne Lee on the OliviaAlex Yahoo mailing list, offers an extreme example of this phenomenon. Known by many as "the never-ending story," "It's Gotta Be Love" reached 1,800 chapters on March 7, 2006 (with no end in sight). The question posed by its story summary—"Just how many tests can two people and their relationship go through?"—is less rhetorical than it might seem. Exemplifying the ongoing process of narrative construction and the resultant textual openness that I'm arguing characterizes Alex/Olivia fan productions in general, "It's Gotta Be Love" implicitly mocks the limited scope and size of its televisual intertext, *SVU*.

The tendency of narratives to transform continuously in the hands of their readers characterizes both the body of online *SVU* fan fiction and the televized text. Much Alex/Olivia fan fiction can be categorized as "missing scene" fiction, a genre that functions to fill gaps between the scenes of particular television episodes. In the process of filling gaps, however, these narratives both draw our attention to the gaps as gaps—revealing the TV episode as incomplete—and alter the televized scenes. Recontextualized, the "before" and "after" scenes mean differently. Moreover, this process of transformation is without end, in a couple of ways. First, suggestive episodes are rewritten repeatedly in multiple missing scene narratives; and second, these missing scene stories resonate with and interrupt each other. Fans often distinguish fan fiction that adheres closely to the TV text from "alternate universe" fan fiction which places series characters in a different place, time, and/or reality. My point here is that fan fiction is always "alternate universe" fiction insofar as it recontextualizes the televisual text, activating a previously unknown future iteration.

Of particular interest for my argument is the perpetual recontextualization of series characters' sexual identities. Since Alex and Olivia are presented by the TV text as having dated men, this history must be accounted for in fan productions. As Jenkins argues with reference to Kirk/Spock slash,[10] whatever form a given character's (fan fiction) sexuality takes, these stories necessarily present sexual identity as fluid and non-binary (1992b: 219). Within Alex/Olivia fan fiction, being a lesbian doesn't preclude sexual encounters with men, and having sex with other women doesn't necessarily mean that one is a lesbian. Moreover, the recognition that individual stories are parts of the (fan fiction) whole—a point that is difficult to ignore if one reads more than one story—makes defining a character's sexuality even more difficult. Some fan fiction readers mention on online forums that they prefer, for example, "first time" stories and that they tend not to read outside of that genre. If this selective reading practice disrupts expectations with regard to narrative coherence (as the Alex/Olivia story is always and repeatedly beginning rather than progressing toward an end), it also, and with significant ramifications, disrupts the notion of sexual identity as stable since each time these characters' sexualities are told, they are told differently. As disorienting as this phenomenon might be, readers clearly take pleasure in this blurring of lines between categories of sexual identity. Alex/Olivia stories ask readers to think about the way the characters' different sexual pasts and presents inflect their relationship with each other. Interest and enjoyment derive from the recognition that these characters' sexualities can be told in many ways and that these different possibilities are not mutually exclusive but rather coexist. How can Olivia's sexuality not register as fluid if we read stories in which she is presented as having a long history of same-sex relationships as well as stories in which she is "straight-until-Alex"? If Olivia is straight, lesbian, and bisexual, a top (who doesn't switch) and a bottom, experienced and inexperienced in BDSM, and if she only has one-night stands, is a serial monogamist, and enjoys threesomes, how can we name her sexuality in recognizable terms?

The blurring of boundaries between sexualities becomes even more confounding in texts that disrupt the usual boundaries between fiction and reality. An emergent genre within Alex/Olivia fan fiction pairs these characters with the actors who portray them. This crossing (of characters and actors) raises questions about the relation between fiction and reality that are implicit in the body of Alex/Olivia fan productions. On one level, these narratives take up viewers' perceptions/fantasies of the actors' on- and off-screen relationships and the actors' attitudes toward the characters they portray. But these stories also evidence a fascination with the realness of the fictional (and the fictiveness of the real) that complicates this reading.

"Fairytales," by giantessmess, slashes Alex Cabot and Mariska Hargitay as well as Stephanie March and Mariska Hargitay, and Alex and Olivia. Yet this list of pairings obscures the narrative's blurring of the boundaries between characters to the extent that it is never entirely clear who is speaking to whom. Much of this uncertainty derives from the lack of a clear distinction between the real and the fictional, actor and character. Reversing the usual relationship between fictional character and real person, this story's Alex tells Mariska that Stephanie is "a fiction someone made up about [Alex]." While Mariska maintains that Olivia is fictional, she implies that Alex is as real as she is when she asks Alex to play Stephanie at premieres and parties. As Alex enters the "real" world (of public appearances) and plays the part of a "real person," the "real" is revealed to be as fictional as a television script. Indeed the "real" seems more fictional than fiction: Alex longs for the "real Olivia" who never called her words "lines" like Mariska does and whose kisses felt real, not mechanical. This character's quest for the real is set up to fail, however, as she (who?) can't discern the boundary between Mariska and Olivia, actor and character. If identity is a construct and a performance, what makes real people more real than fictional characters? Why does it make more sense to ask if a person was really gay all along than it does to ask the same question of a character? What makes TV characters more real than fan fiction characters? And how can we even tell the difference?[11]

Similar questions are posed in another story by giantessmess that pairs Olivia Benson and Mariska Hargitay. "Foreign Bodies" initially proposes that a fictional character such as Olivia has an edge over the real actor who portrays her. Olivia's muscles are "more real" than Mariska's because they are fictionally constructed as real. Olivia realizes, however, that the real and the fictional are not so easily separated, as they constantly transform each other. Mariska and Olivia leave marks on each other: Mariska surfaces to find that Olivia has a piercing and a new tattoo, while Olivia discovers the effects of Mariska's facial treatments and an "uncanny tan [she] can never explain to Elliot [Olivia's partner]." Mariska's tendency to think of Olivia's city as "just a film set" doesn't negate the fact that Olivia is "everywhere she is." While Mariska insists that she is "not like" Olivia, by which she seems to mean neither fictional nor attracted to women, ultimately this story suggests that the distinction between fiction and reality is merely an illusion designed to pacify. As the protagonists of another fan narrative—"It Ain't Her" (by newbie_2u) —learn, the person/character whose identity they seek to resolve is neither Olivia nor Mariska but something in between: "Oliska Hargenson."

By way of conclusion, I turn to an Alex/Olivia fan video that visually, aurally, and narratively foregrounds the dynamically transformative relationship between TV text and fan text. Set to the music of The Divinyls' "I Touch Myself," "Ship" juxtaposes scenes shared by Alex and Olivia to scenes that pair them with other series characters. While the Alex/Olivia narrative is set to lyrics that repeat variations of "I want you," "I want to make you mine," and "When I think about you / I touch myself," competing narratives which feature alternate pairings are accompanied by large, red graphics—X's which swirl, rotate, and drop into the frame and onto the offending characters' faces—and the lyric "I don't want anybody else." This fan video exemplifies the undecidable oscillation of meaning that describes the TV text-fan text relation. It teaches that narratives produced by fans and television production teams alike necessarily suppress other possible narratives while never fully removing them. Such practices of exclusion are finally impossible because all these texts are haunted by the traces of other texts which help to constitute them.

For Jenkins, fans are productive in acts of consumption which reproduce the TV text differently. I have argued that fans are productive in a different sense: They help to produce the TV text itself. Gwenllian-Jones maintains that fan texts extend rather than oppose the logics of the TV text (2002: 89); as a result "relations between the culture industry and online fan cultures are more symbiotic than they are antagonistic" (2003: 171). My reading of *L&O, SVU,* and the productions of these shows' fans demonstrates this symbiosis. These texts can't adequately be understood as presenting opposed meanings because their meanings reside not within a text but rather in relations between texts. This limitless transfer of meaning between TV text and fan text (and between actor and character, reality and fiction) creates crises of boundaries such that it is impossible to tell which is inside and which is outside. Ultimately both the priority of the TV text and its originary status are thrown into question, as the "original" is recast by and so in a strange way becomes subsequent to the text that rewrites it.

Notes

1. For their helpful suggestions during the writing of this chapter, I would like to thank Sarah Lamble, Jennifer Henderson, Marlene Ziobrowski, Suzanne Bailey, Rachel Torrie, Rain Mulyanto, Zailig Pollock, and Charmaine Eddy.
2. See Allen (2000), Morgan (1989), and Orr (2003) for incisive summaries of and interventions into the debates about intertextuality.
3. John Ellis argues that "[t]he form that tends to be adopted by TV fiction . . . is the same as TV news, with a continuous updating on the latest concatenation of events rather than a final ending or explanation" (120). As a result, "segments tend never to coalesce into an overall totalising account" (120).
4. A small sample of shows cited in the pixel challenge includes *Peanuts, Xena, Ellen, Wheel of Fortune, The O.C., C.S.I., The West Wing, Carnivàle, Arrested Development, Lassie, The Amazing Race, Smallville, The Simpsons, Star Trek: DS9, Battlestar Galactica* (2003), and *Postcards from Buster.*
5. One entry depicts Anya, from *Buffy the Vampire Slayer,* spotting a bunny and recoiling in fear, leaving the bunny to ask "Is this because I'm a lesbian?" (watcha). *Survivor Vanuatu*'s Scout is shown reciting The Line as her torch is put out (neptune42). The Line is cited by *Charmed*'s Future Chris after he has been shot (Loco Lady); by Angel as Buffy is sending him to Hell (bellememmers); by *Alias*' Lauren Reed as she is being shot (lotusgt1chick); and by Charlie (hanging from a tree, limp) and the dying polar bear from *Lost* (Frogboy Lives; DaNator). An especially evocative entry uses a screen capture from a *Buffy* episode titled "Seeing Red," in which Willow, covered in her girlfriend Tara's blood, holds her dead body (DaNator). Tara asks "Willow . . . is this because . . . *cough* I'm a . . . *wheeze* . . . lesbian?" An inset image of *Buffy* creator Joss Whedon accompanies his response: "Yes, it is."
6. LiveJournal is a large online community organized around personal journals.
7. In contrast to the subtext-text relationship, which positions the homo beneath the hetero, the hoyay-hetyay dynamic doesn't linguistically subordinate hoyay.
8. A fan narrative by aqua_blur which discusses Olivia and Rebecca's breakup also functions as a meditation on the dangers of intertextuality. In this story, Rebecca explains that if she and Olivia stay together, Olivia will "end up dead" since this is the fate shared by all of Rebecca's "lesbian co-stars." Olivia fights for their relationship by marking a distinction between life and art, actor and character. She insists

that Rebecca's fear is misplaced as it derives from a conflation of real life and "a movie." However, Olivia inadvertently weakens her case when she points out that Rebecca only seems to trail dead lesbians behind her because of her connection to Mary Louise Parker's character in *Fried Green Tomatoes* and, through her, to additional lesbian characters that died in movies starring Mary Louise Parker. This argument confirms Rebecca's fear as it foregrounds the complex and layered web of associations that results from characters and actors carrying their histories with them as they enter new narratives that are in turn transformed by these histories. From this perspective, Rebecca's theory that the dead lesbian narrative will contaminate her life with Olivia makes a certain kind of sense. And Olivia's vow to refrain from calling Rebecca "Idgie" when they are in bed together only reinforces Rebecca's belief in the inevitability of intertextuality and thus in the necessity of ending their relationship.

9. In a one-page story titled "I Do," *People* magazine juxtaposes a wedding photograph of Stephanie March and husband Bobby Flay to an image from the *SVU* episode "Paranoia" that shows Alex and Olivia in a heated discussion. TV fiction here supplements and reframes "reality"; the implication is that the story of March's real-life wedding can only be told through the story of Alex's relationship with Olivia.

10. Jenkins defines slash as "both a set of generic formulas and an ideology about same-sex relationships. Slash stories center on the relationships between male program characters, the obstacles they must overcome to achieve intimacy, the rewards they find in each other's arms" (1992b: 188–189). With the proliferation of slash in the internet era, the term has also come to operate as an umbrella term that includes, as well as male/male pairings, female/female pairings (more specifically termed fem-slash) and sometimes male/female pairings. This broader definition loses the specificity of the earlier sense of the term, but it has the advantage of acknowledging the challenge to heteronormativity that exists within some fan narratives with male/female pairings.

11. Similar questions are raised in dabkey's suggestively titled fan narrative "And Playing the Role of Herself," which follows two female actors from a *Law and Order*-type series who become involved on-screen and off-screen (both in their "real" lives and in fan fiction).

References

add_duck. *Ship*. Retrieved January 29, 2005, from http://www.columbia.edu/~-ai12001/ship.mov

"Ain't No Love." *Law and Order*. NBC. January 12, 2005.

aleatory_6. "The Dyke Strut." Online Image. October 2, 2004. LiveJournal / ob_fangrrl. Retrieved August 15, 2005, from http://www.livejournal.com/community/ob_fangrrl/8546.html?thread=448178#t448178

Allen, G. 2000. *Intertextuality*. London: Routledge.

anomalys. Online Posting. February 22, 2005. Television Without Pity Forum / Old Law and Order Special Victims Unit thread. Retrieved July 27, 2005, from http://forums.televisionwithoutpity.com/index.php?showtopic=2240922&-st=9850

aqua_blur. "Teh Badfic." December 16, 2004. LiveJournal / ob_fangrrl. Retrieved September 2, 2005, from http://www.livejournal.com/community/ob_fangrrl/98367.html#cutid1

Barthes, R. 1975. *The Pleasure of the Text*. Trans. R. Miller. New York: Hill & Wang.

Barthes, R. 1977. *Image, Music, Text*. Trans. S. Heath. New York: Hill & Wang.

bectec. "HoYay Hall of Fame." Online Posting. November 11, 2004. LiveJournal. Retrieved February 23, 2005, from http://bectec.livejournal.com/1770.html

bellememmers. "Buffy Sends Angel to Hell." Online Image. February 1, 2005. Television Without Pity / TV Potluck / Pixel Challenge #147. Retrieved June 20, 2005, from http://forums.televisionwithoutpity.com/index.php?showtopic=3122718&st=45

Bird, S. E. 2003. *The Audience in Everyday Life: Living in a Media World*. New York: Routledge.

Brady, J. 2005. "In Step with Mariska Hargitay." *Parade Magazine*. Retrieved February 13, 2005, from http://www.parade.com/articles/editions/2005/edition_02–13–2005/in_step_with_0

cabenson. "The Case of the Butch and the Blonde." Online Posting. November 12, 2004. LiveJournal / ship_manifesto. Retrieved July 14, 2005, from http://community.livejournal.com/ship_manifesto/43570.html

dabkey. "And Playing the Role of Herself." July 2005. E-Scribblers.com. Retrieved August 16, 2005, from http://www.e-scribblers.com/dabkey/dk-play1.shtml

DaNator. "Dying Polar Bear from *Lost*." Online Image. February 1, 2005. Television Without Pity / TV Potluck / Pixel Challenge #147. Retrieved February 5, 2005, from http://forums.televisionwithoutpity.com/index.php?showtopic=3122718&st=15

DaNator. "Dying Tara from *Buffy*." Online Image. February 1, 2005. Television Without Pity / TV Potluck / Pixel Challenge #147. Retrieved February 5, 2005, from http://forums.televisionwithoutpity.com/index.php?showtopic=3122718&st=30?

Doty, A. 1993. *Making Things Perfectly Queer: Interpreting Mass Culture*. Minneapolis: University of Minnesota.

Ellis, J. 1982. *Visible Fictions*. London: Routledge.

farinacus. "Les Nessman." Online Image. February 1, 2005. Television Without Pity / TV Potluck / Pixel Challenge #147. Retrieved June 20, 2005, from http://forums.televisionwithoutpity.com/index.php?showtopic=3122718&st=15

Fiske, J. 1987. *Television Culture*. London: Routledge.

Frightened Auk. Online Posting. January 16, 2005. Television Without Pity / Old Law and Order Special Victims Unit thread. Retrieved July 25, 2005, from http://forums.televisionwithoutpity.com/index.php?showtopic=2240922&st=9885

Frightened Auk. Online Posting. February 22, 2005. Television Without Pity / Old Law and Order Special Victims Unit thread. Retrieved July 26, 2005, from http://forums.televisionwithoutpity.com/index.php?showtopic=2240922&st=12000

Frogboy Lives. "Charlie from *Lost*." Online Image. February 2, 2005. Television Without Pity / TV Potluck / Pixel Challenge #147. Retrieved June 20, 2005, from http://forums.televisionwithoutpity.com/index.hp?showtopic=3122718&st=150

"Ghost." *Law and Order: Special Victims Unit*. NBC. February 22, 2005.

giantessmess. "Fairy Tales." September 3, 2005. LiveJournal / rpfs. Retrieved September 6, 2005, from http://www.livejournal.com/community/rpfs/35781.html#cutid1

giantessmess. "Foreign Bodies." October 7, 2005. LiveJournal / olivia_mariska. Retrieved October 9, 2005, from http://community.livejournal.com/olivia_mariska_/1295.html#cutid1

GraydonCarter. "L'Espion." Online Image. February 2, 2005. Television Without Pity / TV Potluck / Pixel Challenge #147. Retrieved February 20, 2005, from http://forums.televisionwithoutpity.com/index.php?showtopic=3122718&st=135

Gwenllian-Jones, S. 2000. "Starring Lucy Lawless?" *Continuum: Journal of Media & Cultural Studies 14*(1), 9–22.

Gwenllian-Jones, S. 2002. "The Sex Lives of Cult Television Characters." *Screen* 43(1), 79–90.

Gwenllian-Jones, S. 2003. "Web Wars: Resistance, Online Fandom and Studio Censorship," in M. Jancovich and J. Lyons (Eds.), *Quality Popular Television: Cult TV, the Industry, and Fans* (pp. 163–177). London: British Film Institute.

Hargitay, M. Interview with Conan O'Brien. *Late Night with Conan O'Brien*. NBC. April 24, 2003.

Hargitay, M. Interview with Jay Leno. *The Tonight Show with Jay Leno*. NBC. March 4, 2005.

"I Do." *People*. March 7, 2005, 80.

Jenkins, H. 1992a. " 'Strangers No More, We Sing': Filking and the Social Construction of the Science Fiction Fan Community," in L. A. Lewis (Ed.), *The Adoring Audience: Fan Culture and Popular Media* (pp. 208–236). London: Routledge.

Jenkins, H. 1992b. *Textual Poachers: Television Fans and Participatory Culture*. New York: Routledge.

jfdb. Online Posting. February 23, 2005. Television Without Pity Forum / Old Law and Order Special Victims Unit thread. Retrieved July 28, 2005, from http://forums.televisionwithoutpity.com/index.php?showtopic=2240922&st=12105

kariyaki. Online Posting. January 6, 2005. Television Without Pity Forum / Old Law and Order Special Victims Unit thread. Retrieved July 29, 2005, from http://forums.televisionwithoutpity.com/index.php?showtopic=2240922&st=9480

Learned Hand. Online Posting. February 23, 2005. Television Without Pity Forum / Old Law and Order Special Victims Unit thread. Retrieved February 25, 2005, from http://forums.televisionwithoutpity.com/index.php?showtopic=2240922&st=12195

Learned Hand. Online Posting. November 30, 2004. Television Without Pity Forum / Old Law and Order Special Victims Unit thread. Retrieved July 29, 2005, from http://forums.televisionwithoutpity.com/index.php?showtopic=2240922&st=8385

Learned Hand. Online Posting. February 24, 2005. Television Without Pity Forum / Old Law and Order Special Victims Unit thread. Retrieved July 27, 2005, from http://forums.televisionwithoutpity.com/index.php?showtopic=2240922&st=12270

Loco Lady. "*Charmed*'s Future Chris." Online Image. February 4, 2005. Television Without Pity / TV Potluck / Pixel Challenge #147. Retrieved June 20, 2005, from http://forums.televisionwithoutpity.com/index.php?showtopic=3122718&st=465

lotusgt1chick. "*Alias*' Lauren shot." Online Image. February 2, 2005. Television Without Pity / TV Potluck / Pixel Challenge #147. Retrieved June 20, 2005, from http://forums.televisionwithoutpity.com/index.php?showtopic=3122718&st=210

medicminx. Online Posting. January 16, 2005. Television Without Pity Forum / Old Law and Order Special Victims Unit thread. Retrieved July 28, 2005, from http://forums.televisionwithoutpity.com/index.php?showtopic=2240922&st=9870

Morgan, T. 1989. "The Space of Intertextuality," in P. O'Donnell and R. C. Davis (Eds.), *Intertextuality and Contemporary American Fiction* (pp. 239–279). Baltimore, MD: Johns Hopkins University.

neptune42. "*Survivor*'s Scout." Online Image. February 1, 2005. Television Without Pity / TV Potluck / Pixel Challenge #147. Retrieved August 13, 2005, from http://forums.televisionwithoutpity.com/index.php?showtopic=3122718&st=0

newbie_2u. "It Ain't Her." October 4, 2005. LiveJournal / alex_liv_lovers. Retrieved October 4, 2005, from http://www.livejournal.com/community/ alex_liv_lovers/257750.html#cutid1

newbie_2u, and aleatory_6. "Kissing? We're Not kissing." Online Image. August 30, 2005. LiveJournal. Retrieved August 30, 2005, from http://www.livejournal.com/community/alex_liv_lovers/204946.html

Orr, M. 2003. *Intertextuality: Debates and Contexts.* Malden, MA: Blackwell.

quotidian. "Less Filling." Online Image. February 1, 2005. Television Without Pity / TV Potluck / Pixel Challenge #147. Retrieved June 20, 2005, from http://forums.televisionwithoutpity.com/index.php?showtopic=3122718&st=75

Quinn, K., and Lee, A. 2006. "It's Gotta Be Love." Passion and Perfection. Retrieved March 8, 2006, from http://www.ralst.com/storiesLOI-M.html

rorschachkit, and zuzubailey76. "They're *so* holding hands." Online Image. September 1, 2005. LiveJournal. Retrieved September 1, 2005, from http://www.livejournal.com/community/ alex_liv_lovers/208612.html

Sleestak Hunter. "Lebanese." Online Image. February 1, 2005. Television Without Pity / TV Potluck / Pixel Challenge #147. Retrieved June 20, 2005, from http://forums.televisionwithoutpity.com/index.php?showtopic=3122718&st=45

Sqully. Rev. of "Tension," by jenforvel. June 16, 2005. FanFiction.net. Retrieved August 16, 2005, from http://www.fanfiction.net/r/2439966/0/1/

sravenk. "This Is *Definitely* because I'm a Lesbian." Online Image. February 1, 2005. Television Without Pity / Potluck / Pixel Challenge #147. Retrieved February 5, 2005, from http://forums.televisionwithoutpity.com/index.php?showtopic=3122718&st=10

strangefroote. Online Posting. February 22, 2005. Television Without Pity Forum / Old Law and Order Special Victims Unit thread. Retrieved July 27, 2005, from http://forums.televisionwithoutpity.com/index.php?showtopic=2240922&st=12015

swivel135. "Serena Stole Our Thunder." Online Image. February 1, 2005. Television Without Pity / TV Potluck / Pixel Challenge #147. Retrieved February 5, 2005, from http://forums.televisionwithoutpity.com/index.php?showtopic=3122718&st=90

tenblade. Online Posting. February 23, 2005. Television Without Pity Forum / Old Law and Order Special Victims Unit thread. Retrieved July 28, 2005, from http://forums.televisionwithoutpity.com/index.php?showtopic=2240922&st=12105

watcha. "*Buffy*'s Anya and Bunny." Online Image. 1 February 2005. Television Without Pity / TV Potluck / Pixel Challenge #147. Retrieved February 5, 2005, from http://forums.televisionwithoutpity.com/index.php?showtopic+3122718&st=105

11. Virtual Citizens or Dream Consumers: Looking for Civic Community on Gay.com

John Edward Campbell

> Communities are to be distinguished, not by their falsity/genuineness, but by the style in which they are imagined. (Anderson 1983: 6)

Citizens or Consumers? An Introduction

Arguments surrounding the legitimacy of online communities have largely centered on noncommercial sites evolving organically from the social interactions of their members. Whether these communities emerged out of newsgroups dedicated to popular music (Watson 1997) or soap operas (Baym 1995), chat rooms predicated on sexual identities (Campbell 2004; Correll 1995; Shaw 1997), or MUDs (multi-user domains) constructed for fantasy role-playing (Schaap 2002) or professional networking (Kendall 2002), they were all ad hoc social aggregations. However, a new online social formation representing the peculiar hybrid of community and commerce complicates these discussions by introducing an engineered community—the internet affinity portal. Reflecting the convergence of niche marketing and internet entrepreneurialism, these affinity portals have rendered online communities the hottest commodity in cyberspace. This study explores the political consequences of such commodification.

The keystone of the affinity portal model is the image of community, and by invoking community these portals invite the emotional investment of patrons. However, it is the commercial orientation of these sites that raises concerns regarding their potential for civic engagement and political empowerment. If, as critical theorists contend, the "privatized, commercialized media is instrumentalizing communication and thus undermining the public

sphere" (Dahlberg 2005: 161), then what are the social and political consequences of this commercialization of online communities? This study examines one of the most financially successful affinity portals and the leading
commercial site targeting sexual minorities—Gay.com—in an effort to
address this question. In assessing the potential for these commercial sites to
constitute viable public spheres, this study analyzes the discourse generated
by patrons in response to four polemical news stories reported on Gay.com
with the aim of identifying what civic discourses are promoted or contained
on the site.

What Is an Internet Affinity Portal?

Unable to directly compete with established universal portals (e.g., Yahoo,
AOL, MSN.com), new players entering the internet entrepreneurial arena in
the mid-1990s had to devise a means of distinguishing their portals if they
hoped to garner a share of those elusive online audiences. This need for distinction led to the development of the affinity portal model: specialized portals that "do not aspire to become universal first ports of call," but rather
"are targeted at particular user segments" (*Computer Weekly* 1999: 1).

Targeting specific socio-demographic groups they perceive as being
underserved by universal portals, these affinity portals utilize inviting images
of community to suggest they are more than merely a commercial site. For
instance, the iVillage.com portal presents itself as an online community composed solely of women, using this image of inclusion to attract patrons even
though they may be able to gain access to similar resources through the universal portals. Lisa Chen, Vice President of Business Development at iVil-
lage.com, argues that the success of affinity portals is found in the fact that
people venturing online are most "interested in community" (as quoted in
Liss 2000: 2). Indeed, claims to community are central to the marketing of
these portals whether they are oriented toward women (iVillage.com), baby-
boomers (MyPrimeTime.com), Asian Americans (AsianAvenue.com), African
Americans (BlackPlanet.com), Latinos (MiGente.com),[1] or sexual minorities
(Gay.com and PlanetOut.com).

The primary objective of these affinity portals is no different than that of
the established universal portals: to "structure a total online experience
around the portal" thereby creating a captive online audience for advertisers
(Dahlberg 2005: 164). For those portals targeting politically marginalized
groups, their financial dependence on membership fees and corporate advertising calls into question their potential for political empowerment. In his
examination of affinity portals targeting racial and ethnic minorities, McLaine
(2003) notes that the political commitments of these sites are compromised
by their need to be profitable, commenting that a "company cannot pay staff

with empowerment" (240). This profit imperative begs the question of whether a commercial site can constitute the basis of a viable public sphere in cyberspace. As the preeminent sites targeting sexual minorities in cyberspace, an analysis of Gay.com should provide useful insights regarding the impact of these affinity portals on online civic engagement.

A Brief History of Gay.com

Gay.com was founded in 1994 when Mark Elderkin registered the URL and began distributing a bi-monthly newsletter to paid subscribers. By 2002, Gay.com had more than a million registered members and numerous advertising clients, including IBM, AT&T, and American Airlines.[2] In April of 2001, Gay.com merged with its primary competitor PlanetOut.com to form PlanetOut Inc., and in October of 2004, PlanetOut Inc. went public, trading on Nasdaq and netting $41.6 million during the corporation's initial public offering (*San Francisco Chronicle* 2005: B1). On November 9, 2005, PlanetOut Inc. acquired LPI Media Inc. (the publisher of *The Advocate* and *Out*) for $31.1 million, creating the world's largest gay media company. Critics such as Gamson (2003) express concern over such consolidation, noting that gay media "are now very much modeled on their mainstream counterparts, especially in the trend toward concentrated ownership" (256).

Today Gay.com—PlanetOut Inc.'s flagship site—provides patrons with a vast array of services, including personal ads, chat rooms, online shopping, and news and entertainment reporting. Gay.com organizes its information services into nine distinct headings referred to as "channels," and within each channel patrons are provided with forums in which they can post responses to stories and editorials. This study is based on an analysis of forums accompanying four ostensibly serious news stories appearing on the Gay.com "news" channel. Although anyone visiting the site can read news stories, only those registered with Gay.com can post responses. Thus Gay.com functions much like an online gated community where only those submitting themselves to the inspection process of registration can participate in community discussions. The fluidity of movement that once so characterized cyberspace (Mitra 1997) is now hindered as these commercial sites increasingly regulate entrée through registration processes and membership fees.

Commodification of Communities in Cyberspace

Cyberspace scholars have suggested that emotional investment (Rheingold 1993), social interaction (Mitra 1997), and open channels of communication (Watson 1997) are all vital elements in the formation of online communities. However, Fernback contends that there are additional rudiments involved in constituting a civically engaged community and a viable public sphere. Drawing upon the work of Simmel, Fernback (1997) discusses the essential role played by the dialectic between individual identity and social aggregation, arguing that "the individual cannot be 'actualized' without a sense of contributing to the greater collectivity" (1997: 42). For Fernback a meaningful online community is both a formation in which members are socially and politically invested as well as an "entity of meaning" (1999: 210). That is, as reality is socially constructed, community foremost exists symbolically in the minds of its constituency as a form of "imagined community" (Anderson 1983). Thus, if a community is conceived of as a democratic entity, then it holds the potential to function as a viable public sphere.

However, Fernback expresses concern that the commercialization of cyberspace is changing the very meaning of community, observing that increasingly "community sites are included on the Web for the purpose of selling the notion of communal interaction to a buying public" (2004: 225). For sites such as these the emphasis is less on civic engagement and more on consumption.[3] Dahlberg (2005) argues that this "corporate colonization" of cyberspace recreates "through the internet the dominant discourses and practices of consumer capitalism, marginalizing critical communication central to strong democratic culture" (162).

This increasing domination of cyberspace by the discourses of consumer capitalism is reflected in business literature surrounding online communities. For instance, business authors Hagel and Armstrong (1997) envision online community as "a powerful vehicle for expanding [commercial] markets" (10), proclaiming that "the profit motive will in fact create new forms of virtual communities whose strong commercial element will enhance and expand the basic requirements of community" (xi). In their understanding of community, there is no necessity for civic engagement; there is only the prerequisite that individuals share some mutual affinity by which they can be organized into a viable niche market (Turow 1997). Whereas early pundits on cyberspace saw virtual communities reinvigorating participatory democracy by establishing new venues for radical political dialogue (Rheingold 1993; Watson 1997), Hagel and Armstrong see the most radical potential of online communities being their "impact on the way individuals manage their lives and companies manage themselves" (1997: 216). It is apparent in the business literature that the term "community" has become synonymous with niche market.

The affinity portal is an outgrowth of this corporate perception of community. A cursory examination of these portals supports Fernback's argument that there has been a conceptual shift in understandings of community from an organically evolving social network to a preformulated commodity that can be exchanged in the marketplace. Undeniably these portals offer their patrons immense consumer resources, from online shopping to travel arrangements. Gay.com even offers an online resource developed in cooperation with the Human Rights Campaign for gay job-seekers and consumers interested in the non-discrimination policies of major corporations—the "Corporate Pride Directory."[4] However, such consumer empowerment leaves unanswered how these sites empower their patrons as citizens. As one of the most commercially successful affinity portals, Gay.com provides a useful entry point into a discussion of the implications of these commodified communities for online civic engagement.

Discussing Politics in the Virtual

This study is based on an analysis of 518 postings made by Gay.com patrons in response to four news stories reported on that site. Individual postings ranged from just a few words to several paragraphs in length and were collected between March 1 and April 30, 2005. Stories selection was based on both the unusually high number of patron responses and the distinct political issues each raises—gay civil rights, gay identity politics, the role of organized religion in LGBT life, and sexual representation in the media. The stories include a report on the ban on gay marriage in the state of Kansas, a report on Mary Cheney's book deal, an editorial on the "homophobic legacy" of Pope John Paul II, and finally an announcement of Gay.com's "Come Together" media campaign. This study focuses on forums appearing under the "news" channel as these are the most likely locations where civic discussion will be found.

In evaluating the discourse of Gay.com patrons this study employs an approach from social psychology referred to as "interpretive repertoire" analysis (Potter and Wetherell 1987). This approach is useful in discerning what interpretive strategies Gay.com patrons are employing to make sense of news stories reported on the site. Of particular interest are repertoires that could be characterized as a form of civic engagement. Although tempting to privilege posts making explicit calls for political action, Stromer-Galley (2002) argues that political talk is equally vital to democracy and thus merits due consideration.

Needless to say, postings do not always fit perfectly into one particular interpretive category and a single posting may employ multiple repertoires. The objective here is not to compartmentalize each post discreetly under a single interpretive repertoire, but rather to organize a large body of discourse into recurrent themes which can be understood as "references to underlying meaning systems" (Hermes 1995: 31). These repertoires are not fixed, but rather are derived from patterns of discourse emerging within a particular context. Thus, all the repertoires used here are resultant from the dominant interpretive strategy Gay.com patrons appeared to be using in making sense of these stories and are not reflective of some preformulated listing.

To ensure the anonymity of participants only Gay.com screen names are used in this study. The use of screen names, however, does present ethical considerations for the researcher. Danet, Reudenberg-Wright, and Rosenbaum-Tamari (1997) argue that open online spaces (i.e., those virtual spaces accessible to anyone connected to the internet) are essentially "public" spaces and therefore readily admissible to social science inquiry. In regard to online handles, Danet et al. conclude that "there is no apparent need for researchers to disguise the identity of participants any more than participants have done so themselves" (1997: 8). Although these forums are public venues visited by millions of users, I use actual online handles solely because they represent useful sources of data about how individuals identify themselves within these forums.

Case Study 1: Kansas Voters Ban Gays from Marrying

Published on April 6, 2005, this story reports on Kansas becoming the eighteenth state to ban same-sex marriages. Noting similar bans in Missouri and Louisiana, the story indicates that the amendment banning same-sex couples from the legal rights and benefits of marriage was supported by 70% of the electorate.

Vigorous posting commenced the day the article first appeared in the "news" channel and continued for three consecutive days. In total there were fifty-seven postings with forty-three individuals participating in the discussion. Of those forty-three participants, thirty-six have profiles on Gay.com.[5] In analyzing the posts accompanying this news story, five dominant interpretive repertoires can be discerned. The first and most prevalent can be termed the *comparative repertoire* which is based on comparisons of the citizenry of the so-called "red states" to that of the "blue states," consistently finding the population of "red states" intellectually or morally deficient. This is evident in a post by JohnnyM77, a twenty-eight-year-old male from Minnesota:

> JohnnyM77: The problem with the people in the red states is that they ARE ignorant hicks, otherwise they wouldn't overwhelming vote for ignorant, hateful nonsense like these amendments.[6]

This comparative repertoire often encompassed comparisons of the United State with Canada:

> JohnnyM77: One more reason to move to Canada. You know, the country to the north of us where gays and lesbians are considered human beings?

Interestingly, JohnnyM77's post invokes another interpretive strategy prevalent in this discussion—the *flee repertoire*. In this interpretive tactic, arguments are made for members of the LGBT community to simply move from areas of the country where such anti-gay legislation is enacted, as reflected in this post by soflraver23, a twenty-six-year-old male from Florida:

> Soflraver23: Kansas has nothing to offer any gay person I know. All the more reason to move to a state where we aren't such second-class citizens.

Such posts frequently prompted an opposing interpretive strategy calling for political activism over relocation. This *call-to-action repertoire* generally involved the poster chastizing members of the LGBT community for their politically complacency. Nine of the posts in the forum (approximately 16%) can be characterized as employing this approach, including a post by TattoedTurtel, a thirty-year-old female from Kansas:

> TattoedTurtle: Those who care enough about their rights and their surroundings STAY and FIGHT. We don't relocate—because we want to stay and make things right.

Representative of those employing the call-to-action repertoire, this patron makes an urgent plea for political activism. Many call-to-action posts included some argument for the importance of voting as in a post by Dave018, a 46-yead-old male from Michigan:

> Dave018: What has happen in Kansas, and other states in our country, should be a clear message to the GLBT community. It's time for us to stand up for ourselves. I think too often many of us don't bother to vote, don't bother to talk to our straight friends, about issues such as marriage/union rights.

Some utilizing the call-to-action repertoire cite celebrated civil-rights leaders in making their arguments for political involvement, such as RkyMtnGuy (a thirty-six-year-old male from Colorado), who invokes the words of Martin Luther King Jr. This line of discourse exists in sharp contrast to either the flee or the comparative repertoires which avoid any direct call for civic engagement, leaving unchallenged the political and social status quo.

Two other repertoires appear throughout the discussion: the *personal impact repertoire* which focuses on how this event will effect the patron's personal life, and the *condemning repertoire* which can also be identified as "reap what they sow" line of discourse. This condemning repertoire is apparent in several postings by REXSEX, a forty-four-year-old male from New Jersey:

> REXSEX: this will come back to bite them on the asses—as their beloved President has already been making drastic domestic cuts—like farm subsidies and assistance for poor families etc. (they'll reep what they've sown)

In contrast, those utilizing the "personal impact" repertoire view their posts as an opportunity to communicate feelings they find overwhelming, such as rage or despair. Such posts suggest this forum also serves a therapeutic function for some Gay.com patrons—a place where they can find affirmation and emotional support.

Returning to those key characteristics identified as essential to community formation—emotional investment, communication, and civic engagement—all are evident in the posts examined in this forum. Patrons exhibited a strong emotional investment in the discussion unfolding in the forum suggesting these individuals understand themselves as making meaningful contributions to some broader social collective.

Case Study 2: Mary Cheney Signs Deal to Write Memoir

This report on Mary Cheney's deal with Simon & Schuster to publish her memoirs was published on March 30, 2005. Noting Cheney's $1 million advance from a new subdivision of the publisher devoted to conservative books, the story discusses the "Dear Mary" letter-writing campaign initiated by gay activists to have her publicly acknowledge her sexuality during the 2004 presidential election.

Over the course of a week, seventy-seven posts were made with thrity-seven individuals participating in the discussion. Of those participating, thirty-two had profiles on Gay.com.[7] Whereas the discussion in the prior forum contained several points of consensus, this discussion encompassed strongly divergent interpretations of the political implications of this story. The report of Cheney's book deal essentially functioned as a catalyst for debate surrounding the politics of sexual identity. The discussion was dominated by two distinct repertoires: the *call-to-action repertoire* (an interpretive strategy found in the prior forum) and the *righteous indignation repertoire*. Those assuming the righteous indignation position often used a sarcastic form of parasocial address referred to here as the "Dear Mary" rhetorical strategy. There were, however, a significant number of posts that did not fit neatly within any interpretive repertoire. Many of these posts reflected less an interpretation of the news story and more a response to issues arising within the forum discussion.

The initial posts to the forum reflected the righteous indignation repertoire which generally incorporated three key components: outrage that Cheney is now profiting from her "gay" identity, incredulity that she could have any meaningful contributions to discussions of sexual-minority identity, and resentfulness of her silence during the 2004 presidential election. Often the tone of such posts was sarcastic as reflected in the first post made on the forum:

REXSEX: Well Mary we finally get to hear your long anticipated thoughts, words of deep Meaning . . . after all—These past few months have been life alter-ing for so many fellow gay men and women, and you sat back and said nothing . . . silence was golden, for you.

This form of address was common during the first several hours of posting. In some instances, the anger of users was less veiled by sarcasm, such as in this post by Robinycus, a thirty-one-year-old male in New York:

Robinycus: Shut up Mary! Who cares what you have to say now? Where were you before? Coward. I wouldn't pay for your book nor would I even take it out of the library to read. No thanks.

It is not until the second day of the discussion that the *call-to-action reper-toire* is clearly employed in a patron's posting. Poneystud, a forty-six-year-old male from Pennsylvania, attempts to rally members of the LGBT community to march on Washington:

Poneystud: Why have there not been a march on the white house yet for our rights I would be there, we need to show there are millions of us here and not just a handful who wants this right, [. . .]8 so why don't we fight now and hard for this right, lets get a march planned to the white house.

Poneystud's post had a unifying effect on discussion participants as many of those expressing enthusiastic support for such grassroots political organizing were previously unable to agree on the appropriate response to this story. Tjctoy, a fifty-six-year-old male, builds on Poneystud's post by calling for a boycott of the book:

Tjctoy: THE GAY AND LESBIAN COMMUNITY SHOULD BOYCOTT THIS BOOK AND STORIES THAT FEATURE IT.

Evident in this forum is a vigorous engagement with political topics, in par-ticular the politics of sexual-minority identity. Debated here is the potential impact Cheney's visibility as a lesbian would have had on the election as well as what responsibility she had to the LGBT community by virtue of her sex-uality. This is an engaged, vibrant political discussion, and even those who ostensible share the same political position debate the implications of gay visibility.

Notable is how the discussion is not bounded by the original story. Patrons use the forum to construct a discursive space in which various polit-ical issues surrounding sexual-minority identity are explored. For example, Bookgur199, a twenty-nine-year-old female from Wisconsin, expands the dis-cussion to include a critique of the Republican party:

> Bookgur199: This is a party that claims to care about people, "America," and freedom, yet spends HALF of our tax money on the military, shrinks spending in public schools and public endeavors, pushes for capital punishment, and claims that these choices come from God or the Bible. Ridiculous.

Although initially the discussion centered on Cheney's silence during the election, it comes to encompass debates about the legitimacy of the current presidency and the war in Iraq. Patrons do more than merely post comments on this particular news story; they exploit these online resources to construct a virtual space for political debate. Ultimately, the report of Cheney's deal serves as an entry point into a multi-faceted discussion of the politics of gay identity.

Case Study 3: Legacy of Pope John Paul II

Published on April 2, 2005 only hours before the death of Pope John Paul II, John Gallagher's editorial takes the late pontiff to task for the homophobic policies of his papacy. Gallagher paints the pope as an anti-progressive global force on par with Ronald Reagan or Margaret Thatcher, and warns that if Joseph Ratzinger succeeds John Paul II the Catholic Church would remain an oppressive institution for sexual minorities.

Vigorous postings started within the hour of publication and continued for several days. Due to the vast volume of posts, this analysis will focus on the first 24 hours of posting during which time a total of 305 posts were made with 204 people participating in the discussion. Of those participating, 182 had profiles.[9] Despite the considerable number of individual posts, the overwhelming majority can be sorted into one of two overarching categories: those hostile to the author's position and those sympathetic to the author's argument. Within each faction, a variety of different repertoires were employed in making sense of this story. The initial posts can be characterized as hostile to the editorial, often expressing indignation and defending the legacy of John Paul II. In their defenses some patrons employ the *above reproach repertoire*—an interpretive strategy in which John Paul II is above criticism due either to the frailty of his health or the inviolability of his office. Many of these posts question the tactfulness of writing such an editorial in light of his imminent passing, as exemplified in posts by Noah71250u, a thirty-one-year-old male, and Chjh, a forty-seven-year-old male:

> Noah71250u: as a gay catholic I know it is hard to combine my faith with my lifestyle . . . but to degrade this man in the hour of his death is horrible and in my opinion, shameful of us.

> Ckjh: While most of us gay Catholics do not support and are even troubled by some of his attitudes and teachings, what others clearly fail to appreciate is that

the Pope is our spiritual father . . . or maybe in this case, our "grandfather." Just as you wouldn't take kindly to someone "dissing" your grandfather on his deathbed, no matter how "retrograde" his opinions, so too Catholics don't appreciate attacking our spiritual grandfather.

Such posts make an emotional appeal to the forum regarding the need for discretion in the face of the pope's impending death. In contrast, others employing this repertoire put the pope above admonishment by virtue of his office. The most intriguing, and perhaps troubling, of these posts are those that affirm the hallow status of the pope by condemning homosexuality as "immoral." This is reflected in a post by Mattwm6698, a forty-year-old male from Kansas:

Mattwm6698: The Pope is a great man and a holy man. Homosexuality is immoral, and since he works against things that are immoral, he is against homosexuality. Even I know that my acts of homosexuality are immoral and ungodly.

Most interesting is the contradictions apparent in such posts: many of these individuals express a strong desire to extricate themselves from a "gay lifestyle" and yet continue to patronize a site dedicated to LGBT interests. Though notable, such posts were relatively infrequent and seemed to be largely ignored by other participants.

Some who defend the Pope employ the *reconciliatory repertoire*—an interpretive strategy in which the individual acknowledges the pope's culpability in the homophobic policies of the Catholic Church, and yet compensates for this by promoting his other humanitarian endeavors. This is reflected in a post by Sfrsteel, a thirty-two-year-old male from California:

Sfrsteel: Personally I choose to embrace him for the good he has done, the people he has helped, and the love he has spread. Although I don't agree with some of his teachings, I do respect him for the great things he has accomplished.

These posts attempt to construct a discursive space in which patrons can be both actively Catholic and openly gay. In contrast to those who see homosexuality as immoral, these individuals view same-sex sexual relations as normal and healthy but maligned by the very religious institution they emotionally identify with, as exemplified in a post by Rickyjo, a fifty-two-year-old male from Illinois:

Rickyjo: The Pope is going by his belief's, and I respect him for that. However, it doesn't stop me from going to Mass because I find my spirituality reborn in that celebration. I attend a Mass in Chicago that is sponsored by the Archdiocese of Chicago Gay and Lesbian Outreach group.

Rickyjo's post reflects the complexities involved when sexuality intersects with other axes of identity. Whereas Rickyjo attempts to reconcile his religious and sexual identities, the most overtly hostile posts employ an interpretive strategy dismissing the author's critique of the papacy while calling for some form of reprisal against Gay.com. This interpretive approach can be identified as the *outrage repertoire* and is reflected in a post by Dullessterlingdude, a forty-two-year-old male:

> Dullessterlingdude: I'm incensed by this article. The Legacy of Homophobia is reprehensible, irresponsible and inaccurate. It is so offensive and misleading I am canceling any premium service I have with Gay.com and PlanetOut.

In many such posts, patrons attribute the "inaccuracy" of the article to what they perceive as Gay.com's leftist bias. For instance, Aragorn_117 accuses Gay.com of towing the "party line of the left." Aragorn_177's post reflects many of the characteristics of the problematic "liberal media" argument (Herman and Chomsky 1988) in which commercial media institutions are perceived as promoting the political agendas of the left. Those employing this *liberal media repertoire* interpreted the editorial as inherently skewed, as exemplified in a post by EVTop4Unow, a forty-two-year-old male from Arizona:

> EVTop4Unow: From the comments I see, gay.com should provide some balance in its "news" coverage or it will lose a lot of subscribers! Mr. Gallagher, Get A Life!! I had to smile when I knew what was coming—to bash not only JP2 but the two other punching bags for the left, Ronald Reagan and Margaret Thatcher.

It is not until several hours into the discussion that a significant number of patrons expressed approval of the editorial, often commending Gay.com for providing more critical news coverage than that found in the mainstream media. Employing the *alternative media repertoire,* these patrons saw Gay.com as an invaluable media outlet for marginalized perspectives as evident in a post by Ivyboy1975, a thirty-two-year-old male from New York:

> Ivyboy1975: I am very pleased that someone is telling it like it is. Thank you, gay.com, for providing a reasoned perspective to balance the drollness that TV commentators are dishing out.

Some of these alternative media posts explicitly comment on the importance of gay media outlets. Although only twenty-seven posts (approximately 9%) reflected this alternative media repertoire, these posts made a significant contribution to the forum discussion, often prompting other patrons to acknowledge the importance of the editorial.

What is evident in this collection of posts is the diversity of thought and identification within the LGBT community. Indeed, any notion of the LGBT community as an ideological and cultural monolith is dispelled by the conflicting political positions of those posting to this forum. However, what remained absent was any direct call for offline political action. For the most part, patrons seemed to interpret this story in relation to their own religious convictions and sexual identities. Despite the immense number of posts, there was no significant discussion of civic engagement.

Case Study 4: Gay.com's "Come Together" Campaign

This press release discussing the details of PlanetOut's recent "Come Together" media campaign appeared on the "news" channel on March 1, 2005. Designed for gay-focused print media in key markets (e.g., San Francisco, New York, and Boston), the campaign is composed primarily of images depicting two men in various poses—some physically intimate—involving the American flag.[10] The images relate a narrative of two gay men reconciling their political differences through mutual affection. Notably, the two men appearing in this campaign conform to the predominant paradigm of male attractiveness Locke (1997) found in both mainstream gay and straight media—young, white, lean, and smooth (i.e., lacking body hair). The announcement provided a hyperlink to additional information regarding the creative development of the campaign.[11]

Posting commenced immediately after the campaign was announced and continued throughout the month of March. During this 30-day period, a total of 79 individual posts were made with 72 different individuals participating in the discussion.[12] The majority of posts reflected a negative perception of the campaign with such readings dominated by three interpretive strategies: the *reinforcing gay stereotypes repertoire,* the *disrespectful of the flag repertoire,* and the *unrepresentative repertoire.* Those utilizing the reinforcing gay stereotypes repertoire perceived the campaign as reducing gay men to unidimensional sexual identities, as reflected in this post by Gy_insav, a forty-five-year-old male from Georgia:

> Gy_insav: This is just soft porn to advocate the gay right agenda, which is exactly what the gay rights movement doesn't need!

Those employing this interpretive strategy objected to the campaign on the grounds that it is politically counterproductive, reinforcing oppressive stereotypes of gay men as sexually obsessed. This was evident in a post made by Missprepschool, a twenty-four-year-old female from Vermont:

> Missprepschool: Straight people would not identify with the guys portrayed here, they fit the gay man stereotype too much.

One patron objected on the additional grounds that it reinforces an oppressive paradigm of gay male physical attractiveness. Jojunkiejock, a thirty-two-year-old male from California, expresses concern that the campaign images will prove psychologically damaging to gay men:

> Jojunkiejock: Thanks for perpetuating the myth that one has to look like a model to engage and enjoy gay life. I know my shrink thanks you. And I'm sure al those young, not so perfect boys who see the campaign will thank you for the boots to their mental health and future well being.

Jojunkiejock invoked what has been identified as the "gay male beauty myth" (Campbell 2004), an oppressive index of gay male attractiveness that functions much like the "beauty myth" imposed on women (Wolf 1991). Although Jojunkiejock was the only participant to raise this concern, his post remains significant within the broader context of the discussion.

Another patron, a thirty-five-year-old male from Pennsylvania, who interprets the campaign as politically damaging employs a call-to-action strategy in responding to the campaign:

> John0792: Gay.com is actually owned by PlanetOut, Inc. I urge you to send comments to Jennifer Woodard at the following email . . . jennifer.woodward@ planetoutinc.com This campagne has to be stopped, let's "Come Together" and make it happen.

At the time of the news announcement, Jennifer Woodard was the manager of public relations and her contact information was readily available on the PlanetOut Inc. corporate website. Rburgguy25 builds upon John0792's call-to-action post by presenting a copy of the e-mail he composed to Woodard outlining his grievances with the campaign. Notably, after Rburgguy25 shares his e-mail with the group, several participants post their own calls for stopping the campaign.

Those employing the disrespectful of the flag repertoire based their objections to the campaign on what they saw as the "inappropriate" use of the American flag—an object they view as sacred. This was reflected in a post by Dalguy4you, a forty-year-old male from California:

> Dalguy4you: Show some respect. The flag belongs on a flagpole, not wrapped around naked guys and touching the ground. Who's idea was this anyway? They obviously don't understand how to respect our national symbols.

Those making similar posts expressed greater concerned over the "disrespectful" use of the flag than about the political consequences of the campaign for the LGBT community. In contrast to those employing the reinforcing gay stereotypes repertoire, none of the participants employing the disrespectful of the flag repertoire made any discernable call for political action.

The final group of negative readings employed the unrepresentative repertoire in which the use of two young, thin, white men is seen as denying the diversity of the LGBT community. This pattern of using young white men in advertisements targeting LGBT communities has been noted in other media, including mainstream and specialized magazines (Gluckman and Reed 1997; Sender 1999, 2001). Peñaloza discusses how "pervasive images of white, upper-middle class, 'straight looking' people" often appear at the "expense of those more distanced from and threatening to the mainstream, such as the poor, ethnic/racial/sexual minorities, drag queens, and butch lesbians" (1996: 34). For those employing this interpretive strategy, their objections centered on the campaign's failure to provide representative images of the LGBT community as evident in John0792's initial post:

> John0792: I feel there there's another issue that needs to be addressed: not every gay man is a muscle god. Why not depict real gay men and women to show just how diverse we actually are.

A vocal minority did express their approval of the campaign. Many of those supporting the campaign read the images as ironically playing upon the very stereotypes that oppress sexual minorities. One patron expressing approval, RmyJock, a twenty-seven-year-old male from Ohio, interpreted the campaign from a marketing perspective, seeing the campaign creators as succeeding in their aims:

> RmyJock: Being in marketing myself, I think they did their job. One, they got your attention and put enough fuel into that it made a lot of you think. Not only about what being gay in this country is, but is also made you all ask yourself. What does the flag and everything it stands for, means to me?

In employing this *marketing repertoire*, RmyJock's reading of the campaign aligns with the reading intended by its creative director, Christy Schaefer. In an interview, Schaefer discussed how the campaign was intended to be read ironically, commenting that the use of two "flawless" male models was a play on the "American obsession with all things bright and shiny" (2005). Schaefer also points out that intertextuality was central in the creation of the campaign as the images used play off those visual symbols employed by the Republican Party during the 2004 presidential election. She explains that in creating the campaign the "emphasis shifted from creating brand awareness to creating brand awareness and getting attention to creating brand awareness and making a bold political statement about being gay" (Schaefer 2005). In contrast to the prior forum, there was significantly more consensuses among patrons and even where patrons disagreed there was no heated exchange. The fact that some vociferously defended the campaign is indicative of the sense of safety participants exhibit in expressing their views, even when those views prove unpopular.

Civic Engagement in Commodified Communities: Conclusions

Vibrant debates on a multiplicity of topics—gay civil rights, gay identity politics, the role of organized religion in the LGBT community, media representations of sexual minorities—are evident in each of the forums examined. These politically charged discussions not only demonstrate the diversity of thought and political position among Gay.com patrons, but also could be argued to represent a form of civic engagement. In three of the four forums examined, online discussions led to explicit calls for offline political activism in the form of voting, boycotting, letter writing, or protest marching. The presence of these discourses suggests that even a commercial site can function as a dynamic public sphere in cyberspace, and thus the locus for civically engaged community.

However, this is not a celebratory discussion for these commercial spaces have significant limitations. Though patrons can post responses to the stories reported on Gay.com, patrons cannot publish their own stories. Thus patrons are largely confined to a consumerist role, making selections from what is made available. In this respect, the political discourses occurring in the news forums are contained as Gay.com avoids publishing stories critical of gay marketing or of those commercial sites reserving many of their benefits to those willing and able to pay. In essence, patrons are empowered consumers but not quite full citizens for while they can express their opinions within these forums, they have no vote over what forums will be created.

Although Gay.com cannot determine how news stories will be interpreted—as demonstrated by the varied posts made by patrons—the site can conceivably work towards restricting discussions to select topics. In line with media agenda-setting arguments (McCombs and Shaw 1972), Gay.com influences what will be discussed in the site's forums by regulating what subjects are reported on the site. As a result, the form of civic engagement occurring in these forums is contained within a larger commercial context where discourse critical of capitalism is absent.

Further undermining the potential for a viable public sphere is a business model predicated on surveillance. These portals gather and sell the personal information of patrons to marketing clients (Campbell and Carlson 2002; Campbell 2005). Although these commercial sites are not known to use such information to influence the political activities of patrons, this mined data influences what advertisements and economic opportunities are presented to patrons.[13] This "customizing" of the portal based on consumer profiles hinders the establishment of a truly equalitarian public sphere.

In a final assessment, can these sites be identified as meaningful communities? Fernback holds that community "exists when people invest themselves in social relationships within a group, whether online or offline; but community does not exist where participants are viewed as consumers instead of citizens" (2004: 228). Undeniably, some Gay.com patrons exhibit a sense of personal investment in the discourse manifesting in these forums. However, despite the vibrant political discussions found in these forums, it remains clear that these affinity portals do more to empower their members as consumers than as citizens. Gamson notes in his critique of gay media consolidation that for affinity portals serving "the community and penetrating the market are one and the same" (2003: 265). Indeed, all commercial portals purporting to serve politically marginalized groups beg the question of whether there can be a harmonious balance between the interests of community and the drives of commerce. To this end, McLaine makes an apt observation in his examination of affinity portals targeting racial and ethnic minorities: "Profit and community make curious bedfellows" (2003: 234).

Notes

1. AsianAvenue.com, BlackPlanet.com, and MiGente.com are all enterprises of Community Connect Inc.—a corporation specializing in the construction of online communities targeted at racial and ethnic minorities.
2. http://www.planetoutpartners.com/company/milestones.html
3. Gandy (2002) sees this increasing disparity between audience as citizens with a stake in the public sphere and audience as consumers confined to making choices in the marketplace as the "real digital divide," arguing that new media may only be "widening the distinction between the citizen and the consumer" (448).
4. http://www.gay.com/business/cpd/
5. Of those with profiles, 92% identified as male (thirty-three) and 8% as female (three). This ratio of men-to-women participants was consistent for all of the forums examined here. Considering that PlanetOut Inc.'s marketing kit reports that 85% of their registered members are male, the greater representation of men in this discussion is not necessarily surprising. Of those with profiles, the mean age was thirty-four, with ages ranging from nineteen to fifty-seven. Gay.com personal profiles were the sole sources of demographic information and often key dimensions of a person's social identity—such as race and age—were absent.
6. Posts appear here exactly as they did on the forum at the time of observation, complete with typos, misspellings, and unorthodox uses of grammar.
7. Thirty participants identified as male (94%) and two as female (6%). The reported ages ranged from twenty to fifty-six with the mean age being thirty-six.
8. A portion of this post was omitted due to length constraints.
9. A total of 179 identified as male (94%) and three as female (2%). The mean age was thirty-five with ages ranging from 18 to 101. Again it should be noted that this demographic information was self-reported.

10. The press release comments on the prominent use of the flag in the campaign, proclaiming that the "flag belongs to all Americans, and we are proud to call ourselves Gay Americans" (PlanetOut 2005).

11. In contrast to the many advertisements appearing on the Gay.com portal which are done by external marketing agencies, this campaign represents an in-house creation of PlanetOut Inc.

12. Of those participating, fifty-six had complete profiles on Gay.com, with fifty-five identifying as male and one as female. The mean age was thirty-four, with ages ranging from 18 to 100.

13. In their 2005 sales kit, PlanetOut Inc. proclaims "a thorough knowledge of our members and the ability to target messages to individuals based on the demographic information and usage information we have collected" (6), and that their marketing database allows them "to deliver unique messages directly to specific customers" (7). The PlanetOut Inc. sales kit is available at: http://www.planetoutinc.com/sales/.

References

Anderson, B. 1983. *Imagined Communities: Reflections on the Origin and Spread of Nationalism*. London: New Left Books.

Baym, N. 1995. "The Emergence of Community in Computer-Mediated Communication," in S. Jones (Ed.), *CyberSociety: Computer-Mediated Communication and Community* (pp. 138–163). Thousand Oaks, CA: Sage Publications.

Campbell, J. E. 2005. "Outing PlanetOut: Surveillance, Gay Marketing, and Internet Affinity Portals." *New Media & Society 7*(5), 663–683.

Campbell, J. E. 2004. *Getting it on online: Cyberspace, Gay Male Sexuality, and Embodied Identity*. New York: Haworth Press.

Campbell, J. E., and Carlson, M. 2002. "Panopticon.com: Online Surveillance and the Commodification of Privacy." *Journal of Broadcasting & Electronic Media 46*(4), 586–606.

Computer Weekly. 1999. "Affinity Portals." Computer Weekly November 4, online document available at www.findarticles.com/cf_dls/m0COW/1999_Nov_4/57604021

Correll, S. 1995. "The Ethnography of an Electronic bar: The Lesbian Café." *Journal of Contemporary Ethnography 24*(3), 270–298.

Dahlberg, L. 2005. "The Corporate Colonization of Online Attention and the Marginalization of Critical Communication?" *Journal of Communication Inquiry 29*(2), 160–180.

Danet, B., Reudenberg-Wright, L., and Rosenbaum-Tamari, Y. 1997. "'Hmmm . . . Where's That Smoke Coming From?' Writing, Play and Performance on Internet Relay Chat." *Journal of Computer-Mediated Communication 2*(4). Hypertext publication, retrieved July 4, 1998, from http://cwis.usc.edu/dept/ annenberg/v012/issue4/danet.html

Fernback, J. 1997. "The Individual within the Collective: Virtual Ideology and the Realization of Collective Principles," in S. Jones (Ed.), *Virtual Culture: Identity and Communication in Cybersociety* (pp. 36–54). London: Sage Publications.

Fernback, J. 1999. "There is a there there: Notes towards a Definition of Cybercommunity," in S. Jones (Ed.), *Doing Internet Research: Critical Issues and Methods for Examining the Net* (pp. 203–220). London: Sage Publications.

Fernback, J. 2004. "Community as Commodity: Empowerment and Consumerism on the Web," in M. Consalvo (Ed.), *Internet Research Annual: Selected Papers from the Association of Internet Researchers Conferences 2000–2002* (pp. 224–230). New York: Peter Lang.

Gamson, J. 2003. "Gay media, Inc.: Media Structures, the New Gay Conglomerates, and Collective Sexual Identities," in M. McCaughey and M. Ayers (Eds.), *Cyberactivism: Online Activism in Theory and Practice* (pp. 255–278). New York: Routledge.

Gandy, O. 2002. "The Real Digital Divide: Citizens versus Consumers," in L. Lievrouw and S. Livingstone (Eds.), *Handbook of New Media: Consequences of ICTs* (pp. 448–460). London: Sage Publications.

Gluckman, A., and Reed, B. 1997. "The Gay Marketing Moment," in A. Gluckman and B. Reed (Eds.), *Homo Economics: Capitalism, Community, and Lesbian and Gay Life* (pp. 3–9). New York: Routledge.

Hagel, J., and Armstrong, A. 1997. *Net Gain: Expanding Markets through Virtual Communities*. Boston: Harvard Business School Press.

Herman, E., and Chomsky, N. 1988. *Manufacturing Consent: The Political Economy of the Mass Media*. New York: Pantheon Books.

Hermes, J. 1995. *Reading Women's Magazines: An Analysis of Everyday Media Use*. Cambridge, UK: Polity Press.

Kendall, L. 2002. *Hanging Out in the Virtual Pub: Masculinities and Relationships Online*. Berkeley: University of California Press.

Liss, K. 2000. "Call Them What You Will, 'Portals' Are Here to Stay." *Working Knowledge* (March 7). Online document retrieved June 1, 2005, from http://www.hbsworkingknowledge.hbs.edu/

Locke, P. 1997. "Male Images in the Gay Mass Media and Bear-Oriented Magazines: Analysis and Contrast," in L. Wright (Ed.), *The Bear Book: Readings in the History and Evolution of a Gay Male Subculture* (pp. 103–140). New York: Harrington Park Press.

McCombs, M., and Shaw, D. 1972. "The Agenda-Setting Function of the Mass Media." *Public Opinion Quarterly 36*(2), 176–187.

McLaine, S. 2003. "Ethnic Online Communities: Between Profit and Purpose," in M. McCaughey and M. Ayers (Eds.), *Cyberactivism: Online Activism in Theory and Practice* (pp. 233–254). New York: Routledge.

Mitra, A. 1997. "Virtual Commonality: Looking for India on the Internet," in S. Jones (Ed.), *Virtual Culture: Identity and Communication in Cybersociety* (pp. 55–790). London: Sage Publications.

Peñaloza, L. 1996. "We're Here, We're Queer, and We're Going Shopping! A Critical Perspective on the Accommodation of Gays and Lesbians in the U.S. Marketplace," in D. Wardlow (Ed.), *Gays, Lesbians, and Consumer Behavior: Theory, Practice, and Research Issues in Marketing* (pp. 9–41). New York: Haworth Press.

Potter, J., and Wetherell, M. 1987. *Discourse and Social Psychology: Beyond Attitudes and Behavior*. London: Sage Publications.

Rheingold, H. 1993. *The Virtual Community: Homesteading on the Electronic Frontier*. Reading, UK: Addison-Wesley.

San Francisco Chronicle. 2005. "On the Record: Lowell Selvin." January 23, B1.

Schaap, F. 2002. *The Words That Took Us There: Ethnography in a Virtual Reality*. Amsterdam, Netherlands: Aksant Academic Publishers.

Schaefer, C. 2005. Phone interview on July 29.

Sender, K. 1999. "Selling Sexual Subjectivities: Audiences Respond to Gay Window Advertising." *Critical Studies in Mass Communication 16*, 172–196.

Sender, K. 2001. "Gay Readers, Consumers, and a Dominant Gay Habitus: 25 Years of the Advocate Magazine." *Journal of communication 51*(1), 73–99.

Shaw, D. 1997. "Gay Men and Computer Communication: A Discourse of Sex and Identity in Cyberspace," in S. Jones (Ed.), *Virtual Culture: Identity & Communication in Cybersociety* (pp. 133–145). London: Sage Publications.

Stromer-Galley, J. 2002. New Voices in the Public Sphere: Political Conversation in the Internet Age. Unpublished dissertation, University of Pennsylvania.

Turow, J. 1997. *Breaking Up America: Advertisers and the New Media World*. Chicago: University of Chicago Press.

Watson, N. 1997. "Why We Argue about Virtual Community: A Case Study of the Phish.Net Fan Community," in S. Jones (Ed.), *Virtual Culture: Identity & Communication in Cybersociety* (pp. 102–132) London: Sage Publications.

Wolf, N. 1991. *The Beauty Myth: How Images of Beauty Are Used against Women*. New York: Anchor Books.

12. Life Outside the Latex: HIV, Sex, and the Online Barebacking Community

Sharif Mowlabocus

Since 1984, when the first AIDS-related deaths were reported in the UK, British gay male culture has sought to educate itself about HIV transmission, prevention strategies and treatment regimes. Initial government inaction resulted in voluntary organizations and charities (such as the Terrence Higgins Trust and later, Gay Men Fighting AIDS) being set up by the communities most affected by the virus. Today, the relationship between HIV prevention groups and gay culture remains deeply binding and the gay press continues to provide a platform for awareness campaigns and HIV-related news. Research into HIV awareness among men using cruising grounds in Greater London confirms the important role the gay press has played in terms of HIV education (Scott et al. 1998), and Simon Watney has similarly recognized the function of the gay press during the first ten years of the epidemic (Watney 2000: 113).

Yet while the narrative of HIV develops, both in Britain and across the globe, one shift in Western gay men's sexual practices has proven to be a stumbling block for the gay print media. In 1999, *The Pink Paper* printed an interview with BBC radio broadcaster Nigel Wrench, in which he admitted to having had anonymous unprotected sex since being diagnosed HIV positive. This led to a flurry of responses within the mainstream and gay press. While the former used Wrench's "confession" to highlight the continuing "deviancy" of homosexuality, the latter sought to distance "mainstream" gay culture from such behavior. Responding to Wrench's interview, Mathew Hudson, editor of *Boyz* magazine, was quoted as saying that "I thought if you cared about someone, you'd want to do your best to protect them, not put their lives at risk—or your own" (Wells 2000: 2). While Hudson's response was muted the message was clear; such behavior was not to be tolerated.

Much of the press coverage suggested that barebacking was something new, and Gabriel Rotello has described the term as the glamorizing of unsafe sex claiming that

> the popularization of that term seems to indicate a shift from describing unpro-
> tected sex as unsafe sex, to describing it as sexy and alluring, which the term
> barebacking implies. (Quoted in Mallinger 1998)

The word "bareback" has invested the previously taboo practice of unprotected anal sex between men with a "cool" deviancy that has allowed some to legitimate and eroticize unsafe sexual contact. While the likes of Hudson have sought to separate this new subculture from wider gay culture, others have placed the blame for the rise in barebacking firmly at its door, criticizing it for allowing gay men to construct "lives in ways that enable them—and sometimes even encourage them—to forgo safer sex" (Signorile 1997: 73–74). The hedonistic lifestyle Signorile associates with gay culture may indeed provide a context for unsafe sexual interactions but such criticism often stops short of critically engaging with the cultural formations and prac-tices it attacks. Rarely do such arguments seek to understand why barebacking has become popular; in short, the criticism is never fully contextualized. Contextualizing barebacking reveals it as a by-product of earlier safer-sex campaigns, the same campaigns that successfully saved the lives of millions during the 1980s and the 1990s. And while barebacking appears to be at odds with HIV prevention, it is in fact closely related to such work. One of the most ardent supporters of this argument is Eric Rofes who has sought to re-evaluate the effectiveness of the condom code together with the attitudes gay spokesmen and healthcare professionals have toward contemporary gay male culture. He sees the "state of emergency" reaction to AIDS in the 1980s as being an effective short-term response to the epidemic, but ques-tions its effectiveness in long-term gay men's health work:

> If we created this narrative of gay heroism in the 1980s, fabricating politically
> useful explanations for the decline in new infections in order to win public sym-
> pathy and gain funding for AIDS services, we should not be surprised that it has
> come around to confront us just a few years later. [. . .] the heroic narrative of
> the first decade of AIDS couldn't help but be transfigured into a demonic nar-
> rative in the second decade. (Rofes 1998: 201)

Damon Reaney similarly comments that as a result of "the cast-iron 'wear a condom every time' safer-sex message" unprotected sex has been posi-tioned as a "taboo subject" within gay culture. This silence has been criti-cized by HIV-positive gay men who feel that the " 'black or white' nature of the safer-sex message obscures the particular circumstances of their lives"

(Reaney 2000). While appearing to be the antithesis of HIV prevention programs then, barebacking is in fact the illegitimate child of the condom code. Since the Wrench interview, barebacking has received scant coverage within the British gay press. While other "threats" to safe sex adherence (such as those caused by recreational drug use, "harder" practices such as fisting and S&M, and "heat of the moment" slip-ups) have been recognized and rationally discussed within gay culture, the conscious decision to engage in high risk sexual activities has been dismissed by editors and journalists alike. After the initial condemnation, and in spite of the fact that many commentators are claiming that this practice is on the rise (Signorile 1997: 73–74; Rofes 1998: 187–205; Sheon and Plant 1997) barebacking seems to have been dropped as a subject worthy of attention. Some HIV agencies such as GMFA have succeeded in running brief awareness campaigns in the press, addressing the issue of barebacking, but there has been no sustained discussion of this sexual practice within the press itself, and those engaged in barebacking have rarely been given an opportunity to voice their side of the story. Indeed, when defending[1] their decision to run the "barebacking" advertisement, GMFA cited the "reactionary and ill-informed" attitude toward the phenomenon adopted by the gay press as a reason why such a campaign was needed (MetroM8).

Faced with this media blackout, men who have chosen to bareback have turned to the Internet as their primary method of communication. This in turn has led to the Web being cited as the "home" of barebacking, Michael Scarce commenting that the bareback community "flourishes in private houses and especially on the Internet" (1999). Of course, the Web does not guarantee total freedom of expression, and commercial IRC channels dedicated to barebacking have been closed down due to legal and commercial pressures (Taylor 1999). That said, the Internet has facilitated the creation of spaces dedicated to all aspects of barebacking from the purely pornographic to the political and the instructional.

This chapter develops a reading of two specific Web spaces that critique contemporary understandings of HIV, formulate counter-discourses surrounding safer sex, and renegotiate some gay men's relationship to disease, fear, and queer masculinity. I do not aim to celebrate or demonize either the activities or identities embodied by the term "bareback." More often than not, taking sides in such debates results in a loss of critical rigor as we begin to lose sight of what is really going on. Rather, through these two case studies, I seek to explore how a sexual subculture has utilized the Internet in order to highlight what can be learned from an examination of such spaces within the context of ongoing and future HIV prevention work.

Creating a Space for Barebacking

Type "bareback" into an Internet search engine and the results are likely to list in excess of two million hyperlinks to websites ostensibly catering to the bareback community. Reflecting the fact that sex is the most commonly searched subject on the Web, many of these entries are for pornographic sites offering images and video clips depicting bareback sex. These often appear alongside fetish pornography: to many, bareback sex is a fetish that—like other fetishes—is thrilling because of its deviant status. However, alongside the purely pornographic are links to websites that, while often featuring some pornographic content, do provide a space for barebacking to be discussed, identities and practices negotiated, and (some might say ironically) safer sex information to be disseminated.

That the Internet has been taken up as the preferred method of communication by the barebacking community is of little surprise. Mukerji and Simon have discussed the importance that the Internet holds for groups who have been discredited and/or rejected by wider society. In their study of two marginalized scientific communities, they conclude that

> where authoritative media were undermining the legitimacy of these communities and creating problems of impression management that were both personally and socially difficult to face, computer networks provided participants with opportunities for trying to grapple with their common problems and prepare to re-enter the public sphere as respectable social actors. (Mukerji and Simon 1998: 271)

Similarly, having been presented with two options by the gay press—exile or condemnation—barebackers have turned to the Internet as an important method of communication. However, unlike Mukerji and Simon's scientific communities, barebackers have not fallen out of favor or become stigmatized. Barebacking, as an identity, a practice and a choice has been *formed* as a result of such stigma and condemnation. It is also increasingly tied to the networked communication systems that it utilizes. Any analysis of barebacking must acknowledge the integration of the WWW, bulletin boards, and other digital spaces within this sexual subculture, indeed, barebacking has "emerged" during a period of increasing digital immersion. Of course the practice of unprotected anal sex between men is neither confined to virtual environments, nor confined to this century. The difference between these historical acts and the new practice of barebacking lies in the definition of the latter.

The term "barebacking" was officially recognized at the CHAPS[2] conference in 2002 when it was defined as "non-negotiated unprotected sex where one of the partners is HIV positive and does not know, or care, about the status of his partner" (Carter 2000). This definition raises several questions, particularly surrounding the presumed centrality of HIV to the sex act. Therefore, within the context of this chapter a revised definition of barebacking (as opposed to pre-AIDS gay male sex) is posited. Barebacking signifies male-male anal sex without the use of condoms but within the context of an HIV-informed gay male culture. As a practice and a set of identities it has been formed out of HIV discourses, though it is not governed by them. The erotic economy of barebacking is intimately linked with the condom code, though condoms are consciously eschewed by those who participate in bareback sex, and while many barebackers cite corporeal connection as a primary motivation behind barebacking, it is within the disembodied spaces created by networked communication systems that the subculture associated with this sexual practice has been most vocal.

This definition draws on and is strengthened by studies such as those carried out by Sheon and Plant (1997), Mallinger (1998), Scarce (1999), and Halkitis et al. (2003), all of whom have highlighted the importance of using the Internet as a means of sourcing interview cohorts from the barebacking community. Sheon and Plant state that "the barebacking phenomenon has been most extensively debated on the web" and that the "anonymity of the web" allows "forbidden desires" to be articulated within a relatively safe forum (Sheon and Plant 1997: 3). Scarce also cites the freedom from "stigma attached to openly soliciting unsafe sex" (1999: XX) as being an attractive facet of new media.

However, little has been written about the virtual spaces created by the barebacking community and it is within these spaces that this chapter locates its focus. The two Web spaces discussed here offer a variety of services and membership levels and are more than just pornographic websites. They provide environments in which gay men interested in barebacking can meet and interact with one another. Often the objective of such interaction is sex but there are occasions where advice is sought, or where the fantasy of bareback sex is ultimately the goal. Whatever the type of interaction, in each instance it can be said that gay men are using virtual spaces to interact with the subject in ways that have previously been denied to them.

Kitsch Critique and a "Healthy Combo Platter"
—BAREBACKJACK.COM

Claiming to be the longest-running online space dedicated to the subject, BAREBACKJACK.COM (BBJ) has been providing information, comment, and pornography to barebackers since 1998. While the site has undergone a number of design changes during its lifetime, the current aesthetic is reminiscent of a 1950s American diner. Having entered the site, users are offered a "menu" of different options (the "healthy combo platter," "smorg-ass-board," and "hot spicy links") depending on membership status, and "vintage" pornographic images are juxtaposed with cartoon-style illustrations reminiscent of the period. Similarly the language of the site plays on the discursive style of the 1950s:

> Mmm Mmmm! All sorts of yummy treats can be had when you go for our Homepages. We give you meat and potatoes from around the world (and the men they're attached to), each one with its own home-style flavor [sic] as individual as the guys who cooked 'em up. (Barebackjack.com)

The design is notably different to many gay sex websites and the decision to adopt the kitsch aesthetic style of 1950s Americana runs deeper than a question of taste:

> The mid-century style is more than just retro. It represents a unique period in our culture . . . a period of post-war prosperity, [. . .] massive social, economical, and population growth . . . and all the exuberance and optimism that went along with those times [. . .] I wanted it to represent the exuberance we feel when we liberate ourselves from the 80's mindset by choosing to refuse condoms. (Barebackjack.com)

Moving beyond its aesthetic appeal then, Jack (the Webmaster) draws parallels between this period of economic and technological growth and the decision to bareback. In doing so, barebacking is recontextualized linking it to a time prior to the advent of AIDS (indeed, prior to the formation of a gay community). The reference to a period of Western optimism, growth, and advancement is integral to the way in which the twin issues of bareback sex and condom use are explored within this space: both issues are woven into the very fabric of the website.

This nostalgic twist may appear dangerously naïve, akin to sticking one's head in the sand and dreaming of a time when sex was supposedly "free and simple." But a closer reading reveals quite the opposite. The design of this space supports the development of a sophisticated critique of gay male sexuality and the "condom code," which remains central to HIV prevention strategies in the West. Central to this critique is the way in which chronological time frames are juxtaposed. While the health information pages discuss topics such as HIV, recreational drug use, and safe sex—all subjects to be found within the contemporary gay press—the style and mode of presentation effects a "severing" from contemporary gay culture. In fact there is no reference to a particular gay scene: no suggestion of a gay enclave or ghetto.[3] Whether intentional or not, this collision of contemporary content with an older aesthetic style is highly effective in extracting gay male sexuality from the network of discourses that have governed gay male sexuality since the early 1980s. In doing so, HIV is "cut off" from gay sex: at BBJ the virus no longer "controls" or "dictates" homosexual practices as some barebackers feel it has done. This is not to suggest that the virus is ignored; as the mission statement demonstrates, quite the opposite is true:

> We believe that men can enjoy hot, unprotected sex best if they are informed about the risks involved and what they can do to minimize those risks to themselves and others. We're the only bareback site on the internet that refuses to sweep HIV under the carpet. (Barebackjack.com)

Though inaccurate in it's claim (HIV is discussed on other barebacking websites), BBJ is unique in priding itself on being first and foremost a health information website. Many of the articles linked to the site or written by the Webmaster discuss HIV, and while the 1950s theme harks back to a pre-AIDS era, claims as to the fallacy of the virus or the end of AIDS are absent. However, the severing effect created by the tension between content and form allows bareback sex to operate outside of the rhetoric of the condom code. By placing gay sex outside of contemporary gay culture Jack is able to argue for the right to have bareback sex. He also reminds users that HIV— and by extension, condoms—is an *intrusion* into gay sex not integral to it. In doing so, BBJ creates a space in which the browser is invited to rethink his relationship to sex and realize his choices:

> It seems rather appropriate to the bareback set to reinvestigate this style. [. . .] As gay men who bareback, we also know the forgotten pleasures of no-barrier sex, and feel comfortable carrying on this natural tradition. (Barebackjack.com)

The design of the website looks back to this period of optimism and simultaneously suggests that through this looking back, gay men can "rediscover" bareback sex in the future. This carries with it wider ramifications when we consider the percentage of gay men populating the British and American gay scenes who have come of sexual age under the shadow of HIV. Sean O. Strub notes that a "generation of gay men was defined by AIDS" and while young gay men today are not "immersed [. . .] in the immediacy and the urgency of the epidemic" their sexual identities are still shaped by the virus (Strub 1999: XX); it has become a bodiless specter at the center of gay culture.[4] Alan Sinfield has similarly commented that in Britain, gay men have not "moved beyond" AIDS but rather have yet to pass through it. (1998: 89–91). This disparity between the lived experience of HIV and the specter of AIDS is integral to what Wayne Hoffman has termed the "sexual devolution" of gay male culture (1996: 341). Recognizing this devolution is integral to understanding why the "discovery" of "real" gay sex is perhaps even more tangible—and tempting for those populating the contemporary gay scene.

BBJ does not offer a fantasy of an HIV-free world but it does provide an opportunity to think, talk, and have sex outside of the discourses—and judgments—that surround HIV. The tension between content and form means that at BBJ, the unspeakable gets spoken and new understandings of gay male sexuality are explored and validated. And once more, HIV is positioned as an intrusion, not an integral facet.

> In the hysteria over HIV and AIDS, many people (including healthcare professionals) have apparently forgotten that one person in a sexual encounter must have the virus in order to transmit it. (barebackjack.com)

While HIV agencies acknowledge the need for the virus to be present in order for it to be transmitted, popular discourse has mythologized HIV, transforming it from a virus into a behavioral effect ("bareback sex = HIV infection"). Against this discursive backdrop, and in response to the CHAPS definition, BBJ provides a forum in which unprotected sex can be interrogated using the situated knowledge of the barebacking community: that not all barebackers are HIV positive, and that barebacking does not necessarily involve HIV transmission. BBJ thus offers a competing discourse to that currently in circulation.

Having distanced HIV from gay sex and validated bareback sex ("natural unbarriered sex is true sex"), HIV is re-introduced within a framework of relevant safer sexual health advice. In contrast to the stereotype of the ill-informed, psychologically impaired barebacker who fails to face up to his sexual responsibilities, BBJ demands that users engage with this new framework from the outset. In order to enter the site, browsers are presented with two images, that of a condom and of a brain, and must answer the question "safer sex begins with?" by clicking on the correct image. By asking this question—and demanding that users answer it before gaining access to the website—BBJ establishes a space outside of the condom code in which gay men can identify their own sexual autonomy, something that the Webmaster sees as having been eroded through the condom code.

The site does not position unprotected sex as politically subversive (as perhaps sex radicals such as Tony Valenzuela or Stephen Gendin would) but the very existence of this space serves to critique the effectiveness of the condom code safe sex model. In opposition to this model, it offers a range of relevant and practical sexual health advice tailored to the needs of barebackers. Health awareness is taken seriously here but so is the fact that relying on the condom code will only alienate the barebacking community. While admitting that HIV may well be avoided by other websites, here the bareback community is offered practical information on HIV transmission, ways of reducing risk and hard facts (i.e., "There is no cure for HIV") relevant to their own sexual choices.

This tailoring of appropriate health advice is evident in the Webmaster's discussion of recreational drug use where he makes a distinction between barebackers and "tweakers" (drug users). Jack's discourse echoes recent HIV campaigns, which have identified drug use on the commercial gay scene as leading to high-risk sexual activity. But BBJ comes into its own when it re-contextualizes these messages so that they become relevant to the barebacking community:

> Condom use and/or honest discussion about HIV status is infrequent in these venues, [inhabited by tweakers] Being in control of yourself and your actions is your best weapon against HIV transmission. (Barebackjack.com)

It should however be remembered that while the website provides useful information on HIV, in this space bareback sex and HIV do not go hand in hand—as is implied by the CHAPS definition. In a response to a letter entitled "are there negative barebackers like me?" Jack identifies himself as both a barebacker and HIV negative. He goes on to say:

> I cannot stress enough that barebacking is NOT about passing the virus along to others. Barebacking IS about getting the maximum level of pleasure out of fucking. (Barebackjack.com)

Jack's negative status influences the site content and HIV is positioned as something to be engaged with as an issue but not as an aim. The Webmaster's HIV status is particularly pertinent and he uses his website to communicate not only his desires but his choices and responsibilities: Jack is an HIV negative barebacker who wishes to remain that way. In concluding his response to the letter he states:

> I have been selective in deciding who I'll fuck and under which circumstances, I have managed so far to remain negative. (Barebackjack.com)

This would at first seem poor advice; adopting a strategy of harm reduction based solely upon assumption is both ignorant and irresponsible. However, within the context of the website we learn that BBJ is not promoting a "moderation = safe sex" model of HIV prevention but is reminding the addressee that sex, like any other area of life, is about judgment, and responsibility; Jack does not advocate sexual moderation as a solution to HIV and neither does this model form the bedrock of contemporary HIV strategies. It perhaps should be noted, however, that the call for gay men to form monogamous relationships (and the consequent political lobbying for the right to marriage), together with the adoption of HIV/AIDS as a reason why such coupling should be promoted, pervades the rhetoric of the Gay Right, emanating from the likes of Gabrielle Rotello (1997) and Andrew Sullivan (1989), and groups such as the Log Cabin Republicans and TORCHE (to

name the most notable). Considering the importance of these figures within
contemporary Western gay culture it is unsurprising to see the moderation
model creeping into discussions of safe sex, for all the wrong reasons. While
HIV agencies no longer appear to sanction this rhetoric, it is clear that the
attendant popular discourses such as those found in the gay press continue to
perpetuate such truth-claims.

BBJ uses the medium of networked communications in order to bypass
this rhetoric. In the "fictional" diner, Jack offers users the opportunity to separate sexual choice from moral judgment. The surreal juxtaposition of frank
sexual discussion and kitsch 1950s domesticity not only reveals sex to be con-
trived and discursively constructed, but also validates alternative sexual health
messages that find no avenue for discussion in contemporary gay culture. As
such, BBJ demonstrates the potential of the Internet to put forward arguments that find little or no space for articulation within the offline spheres of
gay men's lives. In response to the singular response to bareback sex given by
the gay press (echoing the gradual move toward a more center-right political
ideology), the Web has become a rich resource for many who wish to challenge the commonly held assumptions of gay culture, the gay media, and
indeed, the average gay man. BBJ does not coerce the user to engage in bareback sex but it does demand an interrogation gay male culture's relationship
to HIV and the condom code.

"Who's Afraid of the Big Bad Bug?"
—BAREBACK.COM

By contrast, BAREBACK.COM (BBC) initially appears to support the claims
made by the tabloid press that new media technologies are responsible for
promoting sexual deviancy. If BBJ is a polemical website that aims to (re)edu-
cate gay men about sexual choice and sexual risk, BBC resembles an SM play-
room that appears to offer little in the way of rational discussion. Members
are invited to take part in the virtual orgy of the website as they throw cau-
tion to the wind in the search of the ultimate sexual high. The mission statement serves to illustrate what the browser can expect to engage with beyond
the site entrance:

> Welcome to the new BAREBACK.COM. We are the premiere home for all you
> studs who crave the feeling only raw sex can provide. Who's afraid of the big,
> bad bug? Not our little piggies. We'll huff and we'll puff and we'll blow your
> Dick Down! Chase those bugs all over town like the horny toad you are. Get
> dangerous and seek out new perversions and new fetishes. (Bareback.com)

The pastel colors and yesteryear cartoons of BBJ are substituted for black
backgrounds and sharp metallic fonts at BBC. And, as with the former space,

the site design reflects the content and attitudes promoted in this environ-ment. Banners, consisting of slogans set against collages of hardcore pornog-raphy, urge users to "leave the Trojans at home, just bring your bone" and promote bareback sex; "no glove? Good, then get ready for hot love." In contrast to BBJ, here users are not asked to *question* their dependence on the condom code, but instead are ordered to *forget* their former beliefs in the pursuit of the ultimate sexual fetish.

It would at first appear that Rotello's assertion—that barebacking glam-orizes what was previously understood as unsafe—holds true. BBC celebrates the deviant, and unsafe sexual contact is positioned as radical, new and—most importantly—sexy. This "devil-may-care" attitude contrasts the discourse of BBJ and the mission statement points toward childish rebellion rather than rational discussion. Such immaturity reveals itself further through the dis-course of BBC, plundering childhood narratives in order to convey a sense of playful libidinality which underscores barebacking in this space. The mission statement appropriates the "Three Little Pigs" fairy tale as the wolf becomes the virus; the Webmaster asking "who's afraid of the big bad bug? Not our little piggies." This may seem crass but it explains how HIV and bareback sex are negotiated at BBC. There is a clear reversal of power relations at the heart of both the fairy-tale narrative and, by extension, the site as whole. Fear over HIV transmission ("the bug") is equated with a child's fear of the fic-tional wolf character and, while HIV is not positioned as similarly fictional, it is decentered via this narrative. "Real" men don't worry about HIV at BBC; here they reclaim their sexuality outside of the dominant "parental" dis-courses of HIV prevention: "Don't tell your mommy, but it's just about time to meet the boy toy of your dreams" (Bareback.com).

Michael, the Webmaster, continues this discursive style throughout the website. In the introduction to the forum he writes as follows:

> Prepare to take your first step out of the condom closet. [. . .] Being mean or lecturing any members of the community is not allowed. Health class was in high school—we have grown up! Rubbers are for women and children on a rainy day[5]—not for a little piggy's bedroom! (Bareback.com)

Ironically, through the use of childhood motifs (fairy-tale characters, ref-erences to "mommy" and high school for instance) Michael isn't suggesting a regression back to childhood (which would subsequently involve forgetting or denying HIV), but is rather advocating *growth*. Gay men are here posi-tioned as immature for allowing themselves to be controlled by the "AIDS Nazis" of gay culture. At BBC, Michael offers a space in which he believes gay men can escape this control and become sexually mature.

To many this will seem ridiculous, not to mention dangerous; stating that barebackers need to come out of the "condom closet" suggests that bareback sex is in some sense more "real," more queerly correct, than adhering to the condom code. However it is possible to plot a course through recent critiques of HIV prevention (and specifically the proscription of bareback sex) in order to identify how Michael reaches this conclusion. Reaney has asserted that the taboo over barebacking "hinders [HIV-positive gay men's] ability to rationalize their desire for bareback sex" (Reaney 2000) and, when commenting on the closure of the Gay.com chat room, Mark Taylor stated that "our health is our own individual responsibility and these guys have the right to risk their lives if they choose to.' He then goes on to make the point that "queers should know better than most how futile it is to try and repress unconventional or unpopular sexual practices" (Taylor 1999: XX).

BBC's use of childhood motifs can be seen as a response to such control. While there is little direct discussion of this response on the website, it is clear that at BBC choice and not rhetoric governs individual sexuality. And, as with BBJ, time frames are central to this environment. While the former involves a collision of contemporary content with historical form, the latter involves a return to childhood in order to critique the condom code, which some feel has restricted gay male sexuality.

But the manipulation of time is not the only similarity between the two spaces. Though BBC ostensibly rejects the "lectures" of the more polemical BBJ the Webmaster *does* offer a similar advice column. The language of Michael's responses differs from Jack's but the content suggests a similar political viewpoint. Most notably, Michael employs a critique of the condom code in order to validate the right to choose bareback sex. In response to a user who questions the risks involved in bareback sex the Webmaster begins by stating:

> No sex act is completely safe. Condoms break, people get caught up in the moment, Shit happens. So you need to get over the idea of safe sex.

He then continues

> Yes, barebacking feels much better. It is the most intimate act of love that can exist between two men. And, despite what Bareback Nazis say there are ways to make it safer without wrapping your crank in latex. (Bareback.com)

Michael provides a list numerous suggestions for safer barebacking, including monogamy, but also the use of lubricant to avoid bleeding, partner selection and the avoidance of semen exchange. Some of these suggestions echo HIV prevention campaigns prevalent in the West since the mid-nineties but with one important difference. They are articulated in a space in which choosing to bareback is socially accepted. Michael appears to be acutely aware of this fact and uses it to his advantage. Having stated that "no sex act is completely safe" he comments that while breeders always preach sa[f]e sex, they seem to have a lot of babies and abortions which means they don't always practice what they preach. (Bareback.com)

This is but one of example of how the Webmaster aligns safer-sex campaigning and the "Bareback Nazis" with heterosexuality—or rather heteronormativity. As quoted above, at BBC, condoms are considered the domain of heterosexual sex ("rubbers are for women") and this heterosexualizing of the tensions at the center of contemporary safe sex campaigns—and by extension barebacking—pervades the advice column. This contrasts the polemics of BBJ, where Jack critiques the gay community as a whole:

It is by exercising responsibility that we can help break down the wall of fear that has others in our gay community and beyond addressing us as reckless, emotionally flawed, or suicidal. (Bareback.com)

While BBJ does not point a finger at any particular group, BBC undermines safe sex campaigns within the context of homophobic anti-sex discourse. Michael uses his advice column to not only "re-educate" the bareback community but also to identify the supposed hypocrisy of heteronormative society's commandment that gay men adhere to the strictures of the condom code. In fact, heterosexuality, and in particular, heteronormative lifestyles, crop up regularly on the website. In his response to another letter he compares HIV infection with pregnancy:

Do you have any idea how many girls have gotten pregnant because their boyfriends promised them they would marry them "if anything happens"? Do you know how many boyfriends actually stayed around after breeding the bitches? (Bareback.com)

This illustrates an important difference between the two spaces in terms of their understanding of bareback sex. At BBJ, barebacking is a specifically homosexual activity, and one of many such activities. The argument for barebacking is premised on validating *all* aspects of gay male sexuality. At BBC, barebacking is compared to heterosexuality in an attempt to validate it as *the* gay sex act above all others. And, according to the Webmaster, barebacking and procreative sex are parallel activities. Not only do they involve unprotected sex, but they also carry risks:

Wake up people!! There is no such thing as safe sex!! It's all a little dangerous!! That's part of what makes it fun! (Bareback.com)

Heteropatriarchy is located as the stuffy parent that must be rebelled against, but somewhat paradoxically this rebellion is paralleled with heterosexual sex. This is rendered visible via another recurring motif within the discourse of the website, namely misogyny. Drawing on the archetypal binary of virgin and whore, women are positioned either as "mommies"—stay-at-home, passive subordinates (as evidenced in the mission statement)—or as "bitches"—sexually promiscuous animal-women who are "punished" through pregnancy for their sexual freedom. Pregnancy and HIV are positioned not only as similar risks, but also as the risk or "problem" for the passive partner only, be that a woman or a "bottom." The passive partner is not overtly feminized by the Webmaster; there is no use of feminine pronouns to describe "bottoms" and the stereotype of the butch male penetrating the femme partner is notably absent. But the passive partner *is* feminized through his objectification. For example, when responding to a reader's enquiry about infecting his (passive) boyfriend during group bareback sex, Michael writes:

> He's your boyfriend! He's your bottom. He's your property. If you want to lend him out to random guys that is your right, but not before you mark your territory first. (Bareback.com)

This objectification of the passive partner can be understood as a process of feminization that borrows from the dominant ideology of hegemonic masculinity. The passive partner (who remains silent) is aligned with Western culture's representation of woman-as-object. This objectification/feminization of the Other is employed here specifically to masculinize the Self: the homosexual sex act is (re)read via dominant understandings of heteronormative relations. Michael speaks "man-to-man" to the correspondent about how to control and manage his "property." The Webmaster subscribes to hegemonic masculinity when he suggests that the correspondent has a duty to his boyfriend, it his job, his task, to infect him with the virus.

And once again HIV is aligned with pregnancy: the active partner has a responsibility to "impregnate" his passive partner in the same way that the heterosexual male must penetrate the woman in order to continue the blood line. This base, animalistic need to penetrate, and the supposedly transcendental nature of such need[6] is identified by Michael. He writes that the correspondent must "mark" his "territory" before he allows any other man penetrate his property, namely his boyfriend. Such a process of objectification and identification (namely of responsibility) serves to frame the homosexual act (barebacking) within a quintessentially heteronormative structure of understanding, and appropriates the power contained within it.

Conclusion

The continuing reluctance of the gay press to address barebacking, together with the difficulties that many HIV agencies face in promoting a discussion of bareback sex, has led to the construction of digital spaces that cater to the desires and needs of those who choose to bareback. The rise in barebacking cannot and—should not—be separated from the history of HIV/AIDS in the West and it is not unreasonable to state that barebacking is in fact a by-product of earlier HIV prevention campaigns. As such the spaces identified here are emblematic of the changing relationship between gay men, sex, and HIV, and are an important resource for future work into the arena of HIV prevention. If we are to gain an understanding of barebacking, we must simultaneously gain an understanding of the virtual environments created by and for this sexual subculture. The importance of the Web to the establishment of a barebacking community also means that it will likely be via networked communication systems that health interventions will most successfully be made. But barebacking must be understood as articulating themes far wider than simply those of disease.

For while BBJ and BBC differ radically in tone, content, and form, both websites foster a belief in gay men's right to choose condomless sex, should they wish: barebacking engenders questions of civil liberties as much as it does issues of sexual health. In neither space is there evidence of peer pressure or recruitment, as perhaps the mainstream press might suggest. Nor is there a failure to engage with the subject of HIV. Instead, what becomes apparent is that both websites seek to disentangle gay male sexuality from what they see as the politicized discourses of disease and protection that have become intimately linked with it since the 1980s. It is interesting to note that both websites employ conflicting time frames and utilize the tension caused by these chronological "ruptures" in order to effect this disentanglement. While this could be understood as a process of denial and regression, as has been demonstrated here this is not in fact the case. Rather, this extricating of gay male sexuality from its contemporary setting suggests that while metropolitan gay culture continues to struggle with the concept of barebacking, the Web is being utilized as space outside of this culture in which such discussions can take place.

Notes

1. Following complaints in the wake of the advertisement, the Advertising Standards Agency (ASA) investigated the GMFA's campaign, though later found no breach of the British Code of Advertising.
2. CHAPS and the CHAPS conference brings together a number of community-based HIV-related health organizations that work with gay men in England and Wales. The Terrence Higgins Trust co-ordinates the partnership and the annual conference provides a space in which recent changes in gay male culture can be discussed from within the context of HIV prevention.
3. If anything the 1950s theme suggests aggressive heterosexual masculinity. This was a period in which the sexual-political climate in both Britain and the United States

was characterized by increased police harassment and judicial interference into the underworld of illegal queer bars and cruising grounds. This state-legitimated homophobia has been documented by Weeks (1990), Jeffrey-Poulter (1991), and Duberman (1994)

4. I call HIV a bodiless specter because for many gay men today HIV is not personified in the death of friends, lovers, or celebrities as it was in the early days of the epidemic.

5. Aside from being slang for condom, the term "rubber" in this context also means Wellington boots. I am indebted to my American friends and colleagues for explaining this secondary level of meaning. What is particularly interesting is that when explaining the meaning of this phrase each person independently remarked that they hadn't heard the term used within this context since childhood.

6. Which draws on heterosexual familial structures of ownership—namely of property, women, and children.

References

Bareback.com. Retrieved August 1, 2003, from http://www.bareback.com

BarebackJack.com. Retrieved January 15, 2003, from http://www.barebackjack.com

Carter, M. (2000, August). "Aids Industry Meltdown?" *Positive Nation*. Retrieved February 12, 2004, from http://www.positivenation. co.uk/issue77/features/feature6/feature6_4.htm

Duberman, M. 1994. *Stonewall*. Middlesex, UK: Plume.

Hoffman, W. 1996. "Skipping the Life Fantastic: Coming of Age in the Sexual Devolution," in Dangerous Bedfellows Collective (Eds.), *Policing Public Sex: Queer Politics and the Future of Aids Activism* (pp. 337–354). Boston: South End Press.

Jeffrey-Poulter, S. 1991. *Peers, Queers & Commons: The Struggle for Gay Law Reform from 1950 to the Present*. London: Routledge.

Mallinger, M. S. 1998. "About Anal Sex. Barebacking: Slogans Aren't Enough." *Badpuppy.com*. Retrieved January 18, 2002, from http://www.gaytoday. badpuppy. com/garchive/viewpoint/040698vi.htm

Mukerji, C., and Simon, B. 1998. "Out of the Limelight: Discredited Communities and Informal Communication on the Internet." *Sociological Inquiry* 68(2), 258–273.

Reaney, D. 2000. "What's Behind Barebacking" *MetroM8 F***sheet* 57 (Aug). Retrieved January 18, 2002, from http://www.metromate.org.uk/fsheet/57/wbb.phtml

Rofes, E. 1998. *Dry Bones Breathe: Gay Men Creating Post-AIDS Identities and Cultures*. Binghamton, NY: Harrington Park Press.

Rotello, G. 1997. *Sexual Ecology: AIDS and the Destiny of Gay Men*. London: Penguin.

Scarce, M. 1999. "A Ride on the Wild Side." *Poz Magazine* (Feb). Retrieved June 18, 2002, from http://www.poz.com/archive/february1999/inside/rideonthewildside.html#safer

Scott, P., Coxon, T., Kirk, M., and Pinson, D. 1998. "Cottaging and Cruising, in Barnet, Brent and Harrow: Final Project report." Retrieved September 3, 2002, from http://www.racoon.dircon.co.uk/bbh/f7.htm

Sheon, N., and Plant, A. 1997. "Protease Dis-inhibitors? The Gay Bareback Phenomenon." *Managing Desire*. Retrieved April 23, 2002, from http://www. managingdesire.org/sexpanic/ProteaseDisInhibitors.html

Signorile, M. 1997. *Life Outside. The Signorile Report on Gay Men: Sex, Drugs, Muscles and the Passages of Life*. New York: HarperCollins.

Signorile, M. 2002. "The "Bareback" Lie" *Signorile.com* (30 July). Retrieved June 12, 2004, from http://www.signorile.com/articles/nyp37.html

Sinfield, A. 1998. *Gay and After*. London: Serpent's Tail.

Strub, S. O. 1999. "Safer Barebacking Is in the Grassroots . . ." *Poz Magazine* (Feb). Retrieved June 12, 2002, from http://www.poz.cpm/archive/archive/February1999/

Sullivan, A. 1989. "Here Comes the Groom: A Conservative Case for Gay Marriage." *New Republic* 28 (Aug). Retrieved October 11, 2005, from http://www.andrewsullivan.com/homosexuality.php?artnum=19890828

Taylor, M. 1999. "Give It to Me Raw Big Boy." *Outcast Magazine*. Retrieved July 22, 2002, from http://www.outcastmagazine.co.uk/13004htm

Watney, S. 2000. *Imagine Hope: AIDS and Gay Identity*. London: Routledge.

Weeks, J. 1990. *Coming Out: Homosexual Politics in Britain from the 19th Century to the Present*. London: Quartet.

Wells, M. 2000. "Sex on the Edge." *The Guardian* (March 2), 14.

Contributors

John Edward Campbell (MS, University of Massachusetts—Amherst, 2001) is a doctoral candidate at the Annenberg School for Communication at the University of Pennsylvania and an instructor at the University of Minnesota-Twin Cities, USA. He is interested in the dynamic between cultural producers and cultural consumers in cyberspace as well as the integration of emerging media technologies into the negotiation of everyday life. His recent focus has been on niche marketing and the commodification of online communities. His book, *Getting It On Online: Cyberspace, Gay Male Sexuality, and Embodied Identity,* was published by Haworth Press in 2004.

Christy Carlson teaches in the English department and the Women's Studies program at Trent University, Canada. Her research interests include pop-cultural appropriation and twentieth-century modernisms.

Carolyn Cunningham is a Ph.D. candidate in the Department of Radio-Television-Film at the University of Texas at Austin, USA. Her research interests include the intersections of gender and communication technology and implications for public policy. She is currently writing her dissertation, which examines technological literacy and democratic communication in an all-girl extra-curricular program.

Debra Ferreday is a lecturer in media and cultural studies at the Institute for Cultural Research, Lancaster University, UK. Her research focuses on aspects of online embodiment, especially relating to the reproduction of gendered subjectivities in new media spaces. She has written on subjects including hate speech and homophobia, pro-anorexic communities, and online shopping. Her current research project, provisionally entitled *Dangerous Femmes,* engages with queer theory and trans theory in order to draw out the relationships and connections between "deviant" feminine identities across a range of sites including transvestite identities, also drag, queer femmes, straight camp, and reproductions of "ironic" femininity.

Andil Gosine is an Assistant Professor in the Department of Sociology at York University, Toronto, Canada. His research examines the collusions of "race," sex and gender in various contexts, including international development, global environmentalism and queer culture.

Irmi Karl is Senior Lecturer in Media and Communication at the University of Brighton, UK. Her research interests include the consumption and use of information and communication technologies (ICTs) in relation to gender and sexual and identities, mobile technologies and social interaction as well as media representations of science and technology. She is currently also working on questions of class representation and reality TV.

Adi Kuntsman has completed her doctorate at Lancaster University, UK, currently completing her doctoral dissertation. Adi's work explores the relations between queer sexuality, violence, and belonging. Her doctoral research traces figurations of nationalism, race, ethnicity, and sexuality in the organizing of Russian-speaking GLBT immigrants in Israel and in cyberspace. Ghostly hauntings of the Soviet past, dreams of Jewish future, Israeli-Palestinian conflict, and on-line flame wars—these are some of the themes discussed in the dissertation. On a theoretical level, her project brings together gay and lesbian studies; cyberstudies; post-colonial and feminist theorizing of nation and nationalism; and anthropological research on violence.

Marjo Laukkanen born 1977 (M.Soc.Sc.) is a post-graduate student in Media Studies in University of Lapland, Finland. She is currently studying sexuality in girls' online conversations, and her doctoral thesis about the subject will be published during 2007.

Simon Lock is currently a lecturer in Computing at Lancaster University, UK. His interests cover a wide range of human factor issues and include the social use of computer systems, both in online spaces and real-world public areas. Simon is especially interested in the use of technologies as building blocks for the construction and development of identity.

Active in the transgender community, he has been involved in various discussion, support, and engagement events, helping to promote public understanding and acceptance. In particular, Simon has been involved in Sparkle (the International Transgender Celebration) where he was in charge of the international film festival.

Simon is also involved in digital art and performance and is director of Big Dog Interactive, a company developing bespoke systems for engagement and interaction. As part of this involvement, he has developed and exhibited artwork addressing issues of gender at various events and exhibitions around the UK.

Shaka McGlotten is an Assistant Professor of Anthropology and Media, Society & the Arts at Purchase College, as well as a faculty member at Goddard College. His research interests explore the vital and volatile intersections of race, desire, and technology. He is currently at work on a book manuscript that details his ethnographic work in real and virtual contexts on queer spaces and sex publics in Austin, Texas.

Sharif Mowlabocus is a lecturer in media and digital media studies at the University of Sussex, UK, where he received his doctorate in 2006. Sharif's research is located at the intersection between gay/queer studies and cyber-cultural studies and his work explores a variety of cultural formations and artefacts currently being produced at this juncture. Such research has included work on the multiple acts of identity formation in gay male web-spaces, the adoption of pornographic discourses in cyberqueer environments and the integration of new media technologies within British gay male culture. Sharif has also published work on film and representation and his interest in the deployment of class within urban gay male environments feeds into both this work, and his main Internet-focused research activities.

Kate O'Riordan is a lecturer in Media and Film Studies at the University of Sussex, UK. She is currently on a research secondment at Lancaster University, where she is completing a co-authored book on *Human Cloning and the Media* (Routledge forthcoming 2007). Her research interests center on the intersections of sexualized and gendered bodies and information and bio-technologies. She has published widely on the dynamics of bodies, identities, and technosciences.

Publications include "Playing with Lara in Virtual Space" in Munt, S. R. 2001 (ed) *Technospaces: Inside the New Media,* Cassell; "Changing Cyber-spaces: Dystopia and Technological Excess" in Gillis, S. 2005 (ed) *The Matrix: Cyberpunk Reloaded,* Wallflower Press; "Technologised Bodies: Transformations in Understandings of Bodies as Natural" in Hargreaves, J. and Vertinsky, P. 2006 (eds) *Physical Culture, Power and the Body,* Routledge; "Women, Feminism and Human Cloning: Re-circulating Concerns and Critiques" in *Feminist Media Studies,* 6: 2, June 2006.

David J. Phillips is Associate Professor of Information Studies at the University of Toronto. He studies the political economy and social shaping of information and communication technologies, especially technologies of privacy, identification, and surveillance. He is the author of "From Privacy to

Visibility: Context, Identity, and Power in Ubiquitous Computing Environments" (in *Social Text*), "Texas 9–1-1: Emergency Telecommunications and
the Genesis of Surveillance Infrastructure" (in *Telecommunication Policy*),
and "Negotiating the Digital Closet: Online Pseudonymity and the Politics
of Sexual Identity" (in *Information, Communication, and Society*), and
numerous other works exploring the relations among information, economics, ideology, policy, culture, identity, and technology.

Nathan Rambukkana is a Doctoral Candidate in the Joint Ph.D. in Communication at Concordia University in Montreal, Canada. He works in the
areas of Cultural and Communication Studies with a focus on queer theory
and discourse analysis, as well as in New Media Studies, with a focus on
sociality and community formation over the Internet. He is particularly interested in places where these two broad fields converge. His current research is
looking into the role of monogamy/non-monogamy in discourse and culture. He has contributions in the *Journal of Bisexuality*, the online journal
Affinities, and the collection *Plural Loves: Designs for Bi and Poly Living*.

Index

Vrooman, Steven, 106

W

Wakeford, Nina: and 'cyberqueer,' 2–3,
    13, 15–16; and technology studies,
    47–48, 51; mentioned, 21
Ward, Katie, 56
Wark, McKenzie, 20, 21; mentioned: 25,
    26
Warner, Michael, 2, 35; mentioned, 4
War on terror, 18, 19
Weed, Elizabeth, 49
Whiteness, 139–141, 148–150
Wittig, Monique, 83
Woodard, Jennifer, 211. *See also*
    PlanetOut
Woolf, Virginia, 96
Wrench, Nigel, 217

X

Xena, Warrior Princess, 186

ϒ

Yahoo, 186–87, 198
Yep, Gust A., 49

www.ingramcontent.com/pod-product-compliance
Lightning Source LLC
Chambersburg PA
CBHW070940050326
40689CB00014B/3281